Anglo-Jewish Poetry from Isaac Rosenberg to Elaine Feinstein

Peter Lawson generously considers the work of six Anglo-Jewish poets and persuades us that their marginality in relation to the central English literary tradition is a blessing.

Dannie Abse

'Anglo-' (not anglophone) – Peter Lawson knows how the hyphen keeps apart what it yokes together: for him the subjects of these six case studies are, yet are not (even quite) English poets. Reading them as Anglo-Jewish, he brings out their contention with English cultural tradition while himself contending with the ways they have been read (or misread – when read at all) in its terms. This book makes an original and unprecedented contribution to the history and criticism of twentieth-century English poetry and should open up a rich field of further enquiry.

Andrew Crozier

To American readers, 'Anglo-Jewish poetry' might seem an oxymoron. The delight of Lawson's ground-breaking study is not that it introduces us to new writers, but that it helps readers understand and identify with six British poets who are an essential part of modern Jewish literature. Clear and cogent, provocative and persuasive, this volume is long overdue.

Rochelle Ratner, Executive Editor, *American Book Review*

This is the first comprehensive account of twentieth-century Anglo-Jewish poetry. The author is to be congratulated for bringing to light a lost tradition that will enhance our understanding of modern British poetry in general.

Professor Bryan Cheyette, Department of English, University of Southampton, and Editor of *Contemporary Jewish Writing in Britain and Ireland* **(1998).**

This is the first detailed investigation of the phenomenon of Anglo-Jewish poetry. As such it forms part of the literary history of the Jews; equally, though, it accounts, at the very least, for a chapter in the history of English poetry in the twentieth century, this having been subject to a multiplicity of ethnic literary influences, not only because of Great Britain's imperial past but also the world status of the English language.

In the present work, Peter Lawson, who has also edited an important anthology of post-1945 Anglo-Jewish poetry (*Passionate Renewal*, 2001) insightfully, i.e. objectively, but also with inner knowledge, focuses on six representative figures, spanning two world wars. His discussion of centrality and marginality, within this particular context has immediate resonances for us, in an age of large-scale involuntary movements of populations.

Arguably, as the late Joseph Brodsky, himself an exile and a Jew, notes, marginality is an inestimable advantage for a poet in our time! Mr Lawson shows also how Jewish poets, from different social strata and cultural backgrounds, struggled to embody native or host sometimes also hostile traditions, enriching the latter in the process and revealing paths that would not otherwise have been taken.

Daniel Weissbort

In this excellent study of a neglected history within the tradition of modern British poetry, Peter Lawson shows us just how vital and important the achievements of Anglo-Jewish poetry have been. He writes with great clarity and insight about a wide range of poems by writers who span the twentieth century, and brings to his analysis a theoretically informed tact that also recognises the individuality of his writers and the significance of their differences. Lawson powerfully demonstrates that their struggles with identity, exile, antisemitism, and the religious authority of the Bible, helped form a developing poetics that is a major contribution to British poetry.

**Professor Peter Middleton,
University of Southampton**

Anglo-Jewish Poetry from Isaac Rosenberg to Elaine Feinstein

PETER LAWSON
University of Southampton

Foreword by
ANTHONY RUDOLF

VALLENTINE MITCHELL
LONDON • PORTLAND, OR

First published in 2006 in Great Britain by
VALLENTINE MITCHELL
Suite 314, Premier House,
112–114 Station Road,
Edgware, Middlesex HA8 7BJ

and in the United States of America by
VALLENTINE MITCHELL
c/o International Specialized Book Services, Inc.,
920 NE 58th Avenue, Suite 300,
Portland, Oregon, 97213-3786

Website: www.vmbooks.com

Copyright © Peter Lawson 2006

British Library Cataloguing in Publication Data

ISBN 0-85303-616-0 (cloth)
ISBN 0-85303-617-9 (paper)

Library of Congress Cataloging-in-Publication Data

A catalog record for this book has been applied for

Typeset by FiSH Books, Enfield, Middx.
Printed in Great Britain by MPG Books Ltd, Bodmin, Cornwall

Contents

In memory of my father
Max Lawson
14 May 1925 – 18 May 2002

Foreword: The Hyphen

It is not Hungary or any other place that is the issue. It
is the inbetweenness. The synthesis is its own voice.

George Szirtes, *The Budapest File*

I suspect that Peter Lawson asked me to write a preface for his new
book because I co-edited an international anthology of Jewish poets,
Voices in the Ark (1980, New York, Avon Books), whose UK section was
the precursor of his own anthology, *Jewish Poetry in Britain Since 1945*
(2001, Five Leaves Press). The interaction between 'Anglo' and
'Jewish' is plainly different for each of the twenty-two UK poets in my
1980 book and the twenty poets in his (eleven poets are in both); there
is, however, enough Jewish specificity in each poet's work to make the
hyphenation existentially significant and our endeavours towards a
collective representation of the works conceptually meaningful and
also, with luck, of interest to various constituencies of readers. The
hyphen is the bridge on which Peter Lawson stands, and delivers.

Lawson begins his measured and thorough critique of Anglo-
Jewish poetry at the beginning, with its grandfather, Isaac
Rosenberg, who on the strength of a handful of poems was as great
a poet as Wilfred Owen and David Jones. I met Rosenberg's
younger brother David in 1974 and this brought home to me in a
forceful way the loss English-language poetry in general, and
Anglo-Jewish poetry in particular, suffered with the death of the
poet in 1918. I have often wondered what it would have been like
to meet Isaac Rosenberg in London or perhaps in Tel Aviv or on a
kibbutz for, unlike Kafka, who also talked about making *aliyah* to
the Jewish homeland, Isaac might well have felt at home in, shall
we say, pre-1967 Israel. I also corresponded with Rosenberg's exact
contemporary, the most Jewish of the best American Jewish poets,
Charles Reznikoff (1894–1975), someone whose work, along with

that of poets such as David Vogel and Paul Celan, is central to any mature consideration of what we mean by diaspora Jewish writing.

Accounts of diaspora Jewish poetry often overlook the UK, squeezing out the indigenous tradition by concentrating on North America, continental Europe and Israel. Furthermore, accounts of minority poetries in the UK often neglect the Jewish one, for the live ethnocultural territory that is neither assimilationist nor religious is not perceived to generate psycho-existential imaginative possibilities for a poetics of Jewish space/time. It is the neglect contained in these two narratives of absence that Peter Lawson seeks to address in his six studies of Anglo-Jewish poets. Isaac Rosenberg and Siegfried Sassoon are already famous, and rightly so, as war poets. Being 'Anglo' *and* 'Jewish' raised issues for both of them, as it did for their much neglected contemporary John Rodker, whose inclusion here will be the most important surprise and discovery even for those already interested in Lawson's literary territory. The problems have changed, however, since 1967 and the Six-Day war, when the existential status of being a post-Holocaust diaspora Jew was brought home to Jewish poets of a later generation, such as the three Lawson discusses in the second half of the book: Karen Gershon, Jon Silkin and the only surviving poet of his six, Elaine Feinstein. English Jews – although they, we, had escaped the fate of continental Europe – could not ignore the passionate arguments involving Israel and the Holocaust. How much the more so since 9/11, with a great debate continuing in various circles, not excluding Jewish intellectual circles, between those who think one of the dangers facing us all lies in the *de facto* coalition between anti-Semites and radical Islam and those who think it lies in the opposing coalition between Jewish neo-Conservatives and reactionary Christian evangelicals.

If they will it, Jewish poets are heirs to an ancient and fascinating heritage, one that for good and for ill has influenced the western world in the form of allo-semitism, Zygmunt Bauman's useful concept (taken from Artur Sandauer) that covers the sometimes mirror image projections of philosemitism and antisemitism, both representing the Jew as Other. More than any other literature, English thanks to the King James Version has the Hebrew Bible as a foundational text, although the tension between Hebraism and Hellenism identified by Matthew Arnold remained an issue for Sassoon, and implicitly for the other poets discussed by Lawson too. Even though there is no law that says Jewish poets are obliged to draw on their heritage or on the impact this heritage has on other groups and individuals, and even though the heritage is open to everybody as a resource (e.g., accentuating the positive, Byron's *Hebrew Melodies*, George Eliot's *Daniel Deronda*, James Joyces's *Ulysses*), it is right there, an open book, ready for access *from the inside*. The 'pressure of history on experience' (Milosz) witnessed in 'excited reverie' (Yeats) by Jewish writers who remain 'prisoners of hope' (Zechariah, IX/12): this is the matrix of the present book by Peter Lawson and of his earlier anthology.

In his conclusion, Lawson argues that Jewish poetry could offer paradigms for other minority literatures in the UK. Perhaps so. But I do think that anthologies of, for example, Anglo-Sikh poetry, Anglo-Irish poetry, Anglo-Muslim poetry, will produce syntheses, abreactions and fault-lines of their own, and that the existential and cultural tectonic plates will shift differently according to the length of settlement in this country, where immigration has been front-page news for about a hundred years. The rules are different in the USA, where the hyphenated identity is built into a new nation even more marked by minority sub-cultures than the UK, notwithstanding the proponents of cultural homogenisation such as Bill Gates, Ronald Macdonald, Rupert Murdoch, and Madonna, whose absurd, debased and dejudaised Kabbala is but one of various syncretic quasi-religious phenomena creating common ground that the USA does not need.

Anglo-Jewish poetry as such has existed for about a hundred years, provided that – despite Elaine Feinstein's poem about her – we read Amy Levy (1861–1889) as a novelist rather than as a poet, a novelist whose death at 27 (only six months older than Rosenberg) entailed an inordinate loss to the cognate hyphenated tradition, Anglo-Jewish fiction. Since 1945 and, even more so, since 1967, Szirtes's 'inbetweenness' has flowered. In the present book, Lawson explores the matrix of that flowering, with his anthology serving as the garden for the flowers. Since the death of Jon Silkin, and with the older Abse sidelined as Welsh-Jewish, Feinstein is, in our time, the dominant productive poet – along with Ruth Fainlight and Daniel Weissbort – with an inner pathway to 'the structures of shared feeling and common perception bequeathed by a dynamic heritage; there are psychic tensions created and psychic energies released (blocked too in certain quarters) by the dialectical components of that heritage', as I wrote in 1980. Such inwardness to the Judaic heritage generates strong poetry and indeed strong Jewish poetry.

Lawson explicates, deploys or implies a number of binary oppositions or pairs, to characterise his chosen poets: otherness and affiliation, territorial and extraterritorial, exile and homeland, secular and religious, Hellenic and Hebraic, I and we, dream and reality, universalist and particularist, metropolitan and peripheral, internationalism and parochialism, modernism and tradition, lyric and story, all these playing their part in the grand dialectical narrative, symbiotic or not, of Anglo and Jewish. He explores the way Rosenberg's vision of Zion faces the future, Sassoon's the past. For Rosenberg it was the Hebrew bible, for Sassoon it was the Old Testament. Lawson discusses John Rodker as a secular Jewish modernist, who conflates Jew and poet in his self-image as an exile. He investigates Silkin's concerns both with metrics and social class, and how this relates to his powerful and influential advocacy of Isaac Rosenberg as a great poet, one who, like himself, is as Jewish as he is Anglo. Lawson does not neglect Karen Gershon's and Elaine Feinstein's novels – both fixing on the Shoah, but Gershon more concerned with Israel, Feinstein with Europe – in his assessment of their significance as Judaeo-centred writers and poets. Lawson, too, is at home with the Jewish hermeneutical tradition, and discusses how it impacts on these writers, although none of the poets in this book (unlike a few in his wider anthology) can be said to have it at the centre or close to the centre of their thematic concerns. Formal renewal in strictly Jewish terms – work that interrogates, perhaps redeploys, Talmudic or Midrashic discourse – is not yet on the agenda.

Peter Lawson's book is non-reductive. He knows that all his poets can be read via other critical templates. He is gratifyingly undogmatic in argument and blessedly non-authoritarian in critical discourse. He rightly takes issue with those who would see the ancient Jewish narrative teleologically, ending either in the Shoah or with Israel. By exploring the local conditions and environment (historical, cultural, psychological, literary and religious) in which his writers have, in the words of Ezra Pound, 'gathered from the air a live tradition' – these writers include Silkin, Fainlight, Feinstein and Weissbort (the latter three now in their seventies) and younger poets such as Richard Burns, Jonathan Treitel and Joanne Limburg, all found in Lawson's anthology – he has produced a book that could educate us, 'speedily and in our days', to identify still more possibilities inherent in the hyphenated accident of Anglo-Jewishness. Maybe other Jewish poets will be inspired by Lawson's work to bring to bear on their Jewishness the energies they bestow on other aspects of their identity, and find ways to transcend in lyric what they subscend in story.

Anthony Rudolf

Acknowledgements

I want to thank Ruth Kartun-Blum of the Hebrew University in Jerusalem for suggesting this book; Jon Glover for his many enthusiastic and informative emails regarding Jon Silkin; Val, Stella and Naomi Tripp for their hospitality and help with Karen Gershon's unpublished manuscripts; Elaine Feinstein for kindly lending me copies of her early novels; and Andrew Crozier for answering difficult questions about John Rodker.

Further gratitude is extended to Bryan Cheyette and Peter Middleton at the University of Southampton; the Arts and Humanities Research Board for funding two years of research and my visit to the Harry Ransom Humanities Research Center at the University of Texas, Austin; the Poetry Library, London, and the Hartley Library and Parkes Institute, University of Southampton.

Quotations from the work of Siegfried Sassoon appear courtesy of the Barbara Levy Literary Agency. In the USA: 'The Redeemer', 'Sick Leave', Their Frailty', from Collected Poems of Siegfried Sassoon by Siegfried Sassoon, copyright 1918, 1920 by E.P. Dutton. Copyright 1946, 1947, 1948 by Siegfried Sassoon. Used by permission of Viking Penguin, a division of the Penguin Group (USA) Inc.

Quotations from the work of Jon Silkin appear courtesy of the Trustees of his literary estate.

Quotations from the works of Karen Gershon appear courtesy of her husband Val Tripp.

Quotations from the poems of John Rodker appear courtesy of Carcanet Press.

Quotations from the poems of Elaine Feinstein appear courtesy of Carcanet Press, and extracts from her novels appear with the author's permission.

1

Introduction

This book surveys the work of six Anglo-Jewish poets active during the twentieth century: Isaac Rosenberg (1890–1918), Siegfried Sassoon (1886–1967), John Rodker (1894–1955), Jon Silkin (1930–97), Karen Gershon (1923–93) and Elaine Feinstein (1930–). To date, just one critical work has considered twentieth-century Anglo-Jewish poetry: Efraim Sicher's *Beyond Marginality: Anglo-Jewish Literature After the Holocaust* (1985).[1] Sicher's book, however, is only partly concerned with poetry, and not at all with literature produced before the Second World War.

By contrast, this book focuses on tensions over the course of the twentieth century between otherness and affiliation in Anglo-Jewish poetry. Concerns with exile, 'Orientalism',[2] extra-territoriality, and a peripheral relationship with 'English and Jewish specifics'[3] are pertinent here. Otherness also relates to what Isaac Rosenberg identifies as the 'ungraspable' nature of poetry itself, and a prevalent sense of secular Jewish identity as similarly uncategorisable.[4]

Countering such displacement is a common affiliation with the diasporic narrative of exile and deferred return to a textually imagined homeland. As Isaac Rosenberg writes: 'she [Zion] fell, / And only left her story.'[5] This is the 'story' of the Hebrew Bible read as literature, and English literature that borrows from the Bible. Biblically inspired poetry by John Milton, for example, engages Anglo-Jewish poets, as do Byron's *Hebrew Melodies* (1815) and William Blake's *Jerusalem* (1815).[6] Several Anglo-Jewish poets invoke nineteenth-century Romantic poetry for precisely its expression of biblically prophetic visions from the peripheries of conventional mores. Indeed, Anglo-Jewish poetry tends to follow a Romantic tradition. This is a universalistic tradition of affiliation with the outsider, the dispossessed and others passed over in silence. Further, Anglo-Jewish poetry evinces a struggle for Romantic transcendence of quotidian circumstances in order to be free of tensions in the diaspora.

In the twentieth century, Modernism continued the Romantic tradition of speaking for those marginalised by English literature and society. Indeed, it might be said that Modernist poetry was, in Terry Eagleton's phrase, produced by 'exiles and émigrés'.[7] Consequently, Anglo-Jewish poets who consider themselves exilic, such as John Rodker and Elaine Feinstein, self-consciously affiliate with Modernism. Isaac Rosenberg and Jon Silkin also engage with an exilic, Anglo-American Modernism.

America is particularly important to these poets, both as a country of immigrants, and as a relatively young country with a poetic tradition which scarcely pre-dates nineteenth-century Jewish immigration to England. Rosenberg, for example, notes of Ralph Waldo Emerson's verse: 'We have here no tradition – no tricks of the trade.' Instead, he discerns 'spontaneity, inspiration'.[8] Jon Silkin is similarly keen to champion American poetry. He applauds the distinction 'between English and American poetry, suggesting that the rhythms of the latter are more delicate, and subtle, than those in English poetry'.[9] Silkin goes on to praise 'Walt Whitman' as 'great'.[10] Indeed, I suggest that Silkin and Rosenberg, like Rodker and Feinstein, learn from the 'spontaneity' of American poets to challenge an English poetic practice which has not traditionally spoken for diasporic peoples.

Anglo-Jewish poets also look to Israel. Isaac Rosenberg and Siegfried Sassoon both write poems set in British Mandate Palestine. Indeed, Rosenberg's final trio of First World War trench poems – 'The Burning of the Temple', 'The Destruction of Jerusalem by the Babylonian Hordes' and 'Through These Pale Cold Days' (1918)[11] – express a Zionist yearning for Jews to return to their ancestral homeland. By contrast, Sassoon's sonnet 'In Palestine' (1918) suggests an affiliation with Jewish identity located firmly in the Old Testament past. After the establishment of the State of Israel in 1948, Silkin and Feinstein wrote poems set in that country. Silkin also translated a collection of verse by the Israeli poet Natan Zach, *Against Parting* (1967), and contributed to various Israeli journals and anthologies.[12] Karen Gershon lived in Israel for six years before returning to England.

Since Isaac Rosenberg was the first avowedly Jewish poet of the twentieth century to reach a wide English readership, this study begins with him. According to Paul Fussell, Rosenberg's 'Break of Day in the Trenches' (1916) is 'the greatest poem of the war'.[13] Yet Rosenberg's patron, Edward Marsh, considered that the poet paid too 'little attention to form and tradition'.[14] For Marsh, 'form and tradition' were non-negotiably English properties. The concept of a Jewish poetic 'form and tradition' was, evidently, beyond his ken. Indeed Marsh, like several other twentieth-century shapers of canonical English literature, was a Cambridge classics graduate.[15] He was educated in a Hellenistically inclined literary tradition. Within this tradition, English poetry principally followed Latin and Greek paths. Hebraically inflected poetry, for example by Milton and Blake, tended to be marginalised in such a literary education.

Meanwhile, Rosenberg was referring to the Old Testament for 'the exclusive atmosphere such as our literature possesses'. In other words, he located his poetic roots in the Bible read non-theologically as *literature*. Like other Modernists, Rosenberg was mining ancient texts for their potential contemporary significance. Those texts he selected were primarily Jewish. Thus Rosenberg was clear about writing within ancient Jewish (Hebraic) as well as Georgian English (Hellenic) literary traditions; and about fashioning something marginal, something eccentric. As he told his friend Ruth Löwy: 'G. B. [Gordon Bottomley] has urged me to write Jewish plays. I am quite sure if I do I will be boycotted and excommunicated, that is, assuming my work is understood.'[16]

In his near-contemporaneous essay 'Tradition and the Individual Talent' (1919), T. S. Eliot expressed his contempt for the dyad of 'new emotions' and literary 'eccentricity'. Not mincing his words, Eliot termed eccentric poets 'perverse'.[17] However, an eccentric is not merely whoever deviates 'from what is usual or customary', displaying 'oddity'. 'Eccentricity' also refers to a peripheral positioning, such as Anglo-Jewish poets occupied in twentieth-century English literature. The eccentric is not 'centrally placed', and is defined, indeed, by his 'distance from the centre'.[18] The relationship between peripheral status and apparent perversity is an underlying concern of this book.

A few months prior to the Great War, Rosenberg wrote to Marsh from Cape Town: 'You are lucky to be in comfortable London and its armchair culture.' In the same letter Rosenberg mentioned his contemporaneous lecture 'Art', in which he stated: 'The French Impressionists were the reaction from the traditional and lifeless. Art somehow had lost touch with nature and lay simpering, cosy and snug, propped up by sweet anecdote and delicious armchair sentiment.'[19]

Clearly, Rosenberg identifies 'armchair sentiment' (which the patrician Marsh epitomises in 'armchair culture') as 'traditional and lifeless'. Far from London, the metropolitan centre of empire, he expresses ambivalence towards such tradition: Rosenberg characterises it, on the one hand, as 'lucky' and 'comfortable' and, on the other, as 'lifeless'. What he empathetically admires in South Africa (though also ambivalently) is its otherness to the metro-politan centre: its 'elemental' rawness, its tangential freshness, its 'barbarous' vivacity. What Rosenberg perceives it to lack is precisely 'tradition', both Hebraic and English. Consequently, Rosenberg returned to London to excavate and deploy 'useable'[20] Jewish and English traditions, and to develop an Anglo-Jewish poetry and poetics. Eccentric to both traditions, Rosenberg strives to express the dynamic tension of his hybrid literary and social situation.

Although Rosenberg's trench poems are set completely *outside* England, they present an Anglo-Jewish space *within* English poetry. In poems such as 'Break of Day in the Trenches' and 'Chagrin' (1915–16), Rosenberg *deterritorialises* English in order to write another, eccentrically located kind of poetry. Once in the French trenches, I want to suggest, Rosenberg feels free to express the vibrant dynamism of his Anglo-Jewish inheritance. Rosenberg told his friend Joseph Leftwich in January 1918: 'After the war, if things go well – I doubt whether I'd live in London.'[21] Away from the metropolitan centre, Rosenberg finds his eccentricity is no longer out of place.

In Jon Silkin's study of First World War poetry, *Out of Battle* (1972), the later Anglo-Jewish poet remarks:

> It is not possible in Rosenberg's *Moses* to determine what emphasis to put upon the ethnic impulse and what on the radical. For Rosenberg, one suspects that the two issues were in common. To be Jewish in England then was to be, in the main, working class.[22]

Silkin's point is that affiliation with both an eccentric ethnicity and a politically marginalised working class was in no way a contradiction for Rosenberg. In 1979 Silkin edited *The Penguin Book of First World War Poetry*, in which he fulsomely praised Rosenberg as the best of the war poets. According to Silkin, Rosenberg remained underrated as a poet because he wrote a different sort of English: an eccentric English. Silkin explained:

> The English that Rosenberg employs is not the English of [Wilfred] Owen, [Herbert] Read, [Siegfried] Sassoon, or yet [David] Jones. Whether it is better or worse is not quite the question here; it is more to do with the sense that English may have plural rather than singular standards. Rosenberg's language, at any rate, is exploratory; his poetry seeks to re-shape culture by introducing new ideas and alignments, and one might say that this aspiration is most apparent in Rosenberg's language.[23]

Rosenberg's English 'is exploratory; his poetry seeks to re-shape culture by introducing new ideas and alignments'. Rather than looking to English 'form and tradition' (Marsh's patrician phrase), Rosenberg attempts to shape a poetry that will give voice to his First World War, Anglo-Jewish and working-class experiences.

Interestingly, Silkin's point concerning 'plural rather than singular standards' in English language and literature chimes with the notion of 'minor literature' proposed by Gilles Deleuze and Félix Guattari. In *Kafka: Toward a Minor Literature* (1975), the French critics ask:

> How many people today live in a language that is not their own? Or no longer, or not yet, even know their own and know poorly the major language that they are forced to serve? This is the problem of immigrants, and especially of their children, the problem of minorities, the problem of minor literature ... How to tear a minor literature away from its own language, allowing it to challenge the language and making it follow a sober revolutionary path? How to become a nomad and an immigrant and a gypsy in relation to one's own language?[24]

Silkin affiliates with his Anglo-Jewish forebear Rosenberg (the child of immigrants) and to an eccentric project of challenging the English 'language and making it follow a sober revolutionary path'. His stance is ethnically and, therefore, linguistically pluralistic. Silkin reads *Englishes* where tradition would inscribe a singular

English literature. Silkin understands that Rosenberg speaks with a minority voice in the literature of the majority. In effect, Silkin implies that he too, as an Anglo-Jewish poet, writes an eccentric 'minor literature' in English.

Indeed, I want to suggest that all the Anglo-Jewish poets in this study feel compelled, sometimes despite their expressed wishes, to negotiate a minority relationship with England's 'major' literature; and in so doing, produce what Deleuze and Guattari term a 'minor literature'.[25] Further, I want to ask what Anglo-Jewish poets do with such marginality. How do they give it voice and make it speak for themselves as Jews, as well as for other, often overlapping marginal groups, such as women, regional peoples and more recent immigrants?

Marginality, I suggest, may be a blessing. It can confer freedom from the prescriptions of a 'major' literary tradition. Of course, it may also lead to silence born of neglect. As Elaine Feinstein remarks: 'The danger of being at the periphery is that you never quite penetrate sufficiently not to disappear into darkness.'[26]

Writing within the 'darkness' of such neglect, Karen Gershon states in the preface to her *Collected Poems* (1990) that she has ceased to compose poetry: 'I stopped … because my poems met with too much indifference.'[27] Gershon attempted to escape marginality by authoring novels. Several of these remain unpublished, and are considered in Chapter 6. Gershon expresses the curse of marginality.

By contrast, Silkin displaces his Anglo-Jewish eccentricity to the north of England, where he finds his Jewish home, or 'new Jerusalem'. As he writes in 'The ship's pasture' (1986):[28]

> Northwards,
> a new Jerusalem with the lamb lies separate,
> its shade dense and lovely.

Moreover, Silkin empathises with northern poets such as Geoffrey Hill and Basil Bunting.[29] In *The Life of Metrical and Free Verse in Twentieth-Century Poetry* (1997), Silkin refers to Bunting's use of accentual poetry: '[Accentual verse is] a form asking to be used, one capable of expressing rhythms with a radiating vitality, often a rugged one, different from the smooth confidence of a verse-line that counts stresses *and* syllables.'[30] Here Silkin deploys traces of a discourse which consistently informs his poetics, whereby 'rugged' vitality is associated with regional (particularly northern) accentual verse, and 'smooth confidence' is located elsewhere (particularly in London, but more generally across the South of England[31]) side by side with accentual-syllabic verse ('a verse-line that counts stresses *and* syllables'). One is reminded of Rosenberg's comments in South Africa about London's 'armchair culture'. Unlike Rosenberg, however, Silkin *chooses* to stay in an eccentric relationship to the metropolitan centre and its dominant 'singular standards'.[32] Rosenberg only *discovered* his eccentric space in the trenches, as it were, by chance.

Interestingly, the spirit of F. R. Leavis hovers over Silkin's poetics. As Francis Mulhern notes in Homi Bhabha's *Nation and Narration* (1990): 'The strategic prize in *Scrutiny*'s contention with the metropolitan elites was the status of "centrality", which Leavis and his collaborators sought to invest with a strictly cultural, rather than "social", meaning.'[33]

Similarly in Silkin's schema, the regions become culturally central, while the metropolitan centre moves to a paradoxically parochial position. As Silkin remarks on the opening page of his autobiographical essay *The First Twenty-Four Years* (1987): 'No-one is so parochial as a Londoner, who, at the same time, adheres to an unshakeable belief that London is the radiating centre of Britain.'[34]

Following a congruous line of reasoning, apparently peripheral Anglo-Jewish (and other minor) poetries begin to assume a culturally central place, while the 'hostile weight'[35] of the major English literary tradition is radically de-centred.

To be sure, neither Isaac Rosenberg nor Siegfried Sassoon perceived themselves as culturally central. When Sassoon reflects on his youthful hunting days in *The Weald of Youth* (1942), he remarks: 'There were moments when I felt that I was an indecisive intruder who had no genuine foothold in either of those apparently incompatible spheres of activity ["Literature and Sport"].'[36]

In Chapter 3, I consider Sassoon's Romantic sense of being 'an indecisive intruder', with 'no genuine foothold' in England. Feeling like a spectator of contemporary life, the First World War poet characterised himself as peripheral: 'the *ruminant onlooker*'.[37] Unlike Rosenberg, who affiliated with a Jewish present and future, Sassoon located Jewishness in an ancient past. Rosenberg orientated his Jewishness towards a Modernist, politically radical future: socialist and Zionist. Conversely, Sassoon was only comfortable with his Jewishness when he viewed it nostalgically as '*in the past already*'.[38]

The Old Testament and Sassoon's ancestral 'Bagdad'[39] provided loci for the poet's articulation of a biblical and orientalised Jewishness. Such past and far-away Jewishness, I argue, tapped into prevalent imperial and Christian discourses which, respectively, constructed the British Empire as the new 'Protestant Israel',[40] and the New Testament as superseding the Hebrew Bible. These discourses allowed Sassoon to displace his (old) Jewishness on to (new) England, while affiliating with the dominant social and literary mores surrounding him. Although he continued to write verse until his death in 1967, Sassoon's poetic reputation remains, justifiably I believe, based on his separately collected war poems.[41] Therefore I focus principally on these, together with Sassoon's war diaries. His later autobiographies are also considered for the retrospective light they throw on Sassoon's Great War poetry.

War is a recurrent theme of this study. Unsurprisingly, two world wars impinge on much poetry written between, and about, 1914–45. Moreover, I contend that a particular, though 'changing',[42] embattlement is evident in twentieth-century Anglo-Jewish poetry. Before 1945, a significant cause of social and psychological embattlement was antisemitism. Deborah Maccoby remarks that Rosenberg 'saw in the trenches his own symbolic world made real'.[43] Maccoby argues that Rosenberg was liberated by the Great War because social and psychological attacks were already familiar to him. Possibly for the first time in his adult life, Rosenberg did not feel marginalised, because he was writing in a war environment. When Sassoon penned his preface to *The Collected Works of Isaac Rosenberg* (1937), he focused on Rosenberg's moral combativeness, praising the poet's verse as 'biblical and prophetic'.[44] However, it is Sassoon rather than Rosenberg who adopts the persona of a Hebrew prophet in several of his Great War poems. In 'The Poet as Hero' (1916),[45] for example, Sassoon writes:

> But now I've said good-bye to Galahad,
> And am no more the knight of dreams and show;
> For lust and senseless hatred make me glad,
> And my killed friends are with me where I go.
> Wound for red wound I burn to smite their wrongs;
> And there is absolution in my songs.

Here, Sassoon deploys Old Testament language to demand that the 'Galahad' of Christian chivalry ('knight of dreams') be put aside for vengeance ('Wound for red wound I burn to smite their wrongs'). Although Christian readings of the Old Testament presented Jewish values as vengeful, I want to suggest that Sassoon found in the Hebrew Bible a positive means of combating English complacency towards the First World War.

Chapter 4 moves forward to the 1920s and the verse of John Rodker. Here, I argue that Rodker is an exemplary *minority Modernist*.[46] Further, Rodker's affiliation with Modernism – as a poet, publisher and editor – allows him to displace his minority Jewishness on to a (non-racial) minority of artists and intellectuals.[47] The poet confesses in his autobiography, *Memoirs of Other Fronts* (1932): 'In Paris I feel English, in London a foreigner.'[48] Feeling exilic as an Anglo-Jew, Rodker affiliates with a group of exiled Modernists in London and Paris. Further, I suggest that Rodker presents his Jewish otherness as the personal freedom of slipping between definitions, and remaining taxonomically 'ungraspable'.[49] Similarly, Rodker's sense of slipping between categories applies to skin colour, and the implications of skin colour within English literature and society. His verse, criticism and autobiography, I suggest, negotiate an indeterminate Jewish position between black colonial subject and white imperial master. As we shall see, Sassoon, Silkin and Feinstein also explore Jewish racial indeterminacy in English literature and society.[50]

Chapter 5 continues into the second half of the century with the poetry of Jon Silkin. As a critic, Silkin begins to consolidate an Anglo-Jewish poetics by harking back to the work of Isaac Rosenberg. He writes: '[Rosenberg] is the tension that exists between the two societies [English and Jewish], and in this, he is truly Anglo-Jewish.'[51]

As the editor of *The Penguin Book of First World War Poetry*, Silkin submits:

> Rosenberg's language then – this may seem strangely put – is more lived in than Owen's. Owen's language narrates or carries the ideas; Rosenberg's language is them, sensuously enacts them, and experiences them. So to this extent it shares some of the 'haecceity' (or thisness) of [David] Jones's language.[52]

According to Silkin, Rosenberg's language is more faithful to the world as it is ('more lived in') than Owen's. It resembles life to such an extent that it (more or less) becomes life ('sensuously enacts', 'experiences', 'shares some of the "haecceity" (or thisness) of Jones's language'). Apparently, Rosenberg affiliates with life through 'language'. He is text-based in his exploration of what 'is the mystical' in experience. In this, Silkin implies, Rosenberg is fundamentally 'Judaic',[53] and follows a Hebrew tradition of reverence for words.[54] Indeed, Silkin appears to read Rosenberg's language as 'exploratory'[55] and Jewish, while implicitly contrasting Owen's as formalistic ('narrates', 'carries the ideas') and Christian.

This dichotomy between Christian (classical) formalism and Jewish (Romantic) exploration can be discerned in two poetry anthologies of the 1950s: *New Lines* (1956) and *Mavericks* (1957). The former, edited by Robert Conquest, launched what came to be known as 'the Movement'.[56] Kingsley Amis, Robert Conquest, Donald Davie, D. J. Enright, Thom Gunn, John Holloway, Elizabeth Jennings, Philip Larkin and John Wain were thus grouped together. Among the poems in *New Lines* was Larkin's 'Church Going' (1954). If there was such an entity as 'the Movement' (something several of its supposed members denied),[57] 'Church Going' raised the question of its 'religious identity'. It appears that Christianity held a powerful position in several of the poets' upbringings and university educations. As Blake Morrison explains: 'The Movement writers tended to come from homes in which religion was still treated as a matter of seriousness and importance.'[58]

At Oxford University, where Larkin, Amis, Holloway, Jennings and Wain were all undergraduates in the 1940s, Christianity occupied a similarly central position. Morrison continues:

> Christianity exerted a powerful influence at Oxford in the 1940s: 'Everybody to whom an imaginative and bookish youth naturally looked up, every figure who radiated intellectual glamour of any kind, was in the Christian camp.' Wain adds that for him Christianity was intimately associated with the literature which he was reading at Oxford.[59]

In discussion with the poet Anthony Thwaite in 1963, Silkin associates 'the Movement' with both Christianity and a 'formal' poetics.[60] Silkin remarks that Larkin's 'Church Going' demonstrates that 'Larkin ... is busy re-integrating himself with the Christian tradition'. He goes on to suggest that such formalism, or 'tradition', risks repetition of the injustices of the past, particularly persecution and murder of Jews. Silkin explains:

I think that perhaps what I try to do – in my York poem ['Astringencies'] – exemplifies what I mean. Here is a situation of a massacre of Jews at York in 1190. At the end of the poem, an exact correspondence with what happened in York is implied with what happened in Europe in this century. And I'm asking, do we want this kind of thing to continue? If we don't then we have to change society.

Thus, the Holocaust makes the need for social change urgent, while the *poem-as-process* intimates such change through its language:

In this poem-as-process you start off with a concept without knowing where it will lead you. Your concept is a reflection of a certain facet of reality that you feel involved with, but where that reality will lead you you don't know, but you explore it through the poem. The poets I can think of who work like this manage to release an enormous amount of energy in their work. Now Rosenberg would be a good example of a poet working through this 'in process' method.[61]

Silkin's perspective is European ('what happened in Europe in this century') and politically radical ('we have to change society', 'where that reality will lead you you don't know, but you explore it'). By contrast, poets associated with 'the Movement' tended to espouse an insular 'Little Englandism'[62] and political conservatism. As the Welsh-Jewish poet Dannie Abse (1923–) remarks:

I felt in opposition to 'the Movement' … There were also certain political undertones with the upraising of the English tradition. It was a feeling that, you know, 'wogs' began in Calais – that foreign poetry was no good … I didn't feel myself to be a Little Englander.[63]

Together with Howard Sergeant, Abse edited the *Mavericks* anthology in reaction to *New Lines*. Unequivocally, Abse espoused Romanticism:

I suppose I am equating the romantic with the Dionysian and the Dionysian with that mysterious, permanent element in poetry that irradiates and moves us and endures … But if, for this reason, I am anti-movement, I'm certainly not opposed to discipline and form and style.[64]

Mirroring *New Lines*, *Mavericks* featured nine poets: Dannie Abse, Anthony Cronin, J. C. Hall, Michael Hamburger, Vernon Scannell, Jon Silkin, John Smith, W. Price Turner and David Wright. Of these, three were Jewish: Abse, Hamburger and Silkin. Indeed, I want to argue that Silkin's dichotomy – between a 'formal' language which 'narrates', and an implicitly 'romantic' language which 'sensuously enacts' – carries traces of a widely disseminated discourse distinguishing between a conservative, Christian Little Englandism and a radical, Anglo-Jewish Europeanism.

In the wake of the Holocaust, both Abse and Silkin empathise with European Jews. Abse writes in 'White Balloon' (1990):[65]

> Dear love, Auschwitz made me
> more of a Jew than Moses did.

Silkin stresses the Shoah's traumatic effect on him:

> I was in London for the holidays, and I discovered a paperback which induced, or confirmed, my worst fears about what it meant to be a Jew. The book offered an account by a concentration camp inmate of his experiences in – I forget which camp. He had escaped but, unable to rid himself of the imprint of the experience, had killed himself.

He continues:

> That conjunction of brutality and humiliation affected me ... I cannot remember in detail what else the inmates endured, but that, I believe, was the mere tip of the ice. The hulk of experience drifted beneath the conscious surface.[66]

'To be a Jew' meant to suffer 'brutality and humiliation' at the hands of fascists. However, it was also to learn the value of resistance. Silkin describes an episode of antisemitism during his evacuation to rural Kent in 1940 as another example of Jewish education. He writes: 'I was about to become a Jew and a wiser human being.' On this occasion, a Jew took a stand against an antisemitic rabble-rouser, and beat him in 'a physical knuckle-hard' fight. Silkin comments:

Then indeed I felt almost sorry for him [the antisemite] and experienced a half-formed dismay and contempt for those whose aggression and prejudice he had fulfilled without their having to do anything but line up behind him. I also learned that a Jew could resist and succeed. I began to think that I, too, must learn to fight could I find the courage, or simply, the audacity.[67]

It is possible that twelve years later, 'beneath the conscious surface' of his declared reasons, Silkin named his little magazine *Stand* as a pugnacious response to such antisemitic 'aggression and prejudice'.[68] In his editorials, essays and poetry, Silkin maintains an unstinting 'fight' against the fascist *Weltanschauung*.

Further, Silkin champions a universalism which is largely defined by opposition to its fascist, antisemitic Other. Such universalism also takes its bearings from the Hebrew Bible. Silkin's first volume of poetry, *The Peaceable Kingdom* (1954), refers to the book of Isaiah and the prophet's paradisaical vision of 'the leopard' lying down with 'the kid; and the calf'.[69] Again, Silkin invokes the 'covenant' of God with Moses as a 'universal compact' between men, as well as between man and his environment. Thus, the poet's socialist and ecological concerns relate to what Jon Glover describes as his 'religious view of the purpose of poetry'.[70] However, Silkin rejects the bounds of Judaic law as parochial. Similarly, he refuses to be delimited as English. His 'ungraspable' universalism invokes 'English and Jewish specifics', but remains at a cosmopolitan distance from both. Seeking to transcend Anglo-Jewish 'tension', Silkin affiliates with an inclusive 'humanism'.[71]

Chapter 6 focuses on the poetry, novels and autobiographies of a refugee from Nazi persecution. Kaethe Loewenthal was sent to England on a *Kindertransport* (children's transport) from Germany in 1938. Throughout her life, Loewenthal continued to express her sense of exile and marginality. Indeed, she changed her name from Loewenthal to 'Gershon', which is Hebrew for 'stranger in a strange land'.[72] Naturally enough, Gershon had no plans to return to Germany. In the wake of the Holocaust, which claimed both her parents, she considered herself in *metaphorical exile* from Israel. This, I suggest, was an idealised *extraterritorial* space, shaped by Gershon's texts into an 'imaginary homeland'.[73]

Interestingly, Gershon turned to First World War poets – including Sassoon – as her 'mentors' in English verse.[74] She articulates her seminal Holocaust trauma, and consequent perceptions of diaspora, in poetry and novels of embattlement. Nonetheless, Gershon remained in the diaspora for all save six years of her life and claimed to be 'reconciled'[75] to England. Anglo-Jewish poetic tradition sanctions such an accommodation.

As a Jewish contemporary, Elaine Feinstein was also affected by the Holocaust. She confesses in an autobiographical essay that her childhood sense of security ended 'When I read what exactly had been done to so many children, as young as I was, in the hell of Hitler's camps. You could say in that year I became Jewish.'[76]

In the final chapter, I consider Feinstein's poetry and novels in relation to the Shoah. When she writes, for example, of paradisaical 'golden hours' in a 'supernatural city',[77] she seems simultaneously to be fleeing 'the hell of Hitler's camps'. Certainly, Feinstein's verse gestures towards escape. As the speaker of 'Out' (1971) enquires:[78] 'Who shall I take for my holy poet// to lead me out of this plain?' Feinstein, I suggest, follows a Romantic tradition of transcendent poetry. Through art, she seeks to transform the social and psychological tensions of Anglo-Jewish reality into something like 'the daylight of the Duc de Berry's golden hours'.[79] Her intoxicated 'flying' or 'rising', however, is counterbalanced by what she terms the 'baggage' of diasporic history.[80] Consequently, lyrics such as 'To Cross' (1971) express both 'respite' from and affiliation with an embattled Jewish 'story', in a tense and ambivalent 'mad calm'.[81]

Like Silkin, Feinstein rejected 'the Movement': 'It couldn't accommodate me. It was as precise and selfish as that. My voice wasn't suited to those traits.'[82] To escape the restrictive formalism of 'the Movement', she became involved with an alternative group of poets, including J. H. Prynne, Lee Harwood and Tom Pickard. Deborah Mitchell explains:

> Their main interest in common was the potential to British poetry in the practice of the Black Mountain poets; but Feinstein found the Cambridge group's insistence on its 'Englishness' incompatible with her growing awareness of the importance of her background to her work and left it after about six months.[83]

Whereas Feinstein looked to American poets such as Charles Olson and Robert Creeley at Black Mountain College for an extraterritorial way out of Little Englandism, the Gentile members of the group were intent on using the American model 'to explore the history of their particular Englishness'.[84] Indeed, Feinstein's family history of Russo-Jewish immigration and acculturation to England over fewer than a hundred years was passed over in silence. The Cambridge group prized an English insularity which excluded Anglo-Jewish, and other diasporic, experience in the twentieth century. To this extent, it bore a striking resemblance to the similarly insular 'Movement'.

From Isaac Rosenberg to Elaine Feinstein, Anglo-Jewish poetry repeatedly conveys a struggle to reconcile embattled English experience and pacific Jewish visions, metaphorical exile and 'imaginary homelands'.[85] Like the other poetry considered here, Feinstein's lyrics engage with the tensions of diasporic 'inbetweenness' – which is neither literal exile nor a specific home – and gesture towards Romantic transcendence.[86]

NOTES

1. See Efraim Sicher, *Beyond Marginality: Anglo-Jewish Literature After the Holocaust* (Albany: State University of New York Press, 1985).
2. See Edward Said, *Orientalism* (1978; London: Penguin, 1991), p. 73: 'I have been using the word [Orientalism] to designate that collection of dreams, images and vocabulary available to anyone who has tried to talk about what lies east of the dividing line.'
3. Jon Silkin, 'Anglo-Jewish Poetry', *The Jewish Quarterly* (spring 1967), pp. 22–4.
4. Ian Parsons (ed.), *The Collected Works of Isaac Rosenberg* (1979; London: Chatto & Windus, 1984), pp. 151, 238. In Rosenberg's verse drama *Moses* (1916), the eponymous hero speaks of fashioning the Jewish people into 'a thing, / Ineffable and useable' (line 464); and Rosenberg describes poetry similarly in a letter of 1916 to Gordon Bottomley as 'understandable and still ungraspable'.
5. Rosenberg, 'Zion' (1906), in Parsons (ed.), pp. 3–4.
6. See William Blake, 'Jerusalem', in Alicia Ostriker (ed.), *The Complete Poems* (Harmondsworth: Penguin, 1979), pp. 635–847; and George Gordon Byron, 'Hebrew Melodies', in Frederick Page (ed.), *Poetical Works* (1970; Oxford: Oxford University Press, 1979), pp. 77–84.
7. See Terry Eagleton, *Exiles and Emigrés: Studies in Modern Literature* (London: Chatto & Windus,1970).
8. Rosenberg, 'Emerson' (1913), in 'Parsons (ed.), pp. 288–9.
9. Jon Silkin, *The Life of Metrical and Free Verse in Twentieth-Century Poetry* (Basingstoke: Macmillan, 1997), p. 187.
10. Ibid., p. 22: 'Whitman, like other great poets (America's only one, so far) has that interacting of opposites which makes, not a simulation of energy, but a living tissue of strength and delicacy.'
11. Parsons (ed.), pp. 115–17.
12. Natan Zach, *Against Parting*, trans. Nathan Zach and Jon Silkin (Newcastle: Northern House, 1967). See also, for example, *The Tel Aviv Review* 2 (fall 1989/winter 1990), pp. 166–76 and *The Jerusalem Review* 4 (2000), pp. 174–7. See further Moshe Dor and Natan Zach (eds), *The Burning Bush: Poems from Modern Israel* (London: W. H. Allen, 1977).
13. Paul Fussell, *The Great War and Modern Memory* (New York: Oxford University Press, 1975), p. 250.

14.   Christopher Hassall, *Edward Marsh: Patron of the Arts* (London: Longman, 1959), p. 402.
15.   See Joseph Cohen, *Journey to the Trenches: The Life of Isaac Rosenberg 1890–1918* (London: Robson Books, 1975), p. 140.
16.   Parsons (ed.), pp. 287, 247.
17.   T. S. Eliot, 'Tradition and the Individual Talent', in *Selected Essays* (1932; London: Faber, 1966), p. 21 and pp. 13–22.
18.   See *The Oxford English Dictionary*, second edition, vol. V (1989; Oxford: Clarendon Press, 2001), p. 49.
19.   Rosenberg, 'Art' (1914), in Parsons (ed.), p. 296 and pp. 289–97.
20.   Rosenberg, Letter to Edward Marsh, dated 24 July 1914, and *Moses* (1916), respectively, in Parsons (ed.), pp. 205, 151.
21.   Rosenberg, Letter to Joseph Leftwich, dated 8 December 1917, in Parsons (ed.), p. 267.
22.   Jon Silkin, *Out of Battle: The Poetry of the Great War* (1972; Oxford: Oxford University Press, 1978), p. 263.
23.   Jon Silkin (ed.), *The Penguin Book of First World War Poetry* (Harmondsworth: Penguin, 1979), pp. 36–7.
24.   Gilles Deleuze and Félix Guattari, *Kafka: Toward a Minor Literature* (1975; Minneapolis: University of Minnesota Press, 1986), p. 19.
25.   Deleuze and Guattari, pp. 19, 28: 'A major, or established, literature follows a vector that goes from content to expression. Since content is presented in a given form of the content, one must find, discover, or see the form of expression that goes with it. That which conceptualizes well expresses itself. But a minor, or revolutionary, literature begins by expressing itself and doesn't conceptualize until afterward ("I do not see the word at all, I invent it") [.]'
26.   Peter Lawson, 'Way Out In the Centre: In Conversation with Elaine Feinstein', *The Jewish Quarterly* (spring 2001), pp. 65–9.
27.   Karen Gershon, *Collected Poems* (London: Papermac, 1990), p. 3.
28.   Jon Silkin, *The Ship's Pasture* (London: Routledge & Kegan Paul, 1986), p. 84.
29.   See Silkin, *The Life of Metrical and Free Verse*, pp. 240–1: 'In the end Lawrence brings together his background with his life as a writer'; 'Bunting homes to Northumberland'. See also 'The Small Magazine since 1960: a recorded conversation with Jon Silkin', in Michael Schmidt and Grevel Lindop (eds), *British Poetry Since 1960: A Critical Survey* (South Hinksey: Carcanet, 1972), p. 199: 'And thinking of his [Geoffrey Hill's] "Funeral Music" – which, as you know, we [*Stand*] published – there is that harsh, unremitting quality, a sense of the tragic nature of human conflict, of the way in which human beings seem to have to excoriate one another. That kind of abrasive quality is essentially a part of "Funeral Music" – not necessarily the central quality, but almost; and, in many ways, a northern experience.'
30.   Silkin, *The Life of Metrical and Free Verse*, p. 271.
31.   Silkin dismisses the poetry of Charles Tomlinson (who wrote in Bristol, within the centralising and empowered South of England) as 'predicating intellectual certainties validated in a Latinate diction rather than enacted in the more immediate Anglo-Saxon words of physicality that express the more uncertain condition of bodily experience and response': see Silkin, *The Life of Metrical and Free Verse*, p. 311.
32.   Silkin (ed.), *The Penguin Book of First World War Poetry*, p. 36.
33.   Francis Mulhern, 'English Reading', in Homi K. Bhabha (ed.), *Nation and Narration* (London: Routledge, 1990), pp. 250–64.
34.   Jon Silkin, 'The First Twenty-Four Years', in *Contemporary Authors Autobiography Series*, vol. 5 (Detroit: Gale, 1987), p. 243 and pp. 243–65.
35.   Silkin, *Out of Battle*, p. 271.
36.   Siegfried Sassoon, *The Weald of Youth* (London: Faber, 1942), p. 214.
37.   'Unpublished papers in the hands of a private collector:' see Jean Moorcroft Wilson, *Siegfried Sassoon, The Making of a War Poet* (1998; London: Duckworth, 1999), pp. 526, 582.
38.   Wilson, *Siegfried Sassoon, The Making of a War Poet*, p. 526.
39.   Siegfried Sassoon, 'The Fathers' (1917), in Rupert Hart-Davis (ed.), *Siegfried Sassoon: The War Poems* (London: Faber, 1983), p. 93.

40. Linda Colley, *Britons: Forging the Nation 1707–1837* (London: Yale University Press, 1992), pp. 368–9.

41. See, for example, Hart-Davis, *Siegfried Sassoon: The War Poems*. See further Wilson, *Siegfried Sassoon, The Making of a War Poet*, and Patrick Campbell, *Siegfried Sassoon: A Study of the War Poetry* (Jefferson: McFarland, 1999).

42. Jon Silkin (ed.), *Poetry of the Committed Individual: A Stand Anthology of Poetry* (Harmondsworth: Penguin, 1973), pp. 20–1. Here, Silkin urges that 'preparations be made for a continuingly vigorous and changing culture'.

43. Deborah Maccoby, *God Made Blind: Isaac Rosenberg, His Life and Poetry* (London: Symposium Press, 1999), p. 162. See further 'Isaac Rosenberg's English', in Adam Phillips, *On Flirtation* (London: Faber, 1994), p. 187 and pp. 175–95: 'For Rosenberg... to enlist was to make vivid in a peculiarly literal way the dilemmas that constituted the struggle of his life.'

44. Parsons (ed.), p. ix.

45. Hart-Davis (ed.), *Siegfried Sassoon: The War Poems*, p. 61.

46. See Deleuze and Guattari, p. 16: 'A minor literature doesn't come from a minor language; it is rather that which a minority constructs within a major language.'

47. See Nancy Cunard, *These Were The Hours: Memoirs of My Hours Press, Réanville and Paris 1928–1931* (Carbondale: Southern Illinois University Press, 1969), p. 142: 'He had learned printing and publishing years before at his Ovid Press, in London, which he had founded "to bring before the public work that was considered advanced". Its first book was T. S. Eliot's *Ara Vos Prec*.' Rodker replaced Ezra Pound as London editor of *The Little Review* in 1919. See Margaret Anderson, 'Editorial Note', *The Little Review* 6:2 (June 1919), p. i: 'Ezra Pound has abdicated and gone to Persia. John Rodker is now the London Editor of the Little Review.'

48. John Rodker, *Memoirs of Other Fronts* (London: Putnam, 1932), p. 16.

49. Rosenberg, Letter to Gordon Bottomley, dated 23 July 1916, in Parsons (ed.), p. 238.

50. See Bryan Cheyette, 'Neither Black Nor White: The Figure of "the Jew" in Imperial British Literature', in Linda Nochlin and Tamar Garb (eds), *The Jew in the Text* (London: Thames and Hudson, 1995), pp. 31–41.

51. Jon Silkin, 'The Poetry of Isaac Rosenberg', in *Isaac Rosenberg 1890–1918: A catalogue of an exhibition held at Leeds University May–June 1959, together with the text of unpublished material* (Leeds: Partridge Press, 1959), p. 3.

52. Silkin (ed.), *The Penguin Book of First World War Poetry*, p. 52.

53. Ibid., p. 52: 'In Judaic terms,' Silkin explains, 'although the soul may be nucleated by God's essences, humanity can only experience these through the body, that is, the total being; for in earthly life body and essences are inseparable.'

54. See Susan A. Handelman, *The Slayers of Moses: The emergence of Rabbinic interpretation in modern literary theory* (Albany: State University of New York Press, 1982), pp. 17, 30, 39.

55. Silkin (ed.), *The Penguin Book of First World War Poetry*, p. 36.

56. Blake Morrison, *The Movement: English Poetry and Fiction of the 1950s* (Oxford: Oxford University Press, 1980), p. 3: '*New Lines* (1956), edited by Robert Conquest, contained the same eight poets [as D. J. Enright's *Poets of the 1950's* (1955)] and added one more: Thom Gunn. In the years since 1956, the term "the Movement" has come to be taken to mean these nine poets.'

57. Morrison, p. 4: 'Larkin has said that he had "no sense at all" of belonging to a movement. Amis in a 1960 essay referred to "the phantom 'movement'". Gunn comments: "I found I was in it before I knew it existed ... and I have a certain suspicion that it does *not* exist." Enright remarks very similarly: "I don't think there was a movement back in those days, or if there was I didn't know about it." Jennings argues that "it is the journalists, not the poets themselves, who have created the poetic movements of the 'fifties." Conquest has claimed that, in editing *New Lines*, he "was not trying to assemble a movement".'

58. Morrison, pp. 226, 227.

59. Morrison, p. 228. Morrison quotes from John Wain, *Sprightly Running: Part of an Autobiography* (1962; London: Macmillan, 1965), p. 142.

60. See Jon Silkin and Anthony Thwaite, 'No Politics, No Poetry?', *Stand* 6:2 (1963), pp. 7–23.

61.   Silkin and Thwaite, pp. 7–23.
62.   See Neil Corcoran, *English Poetry Since 1940* (Harlow: Longman, 1993), p. 84: 'The attitudinising associated with a "little Englandism" in the Movement has always come under suspicion [in Silkin's oeuvre].' See further Peter Conradi, 'Elaine Feinstein', in *Dictionary of Literary Biography, volume 14: British Novelists Since 1960, Part 1: A–G* (Detroit: Gale, 1983), pp. 293–4: '[Feinstein's] roots, if she had them and was not nomadic, were certainly not to be discovered in a nationalist version of "Little Englandism".'
63.   Elaine Feinstein, 'Writers in Conversation: Dannie Abse' (London: ICA Video, 1987).
64.   Howard Sergeant and Dannie Abse (eds), *Mavericks: An Anthology* (London: Poetry and Poverty, 1957), p. 10.
65.   Dannie Abse, *Remembrance of Crimes Past* (London: Hutchinson, 1990), p. 34.
66.   Silkin, 'The First Twenty-Four Years', p. 254. Silkin's senior, the Anglo-Jewish poet Emanuel Litvinoff (1915–), also experienced the Shoah as an education in the Jewish predicament: 'I am concerned here with my education as a Jew, and it was the *churban*, the destruction, which largely completed it': see Emanuel Litvinoff, 'A Jew in England', *The Jewish Quarterly* (spring 1967), p. 12.
67.   Silkin, 'The First Twenty-Four Years', pp. 248, 249.
68.   Silkin explains his reasons for the name *Stand* as follows: 'For besides the fact that hardly anyone would publish me, I also felt that there was an apathy in England, both in social relations and towards new writing. I therefore called the magazine *Stand*, because it was meant as a *Stand* against this double malaise': Silkin, 'The First Twenty-Four Years', pp. 260–1.
69.   Jon Silkin, *The Peaceable Kingdom* (London: Chatto & Windus, 1954), p. 3; Silkin, *The Life of Metrical and Free Verse*, p. 211. See also Isaiah, in *The Holy Bible* (Oxford: Oxford University Press, 1862).
70.   Jon Silkin, 'What Can We Mean?', in *The Little Time-Keeper* (Old Woking: Carcanet, 1976), p. 66; Jon Glover, 'The Critic as Poet', *Poetry Review* 69:4 (1980), pp. 16–20.
71.   Parsons (ed.), p. 238. Silkin, 'The Poetry of Isaac Rosenberg', p. 3. Silkin, 'Anglo-Jewish Poetry', *The Jewish Quarterly*, pp. 22–4.
72.   See director John Pett's television documentary about Karen Gershon, *Stranger in a Strange Land* (Channel 4, 1990).
73.   See Bryan Cheyette, '"Ineffable and usable": towards a diasporic British-Jewish writing', *Textual Practice* 10:2 (1996), p. 303 and pp. 295–313.
74.   See 'Foreword', in Gershon, *Collected Poems*, p. 2, and Karen Gershon, *A Tempered Wind: autobiography* (unpublished, 1992), pp. 163–4.
75.   Karen Gershon (ed.), *We Came as Children: a collective autobiography* (1966; London: Papermac, 1989), p. 9.
76.   'Elaine Feinstein', in *Contemporary Authors Autobiography Series*, vol. 1 (Detroit: Gale, 1984), pp. 215–24.
77.   Elaine Feinstein, 'Renaissance Feb. 7' (1971), in *Selected Poems* (Manchester: Carcanet, 1994), p. 66.
78.   Feinstein, *Selected Poems*, p. 27.
79.   Feinstein, 'Renaissance Feb. 7' (1971), in *Selected Poems*, p. 66.
80.   Feinstein, 'Aubade for a Scientist' (1966) and 'At Seven a Son' (1966), in *Selected Poems*, pp. 8, 10. Elaine Feinstein, *Dreamers* (1994; Basingstoke: Pan, 1996), p. 176.
81.   See note 5 above. See also Feinstein, *Selected Poems*, p. 47.
82.   Lawson, 'Way Out In the Centre: In Conversation with Elaine Feinstein', pp. 65–9.
83.   Deborah Mitchell, 'Elaine Feinstein', in *Dictionary of Literary Biography, volume 40: Poets of Great Britain and Ireland Since 1960, Part 1: A–L* (Detroit: Gale, 1985), p. 118 and pp. 116–21.
84.   Conradi, pp. 293–4.
85.   See Salman Rushdie, 'Imaginary Homelands' (1982), in *Imaginary Homelands: Essays and Criticism 1981–1991* (London: Granta Books, 1991), pp. 9–21.
86.   Silkin, *The Life of Metrical and Free Verse*, p. 61; George Szirtes, *The Budapest File* (Newcastle: Bloodaxe, 2000), p. 15. Szirtes, an Anglo-Hungarian-Jewish poet, came to England as a refugee in 1956. He remarks: 'It is not Hungary or any other place that is the issue. It is the inbetweenness.'

2

Isaac Rosenberg: Roots
and Regeneration

Isaac Rosenberg (1890–1918) is primarily read today as a poet of the
First World War.[1] However, I argue here that Rosenberg is most
rewardingly approached as an Anglo-Jewish poet engaged with social
and literary hybridity. As Simon Featherstone has astutely remarked:
'Rosenberg's wartime work is as much a struggle for social and
cultural self-definition as a record of military experience.'[2] Rosenberg
was already embattled before he stepped into the trenches.

Living in Stepney, east London, Rosenberg was simultaneously
at the centre of the Jewish ghetto and the British Empire. As David
Englander notes: 'In an area of less than two square miles [in east
London] lived nine tenths of the Jewish population of late Victorian
Britain.'[3] This is the milieu that Rosenberg experienced from the age
of six, when the family moved from Bristol. In what has been
described as an 'open' ghetto,[4] Rosenberg grew conscious of a
hybrid identity which consistently resisted assimilation, while
simultaneously experiencing British acculturation. I use
'acculturation' in the sense of 'an accommodation to non-Jewish
standards that was less complete than assimilation, in which Jewish
religion or culture was not renounced'.[5]

In such a milieu, radical socialist views were by no means
inconsistent with ethnic affiliations. On the streets of Stepney,
Rosenberg was exposed to 'the Russian revolutionary tradition' and
ideologically charged 'anarchism among the immigrant
intelligentsia'. Significantly for the poet, 'the movement they
created was internationalist in outlook and secular in tone'.[6]
Rosenberg's internationalist perspectives were further honed by
developments in European art, which influenced both his painting
and his poetry. On his canvases, Rosenberg moved away from the
precise hyper-realism[7] of Pre-Raphaelite art, and fell under the
influence of Post-Impressionists such as Cézanne and Whistler

immediately before the outbreak of the First World War. I suggest that Post-Impressionism liberated Rosenberg's poetry and poetics in a similar fashion.[8]

Moreover, Rosenberg's theory of an 'ungraspable'[9] poetry relates both to the traditional Jewish conception of an unrepresentable God and to an 'ineffable',[10] or indefinable, Anglo-Jewish identity. Rosenberg learnt from the Old Testament and Judaic hermeneutic tradition that a continuous process of textual interpretation formed the basis of Hebraic poetry and poetics, whereas his Gentile Georgian patrons more often favoured the Hellenic and Christian traditions prioritising unambiguous images.

Rosenberg's situation as a first-generation English Jew is significant. Unlike his parents' generation of immigrants, who generally spoke Yiddish and were religiously observant, Rosenberg's generation tended to speak English as their first language and to be less observant. Thus, Rosenberg crossed traditional linguistic and religious boundaries in his life and poetry. His cultural hybridity led to what Gilles Deleuze and Félix Guattari have termed the 'minor literature' which a 'minority constructs within a major language'.[11] Though it is true to say that Modernism as such was very much a minority affair, I want to argue that Rosenberg's 'minor' Modernist verse differs from mainstream Modernist practice and is most usefully read as *minority Modernist* poetry.

Finally, this chapter considers Rosenberg's Zionist poems as attempts to impose closure on the Jewish narrative of exile by affiliating with the happy ending of an idyllic Israeli future. Such a future seemed to promise escape from the tension of 'being a hyphenation'[12] between Englishness and Jewishness.

THE POETRY OF ISAAC ROSENBERG

From his earliest poems, Rosenberg explored memories, traditions and sources of identity. Roots, and their relationship to Jewishness, feature repeatedly in Rosenberg's oeuvre. Indeed, roots figure in poems as otherwise diverse as 'O, be these men and women' (1913) ('famished flames that fly/ On a separate root of fire/ Far from the nurturing furnace'), 'A Warm Thought Flickers' (1913) ('Being is one blush at root') and 'Chagrin' (1915–16) ('We ride, we ride, before the morning / The secret roots of the sun to tread').[13] What such poems intimate is new growth from an old root.

Yet the bloom to be expected from plant roots is somehow stunted when metaphorically applied to Jewish roots. 'At Night' (1914) – with lines later incorporated into 'Chagrin' – presents 'secret roots' touched by 'venom':

> Star-amorous things that wake at sleep-time
> (Because the sun spreads wide like a tree
> With no good fruit for them)
> Thrill secrecy.
>
> Pale horses ride before the morning
> The secret roots of the sun to tread,
> With hoofs shod with venom
> And ageless dread,
>
> To breathe on burning emerald grasses,
> And opalescent dews of the day,
> And poison at the core
> What smiles may stray.[14]

Echoing William Blake's 'A Poison Tree' (1792), in which a poisoned apple, watered 'in fears', kills the narrator's foe – 'When the night had veil'd the pole' – the 'secret roots' of 'At Night' similarly produce 'venom / And ageless dread'.[15] Here is 'no good fruit', but 'poison at the core'. Rotten fruit in 'secrecy' is juxtaposed with growth and openness: 'smiles', 'day', 'the sun spreads wide like a tree'. As regards Jewish roots, 'At Night' implies that they too will be stunted unless allowed to move beyond the superseded position allotted to Judaism by Christianity.

In 'Creation' (1913), roots and religion are explicitly associated: 'Your roots are God, the pauseless cause.' Continuing to deploy plant imagery, Rosenberg considers the growth of Christianity from the 'seed' of Judaism:

> Moses must die to live in Christ,
> The seed be buried to live in green.
> Perfection must begin from worst.
> Christ perceives a larger reachless love
> More full, and grows to reach thereof.
> The green plant yearns for its yellow fruit.
> Perfection always is a root.

These lines express both a Judaised Christianity and a Christianised Judaism, a Judaeo-Christian synthesis through the metaphor of natural growth. Moreover, far from positing a traditional Christian consummation of Judaism, the poem anticipates a further growth:

> A sun, long set, again shall rise,
> Bloom in annihilation's skies.[16]

This anticipated new phase of 'Creation' is post-Judaeo-Christian. Thus, modernity is shown to offer Judaeo-Christianity a means both to 'bloom' and to retain its 'root'. The 'root' is Judaic ('Moses') and universal ('Perfection always is a root'). It also relates to 'Auguries' (1914), with its Jewish messianic anticipation:

> The broken stem will surely know
> And leap unto its leaf.
> No blossom bursts before its time
> No angel passes by the door
> But from old Chaos shoots the bough
> While we grow ripe for heaven.[17]

Here too 'blossom' is inevitable, a natural event ('The broken stem will surely know/ And leap unto its leaf'). Like Elijah, the herald of the messiah in Judaism,[18] the 'angel' points the way to 'heaven'. The rhetorical repetition of 'No' in the two lines preceding the turn of 'But' suggests a linkage of 'blossom', 'angel' and personal growth ('shoots the bough', 'we grow ripe'). Such growth is imagined Judaically. From roots – of night, secrecy and Mosaic perfection – a new bloom is confidently awaited. Some new cultural formation will free Jews for personal and collective development. Hence, the lines from 'On Receiving News of the War' (1914) – 'Give back this universe / Its pristine bloom' – suggest both a continuity of messianic anticipation in Rosenberg's oeuvre and renewed hope offered by the outbreak of the First World War.[19]

Similarly, Rosenberg uses images of pregnancy and birth to suggest fresh starts. 'Creation' opens with the lines: 'As the pregnant womb of night / Thrills with imprisoned light.' Again, 'The Jew' (1916) recalls 'Creation' in its positioning of Moses as the progenitor of Judaeo-Christian faith:

Moses, from whose loins I sprung,
Lit by a lamp in his blood
Ten immutable rules, a moon
For mutable lampless men.[20]

Faith and life for everyone ('For mutable lampless men') spring
from virile Judaism ('Moses, from whose loins I sprung'). Nature,
religion and mankind share one creative impulse with the poet. As
Rosenberg wrote in a letter to the novelist Sydney Schiff: 'Is the
novel growing? I am a bad midwife to ideas just lately and only
bring out abortions.' Works of art must gestate like embryos: the
new is enacted and ensured through them. Rosenberg's verse-play
Moses (1916) retraces the poet's ethnic roots ('Here are the springs,
primeval elements, / The roots' hid secrecy, old source of race') in
order to posit 'some newer nature'. The poet chooses to dramatise
the roots of his Jewishness in order to promulgate some 'useable'
(*Moses*, l. 464) future: a new socio-cultural birth.[21] Rosenberg's
emphasis on newness calls to mind Ezra Pound's adage 'Make it
new!'[22] Indeed, the very titles of poems such as 'Creation' and
'Dawn' (1914) point to the Modernist credo of new beginnings.
However, Rosenberg's Modernism is expressive of a Jewish
yearning for initiatives not dominated by a *de facto* Christian
culture. In this sense, it combines Modernist universalism with
Jewish minority aspirations in what Chana Kronfeld has termed
'minor modernism'.[23]

'Dawn' was written in South Africa (as were 'Auguries' (1914)
and 'On Receiving News of the War') when Rosenberg was staying
in Cape Town between June 1914 and February 1915. The poem
presents South Africa's economic culture of gold mining as
shamelessly sensual and decadent: 'While naked day digs goldly
deep / For light to lie uncovered'; and recalls Rosenberg's letter to
Edward Marsh about South Africans being 'dreadfully clogged up;
[with] gold dust, diamond dust, stocks and shares, and heaven
knows what other flinty muck'.[24] Although there was a welcoming
Jewish community in Cape Town,[25] the place clearly did not offer
the sort of newness Rosenberg sought. Roots in this society,
apparently, went no deeper than gold ('goldly deep'). The present
seemed a sterile dialogue with the idolatrous Golden Calf of the
Book of Exodus, rather than the Decalogue of Moses, and
consequently offered no possibilities for socio-cultural change:
'Though they are millions of years behind time they have yet

reached the stage of evolution that knows ears and eyes', Rosenberg wrote to Marsh.[26] He comments on South Africans' evolutionary success ('ears and eyes') with ironic surprise, since the populace appeared to have forgotten their aesthetic and spiritual senses ('these passages are dreadfully clogged up'). Fleeing 'gold dust' and a dead culture – 'And all her dreams lay somewhere dead' ('Dawn') – in February 1915, Rosenberg left Cape Town and embarked for life, and rejuvenation, in London.

Later that year, Rosenberg wrote to Schiff: 'I am enclosing a sketch for a play, which may interest you.' His verse-drama *Moses* had been conceived, although it did not see the light of day until 1916. Moses was the virile source ('Moses, from whose loins I sprung' – 'The Jew') from which some newer nature was to grow. The eponymous hero meditates on the Jewish slaves in Egypt:

> Their hugeness be a driving wedge to a thing,
> Ineffable and useable, as near
> Solidity as human life can be.
> So grandly fashion these rude elements
> Into some newer nature, a consciousness
> Like naked light seizing the all-eyed soul,
> Oppressing with gorgeous tyranny
> Until they take it thus – or die.

It is not unreasonable to ask whose 'newer nature' Rosenberg is articulating here. In a letter written to the Georgian poet Lascelles Abercrombie during the composition of the play, Rosenberg states: 'Nobody but a private in the army knows what it is to be a slave.'[27] Thus, it is feasible that the liberation of slaves in *Moses* refers also to First World War soldiers and the working class of which they were largely composed.[28] Significantly, when Rosenberg was offered promotion to lance corporal in December 1915, he 'declined'.[29] It seems that he preferred to remain unaffiliated to the army hierarchy, and not to 'become an authority' over his fellow working-class privates.[30]

David Feldman notes that for late nineteenth- and early twentieth-century Anglo-Jews, such as Isaac Rosenberg, the Jewish working class was a social fact, since approximately '71 per cent' of Jews were wage-earners 'engaged in manufacturing, mechanical or labouring occupations'. Feldman continues, 'The emergence of the Jewish working class in the 1880s coincided with an expansion of the labour movement and with the appearance of socialism as a current within it.'[31] Socialist politics found adherents among working-class Jews concerned to alleviate the poor conditions they shared with fellow wage-earners. Considered in its socio-economic context, it is perhaps no surprise that *Moses* lends itself to a socialist reading.

Another possible reading is Zionist. Indeed, the founder of modern Jewish nationalism, Theodor Herzl, saw himself as a Mosaic leader: 'On 7 June [1895] he [Herzl] had noted in his diary: "The Exodus under Moses bears the same relation to this project [Zionism] as a Shrovetide play by Hans Sachs does to a Wagner opera."'[32] Supporters also compared Herzl to Moses. For example, David Wolfson urged, '"Hold your hands high, dear Doctor," ... to encourage him and to remind him of Moses whose flagging arms were held high by his men until the battle between the Israelites and Amalek had been won.'[33] Following Herzl's death in 1904, comparisons with Moses appeared even more appropriate to many Zionists. At the Tenth Zionist Conference in Basle (1911), for instance, a 'full-length picture of Herzl' showed him 'standing on a mount overlooking the Holy Land' he was destined never to enter.[34]

Possibly, Rosenberg recognized in Herzl a fellow visionary poet, since the Zionist leader had often described himself as such.[35] Herzl's famous dictum 'Wenn ihr vollt, Ist es kein Märchen' ('If you will it, it is not a dream')[36] emphasises that Zionist determination can transform poetry ('a dream') into fact. Similarly, *Moses* offers an exhortation to action through poetry.

Further, *Moses* announces itself as a primarily Jewish play by both its title and its reactivation of what Rosenberg, in an art review for the *Jewish Chronicle* in 1912, referred to as 'the exclusive atmosphere such as our literature possesses': meaning, a biblical literature.[37] Rosenberg also admired poets such as Heinrich Heine precisely because they wrote what he perceived to be a modern Jewish literature. As he explained to Schiff: 'Heine, our own Heine, we must say nothing of. I admire him more for always being a Jew at heart than anything else.'[38] Thus, Rosenberg was clear about affiliating with a Jewish literary tradition. Significantly, he presents such a tradition as universalistic. *Moses*, for example, is universalistic in so far as it implies a contemporary liberation of all marginalised and oppressed groups.

To be sure, Rosenberg's evocation of Moses is consistent with his mining of the Old Testament and Jewish history in order, modernistically, to make Jewishness new. From Rosenberg's first extant poem, 'Ode to David's Harp' (1905), to his final trio of poems 'The Burning of the Temple', 'The Destruction of Jerusalem by the Babylonian Hordes' and 'Through These Pale Cold Days' (1918), a continuing *midrash*, or investigation, of biblical texts is discernible.[39]

Rosenberg wrote 'Ode to David's Harp' at the age of fifteen. Its Hebraic theme is filtered through Byron's 'The Harp the Monarch Minstrel Swept', from the Romantic poet's *Hebrew Melodies* (1815).[40] Here, Rosenberg taps into the Bible, and looks to English poetry with biblical affiliations, in order to write a hybrid Anglo-Jewish and 'minor' poem.[41] Moreover, 'Ode to David's Harp' lends itself to a Zionist reading:

> Awake! Ye joyful strains, awake!
> In silence sleep no more;
> Disperse the gloom that ever lies
> O'er Judah's barren shore.

Despite this invocation, the poem concludes on a 'plaintive sad' note:

> O! when again shall Israel see
> A harp so toned with melody?

Rosenberg appears to associate the revival of a Jewish poetry with the success of Jewish nationalism: 'One chord awake – one strain prolong / To wake the zeal in Israel's breast.' In 1905, however, 'Israel' was a distant Zionist prospect. Indeed, it stands in 'Ode to David's Harp' rather as an inclusive term for contemporary Jews seeking a common future from a past trajectory. In 'Zion' (1906), Rosenberg refines his definition of this 'useable' Jewish past when he notes: 'she [Zion] fell, / And only left her story.'[42] What the Jewish people seem to share here is a diasporic narrative ('story') of exile from Zion, without promise of imminent Zionist closure.[43]

By 1918, things had changed. When Rosenberg penned his final three lyrics, Zionism was British government policy. The Balfour Declaration of 2 November 1917 stated, 'His Majesty's Government view with favour the establishment in Palestine of a national home for the Jewish people, and will use their best endeavours to facilitate the achievement of this object.'[44] That month, Rosenberg wrote to his mother that he had 'applied for a transfer about a month ago'. In a letter to Marsh of March 1918, he expounded: 'I have now put in for a transfer to the Jewish Batt – which I think is in Mesopotamia now.' In his final letter to Marsh, Rosenberg enthused: 'I wanted to write a battle song for the Judaens but can think of nothing strong and wonderful enough yet.'[45] As Joseph Cohen explains, the 'Judaens' (or Judains) was 'the Jewish Battalion which Vladimir Jabotinsky had organised, then serving in Egypt and Palestine. It was composed entirely of Russian Jews who had immigrated earlier to England and the United States'.[46]

Clearly, Rosenberg was keen to fight with 'Jewry's first military force in two millennia'.[47] Though concerned with working-class oppression, and in correspondence with R. C. Trevelyan, the writer of 'Revolutionary literature', Rosenberg's reaction to the Russian Revolution is tellingly ethnocentric. He tells his mother, 'I hope our Russian cousins are happy now. Trotsky, I imagine will look after the interests of his co religionists.' Of course, this is a reference to relatives: 'cousins'. Rosenberg was always concerned with love for family, 'the natural ties of sentiment with one's own people'.[48] However, it also refers to Russian Jews in general: Trotsky's 'co religionists'. Indeed, Rosenberg's ethnic affiliations appear to be an extension of family love, with revolutionary sentiments only relevant where they overlap with the former.

If Rosenberg had survived the war, he probably would have emigrated. As he wrote to the poet Joseph Leftwich in January 1918, one month after General Allenby had entered Jerusalem as its British conqueror: 'After the war, if things go well – I doubt whether I'd live in London.'[49] Zionist *aliya*[50] (emigration to Palestine), rather than a new life in Soviet Russia, remained Rosenberg's more likely preference.

Once Zionism became a practical political possibility, Rosenberg returned to the themes and lyrical style of Byron's *Hebrew Melodies*. His 'The Burning of the Temple' and 'The Destruction of Jerusalem by the Babylonian Hordes' echo, in particular, Byron's 'On the Day of the Destruction of Jerusalem by Titus' and 'By the Rivers of Babylon We Sat Down and Wept'.[51] Significantly, Rosenberg's poems juxtapose the Great War with the destruction of the First Temple and the Babylonian Exile to suggest the continuity of Jewish history. 'The Burning of the Temple' addresses Solomon in its first stanza:

Fierce wrath of Solomon
Where sleepest thou? O see

> The fabric which thou won
> Earth and ocean to give thee –
> O look at the red skies.

Here, the fires along the Western Front are trans-historically super-imposed on the fires which destroyed Solomon's Temple ('O look at the red skies'). In the second stanza, the conflagration is envisaged as a potentially apocalyptic reanimation of a disastrous moment in Jewish history:

> Or hath the sun plunged down?
> What is this molten gold –
> These thundering fires blown
> Through heaven – where the smoke rolled?
> Again the great king dies.

Like the post-Solomonic exiles ('Again the great king dies'), diaspora is the cataclysmic fate ('These thundering fires blown / Through heaven') of contemporary Jews. The poem's final stanza summarises the destruction of the dreams of Zion:

> His dreams go out in smoke,
> His days he let not pass
> And sculptured here are broke
> Are charred as the burnt grass
> Gone as his mouth's last sighs.

Significantly, Rosenberg's poem differs from Byron's 'On the Day of the Destruction of Jerusalem by Titus' in referring to Solomon's Temple. Unlike Byron's lyric, 'The Burning of the Temple' does not deal with the destruction of the Second Temple, which led to the 2000-year diaspora of the Jewish people. Rather, Rosenberg focuses on the destruction of the First Temple (Solomon's Temple) which led to the Babylonian Exile, from about 586 BCE to 538 BCE.[52] Thus, beyond the present destruction lies the implicit realisation within a few generations of the deferred 'dreams' of Zion ('Solomon / Where sleepest thou?'). Jews, Rosenberg suggests, will return to their Promised Land some fifty years after this current destruction and, perhaps, in the wake of the poet's demise ('his mouth's last sighs').

Similarly, 'The Destruction of Jerusalem by the Babylonian

Hordes' evokes 'Solomon's towers crashed between / The gird of Babylon's mirth.' The poem describes destruction; but beyond that is implied restitution through a return to Zion.[53] Rosenberg's final work, 'Through These Pale Cold Days', conveys an explicit yearning for such a Zionist return from exile:

> Through these pale cold days
> What dark faces burn
> Out of three thousand years
> And their wild eyes yearn,
>
> While underneath their brows
> Like waifs their spirits grope
> For the pools of Hebron again –
> For Lebanon's summer slope.
>
> They leave these blond still days
> In dust behind their tread
> They see with living eyes
> How long they have been dead.

The poem takes as its point of historical reference the beginning of the Kingdom of Israel in the tenth century BCE ('Out of three thousand years').[54] Further, this history is rendered somatically present in the 'living eyes' and ethnically signified 'dark faces' of Jews who 'yearn' to leave the 'pale' and 'blond' population of semi-foreign England. Such Zionist yearning, moreover, confirms a continuity of the diasporic Jewish 'story'.[55]

Indeed, all three poems – 'The Burning of the Temple', 'The Destruction of Jerusalem by the Babylonian Hordes' and 'Through These Pale Cold Days' – may be Rosenberg's attempts to write a 'strong and wonderful' song for the Judaens.[56] As Michael Berkowitz has noted, songs 'remained of vital importance' for pre-First World War Zionists, and frequently featured 'images of the ruins of Zion and new life in Palestine'.[57] Rosenberg's poems reanimate such lyrical Zionist tropes.[58]

Simultaneously, these poems evoke Jewish alienation in England. Deborah Maccoby notes further that there is a reference in *Moses* 'to the biblical legend that Moses suffered from a speech impediment', and cites lines 247–50 from the verse-drama:

> The streaming vigours of his blood erupting
> From his halt tongue is like an anger thrust
> Out of a madman's piteous craving for
> A monstrous baulked perfection.[59]

Maccoby continues:

> We are reminded also of descriptions by Rosenberg's friends
> of his own speech problems: 'He stutters and his voice is
> monotonous' wrote Leftwich, and Binyon described him as
> 'shy of speech'. 'I've discovered I'm a very bad talker,'
> Rosenberg wrote to Miss Seaton in 1911. 'I find it difficult to
> make myself intelligible at times; I can't remember the exact
> word I want, and I think I leave the impression of being a
> rambling idiot.'[60]

Other examples of awkwardness and taciturnity pepper
Rosenberg's texts. In a rare prose fiction, *Rudolph* (1911), Rosenberg
explains that the eponymous hero suffers from 'a super-
selfconsciousness, a desire not to frustrate expectation' and is
'perpetually on the strain to say something clever' among cultured
people.[61] In this short story, the impoverished Rudolph is Other to
the 'wealthy' poet who invites him to supper. His friend Dave (the
name belongs to one of Rosenberg's brothers[62]) warns Rudolph that
among such people 'if you don't look as if you'd just stepped out of
a fashion plate you're a pariah'. Rudolph has no wish to be 'a
pariah', but cannot stay at home with his (Jewish) family. As he
explains to the wealthy poet's mother, Mrs Harris: 'I am the first to
scandalise the family with a difference. They consider it perfectly
immoral to talk and think unlike them.'

Thus, Rudolph is caught on the horns of a dilemma: he cannot
talk to his (Jewish) family, and has 'a feeling of general discomfort,
and that they were all looking at him' among the (Gentile) literati.
Other both within his (Jewish) home and 'amongst those of more
affinity to himself', perhaps it is unsurprising that Rudolph feels
'socially isolated'.[63] Rosenberg describes himself, in a letter of early
1914, as similarly isolated: 'Whether it is that my nature distrusts
people, or is intolerant, or whether my pride or my backwardness
cools people, I have always been alone.'

Here, his self-blame and 'super-selfconsciousness' convey an
apologetic tone which embarrasses Rosenberg into further apology

and embarrassment: 'Forgive this little excursion into the forbidden lands of egotism.'[64] Combining apologetic Anglo-Jewishness[65] with a diasporic sense of possessing no country apart from 'the forbidden lands of egotism', Rosenberg's letter to Miss Seaton articulates the awkward, tongue-tying tension between desires to suppress and discuss Anglo-Jewish otherness.

According to Dennis Silk, 'Rosenberg is nowhere more Jewish, or rather Hebraic, than in the active and dynamic quality of his thinking'. Silk goes on to essentialise such 'Israelite' thinking and to juxtapose it with Greek modes of thought, using a definition of Thorlief Boman:

> If Israelite thinking is to be characterized, it is obvious first to call it dynamic, vigorous, passionate, and sometimes quite explosive in kind: correspondingly, Greek thinking is static, peaceful, moderate and harmonious in kind.[66]

Certainly, Rosenberg's attempts to formulate a dynamic, Anglo-Jewish poetry and poetics did not endear him to the Cambridge classics graduate Edward Marsh.[67] Marsh, editor of the five *Georgian Poetry* anthologies which appeared between 1912 and 1922, was adamant that the Jewish poet 'renounce the lawless and grotesque manner in which he usually writes, and pay a little attention to form and tradition'.[68] Indeed, Marsh's adherence to Greek models of static clarity restricted Rosenberg's contribution to the dominant English literary 'tradition'. For example, the only poem by Rosenberg which Marsh published – in *Georgian Poetry 1916–17* – was the 'Ah! Koelue!' speech from *Moses* that featured 'embalmed' beauty and 'amorous sculptures' kept 'fixed' in time.[69] Possibly, the echoes of Keats' 'Ode on a Grecian Urn' (1820)[70] appealed to Marsh's Hellenic proclivities.

Otherwise, Rosenberg was left to plead for Marsh's understanding. 'Don't say they're obscure,' he wrote in 1915; 'The idea in the poem I like best ["God Made Blind"] I should think is very clear.'[71] Rosenberg's letter proceeds to gloss the poem, and ends by reiterating the defensive plea: 'I think myself the poem is very clear.' Clearly enough, 'God Made Blind' presents a syllogism to justify a lovers' relationship. Moreover, the poem appears to reappropriate and subvert traces of antisemitic language such as 'cheat' (which is repeated three times), together with the associated 'God-guiling'. 'Gloom' is turned to 'joy' in the light of the logical impossibility of God hating himself (a 'self-hate' consequent on hating the lovers who 'are God grown'). Thus, the poem asserts a secular and logical mode of Jewishness, Other to both traditional Judaism and the language of antisemitism.

'God Made Blind' follows the style of the seventeenth-century metaphysical poet John Donne.[72] To a degree, Rosenberg empathises with Donne as a London-based poet.[73] This was the city that, Rosenberg wrote to Miss Seaton, caused 'the peculiar feeling of isolation I believe most people have in London'. In the same letter, Rosenberg confessed: 'I have always been alone.' Consequently, Rosenberg looked to other London-based poets – including 'Donne' and 'Milton'[74] – to find, precisely, a tradition of otherness ('isolation') in English poetry.

Following Milton, who penned a Protestant epic for the English Revolution, Rosenberg undertakes in *Moses* a Judaic epic for similarly turbulent times. Rosenberg writes of Milton, 'How dignified he is! How grand, how healthy! What begins in a mere physical moan, concludes in a grand triumphant spiritual expression, of more than resignation, of conquest.'[75] Such 'triumphant spiritual expression' is emulated in *Moses*, employing an epic register which may well owe a debt to *Paradise Lost* (1667). Drawing on Graeco-Roman and Hebrew texts, Milton had fashioned an epic anglophone poetry pertinent to his individual and collective situation as an English Puritan. Similarly, Rosenberg draws on the Miltonic epic and Old Testament to express his individual and collective situation as an English Jew. Such hybrid poetries complement Rosenberg's hybrid Anglo-Jewish identity. Interestingly, his praise for a Miltonic poetry of 'conquest' in 1912 suggests Rosenberg's sense of personal embattlement years before the First World War. It seems that Rosenberg was resolved to overcome the obstacles, and to grasp the opportunities, that England's dominant culture set before him.

Rosenberg's enthusiasm for Milton is matched by his encomia for poets of the New World. As a young country founded on immigration, America presents Rosenberg with the extraterritorial space in which to find his 'real voice', free of the 'echoes' of England's past. Writing of Ralph Waldo Emerson, Rosenberg notes how 'it not infrequently happens that the real voice, sickened by echoes and shy of its own sound, withdraws'. Rosenberg's own 'shy' stuttering and self-conscious otherness in England come to mind. By contrast, the absence of a sickening tradition of 'echoes' in America permits enthusiastic affiliation for this child of immigrants: 'We have here no tradition – no tricks of the trade.' Instead, we see 'spontaneity, inspiration'. Rosenberg espouses the 'spontaneity' of Emerson and Whitman in order to bypass the dominant English literary tradition, behind which his own voice stutters and is 'shy of its own sound'.[76]

Moreover, Rosenberg struggles to unite such American 'newness' with 'the elemental' in order to formulate a 'useable' minority Modernist poetics.[77] Significantly, this old–new synthesis resembles the unification of ancient Jewish roots with contemporary 'bloom'[78] which Rosenberg championed in both his poetry and his socialist-Zionist politics.[79]

Rosenberg's 'Art' (1914), a lecture delivered in South Africa, also champions the new. It praises Rembrandt's 'new combinations', the 'vehement spontaneity' of the Post-Impressionists, and the Futurist – 'a new being' – for his 'dynamic force'. Rosenberg continues:

> The French Impressionists were the reaction from the traditional and lifeless. Art somehow had lost touch with nature and lay simpering, cosy and snug, propped up by sweet anecdote and delicious armchair sentiment. It was the day of Dickens' slime and slush.

Similarly, in his collection of prose fragments 'The Slade and Modern Culture' (1911–12), Rosenberg notes:

> Whistler, exquisite, dainty and superficial, dandied through the slushy sentimentalism that had saturated English art, and taught Art not to despise the moods of nature; that a pigsty in twilight was a poem, and even a church could be hallowed – by a fog.[80]

Rosenberg's references to 'slime and slush', 'a pigsty in twilight' and 'a church ... hallowed – by a fog' are usefully read in the context of early twentieth-century literary constructions of the 'slimy' Jew, the Jew who was considered a threat precisely because he was 'impossible to contain in any one category'.[81] In T. S. Eliot's 'Burbank with a Baedeker: Bleistein with a Cigar' (1920), for example, Bleistein's 'lustreless protrusive eye / Stares from the protozoic slime'.[82] Here 'semitic "sliminess"'[83] semantically resembles the smoke from Bleistein's cigar, which obfuscates the classical clarity of 'a perspective of Canaletto'. Like Marsh, Eliot was principally concerned with (Hellenic) 'form and tradition', and judged (Hebraic) deviations from such to be (as Marsh remarked of Rosenberg's verse) 'lawless and grotesque'.[84]

According to Eliot, any work which culturally deviated from the 'ideal order' of European art – from the legacy of 'Shakespeare, or Homer, or the rock drawing of the Magdalenian draughtsmen' – demonstrated 'eccentricity' and was 'perverse'.[85] Eliot's Greek and Christian references ('Homer', 'Magdalenian') emphasise his conviction that art is essentially non-Judaic. Indeed, secular Jews are excluded from Eliot's 'tradition', since 'Tradition and the Individual Talent' (1919) is addressed to an English collective which is conceived in terms of 'race'.[86]

Rosenberg's definitions of art counter such notions of a European tradition which is hermetically Hellenic and Christian. Instead, Rosenberg suggests that all art is essentially uncategorisable. Dickens is Victorian 'slime and slush', rather than one of Eliot's fixed and bounded 'monuments'.[87] Similarly, Whistler's 'fog' lacks the clear boundaries of the 'church' it obscures, while suggesting the supersession of christocentric perspectives on art. Moreover, the mutable 'fog' replaces an English 'slushy sentimentalism' which was itself metaphorically open to shifting between forms: to freezing as ice, flowing as water, or simply remaining for a while unclassifiable as either 'slushy' water or ice. From Cape Town, Rosenberg urged Marsh, 'Do write to me – think of me, a creature of the most exquisite civilization, planted in this barbarous land.'[88] The term 'exquisite' links Rosenberg to Whistler, similarly described ('exquisite, dainty and superficial') as a post-Christian artist. Further, Rosenberg's preference for the 'ineffable' and 'ungraspable'[89] qualities of Impressionist art possibly relates to the Old Testament conception of an unrepresentable God. Unlike Christianity, which can be clearly signified by a representation of Christ, no such representation of Yahweh (God) is permitted in Judaism. Indeed, attempts at depicting *anything* are forbidden by the Second Commandment as akin to idolatry:

> Thou shalt not make unto thee any graven image, or any likeness *of any thing* that *is* in heaven above, or that *is* in the earth beneath, or that *is* in the water under the earth. Thou shalt not bow down to them, nor serve them: for I the LORD thy God *am* a jealous God.[90]

Consequently, there is no tradition of portraying God in Judaism. Yahweh remains, as it were, Impressionistic. Rather like Whistler's 'fog', he is 'ineffable' and 'ungraspable'.

As we will see in the next chapter, Siegfried Sassoon felt quite differently towards art and identity. An Anglo-Jew affiliated to the Anglican Church, he strove for clarity, and eventually converted to Catholicism. Clarity was reflected in Sassoon's regular stanzaic forms, and eschewal of Modernistic free verse. Semantic clarity, in such later collections as *The Heart's Journey* (1928), *Vigils* (1934) and *Sequences* (1956), becomes Sassoon's means of mimetically expressing Christian purity of soul. *The Heart's Journey*, for example, opens:

> Song, be my soul; set forth the fairest part
> Of all that moved harmonious through my heart;
> And gather me to your arms; for we must go
> To childhood's garden when the moon is low.[91]

Here, Augustan couplets lend complementary form to the poem's articulation of the 'harmonious', which, in turn, is associated with a circumscribed 'childhood's garden'. Such boundaries contain 'the fairest part' of the 'soul', representing the security and safety ('gather me to your arms') offered to the devout Christian.

Not so circumscribed, Rosenberg writes to Marsh of the praise heaped upon him by the poet and critic Lascelles Abercrombie in 1915, and concludes, 'All this must seem to you like a blur on a window, or hearing sounds without listening while you are thinking. One more blur and I'll leave you a clean window – I think we're shifting to Shoreham in a week.'[92] Here Rosenberg juxtaposes the unbounded opacity of his life and oeuvre ('a blur', 'shifting') with the framed clarity sought by Marsh ('a clean window'). He imagines himself dismissed by Marsh because the latter is limited to 'thinking' of words as transparent ('a clean window'), rather than concentrating ('listening') on their 'shifting' meanings. By contrast, Rosenberg affiliates with the Romantics in prioritising 'the concealed poetic power in words' and an unprescribed process, or 'original impulse'.[93] According to the poet, boundaries limit neither 'the active vital spirit' of 'spontaneous and intelligent understanding'[94] nor, by implication, the 'shifting' mixture of religion, race and English acculturation which informs his Anglo-Jewish poetics. Thus Romanticism, biblically inspired poetics and an indefinable Jewish identity are merged in Rosenberg's sense of seeming 'like a blur'.

Meanwhile, Marsh's characterisation of Rosenberg's style as 'lawless and grotesque' suggests that he considered the poet a somewhat 'barbarous'[95] creature. Indeed, as Bryan Cheyette has noted, Jews in the early decades of the twentieth century were often culturally signified as hybrid creatures, simultaneously modern cosmopolitans and primitive savages.[96] Nor was Rosenberg insensitive to this patronising attitude. When Gordon Bottomley wrote to Rosenberg in 1916, praising his work, Rosenberg mentioned Marsh in his reply: 'People are always telling me my work is promising – incomprehensible, but promising, and all that sort of thing, and my meekness subsides before the patronizing knowingness.' A few lines on, he comments *en passant*: 'Mr Marsh told me of your plays.'[97] Thus, Rosenberg hints at whose 'patronizing' he has in mind.

Additionally, Rosenberg had to contend with Jewish patrons. In 1912, his middle-class Anglo-Jewish patron at the Slade, Mrs Cohen, urged Rosenberg to stop experimenting in art and to follow a traditional 'healthy style of work'.[98] Like Siegfried Sassoon, Mrs Cohen was apparently concerned to affiliate with Georgian notions of national health.[99] Rosenberg, however, was quite dumbfounded by her philistinism. 'God knows what she [Mrs Cohen] means by a more healthy style of work,' he wrote to Ruth Löwy. 'Do you feel ill when you see my work [?] I know some people faint looking at a Michel Angelo.'[100] Evidently, Rosenberg was considered wrong-headed by his assimilated Anglo-Jewish, as well as Gentile, patrons. Berated on the one hand by philistine Anglo-Jews, and patronising Gentiles on the other, it is perhaps unsurprising that Rosenberg remarks: 'I have always been alone.'[101] Further, his expressions of isolation may derive partially from a sense of suspension between Englishness and Jewishness – like the 'hyphenation' in 'Anglo-Jewish'.[102] Such suspension is effectively evoked in 'Chagrin' (1915–16):

> Caught still as Absalom,
> Surely the air hangs
> From the swayless cloud-boughs,
> Like hair of Absalom
> Caught and hanging still.

From the imagined weight
Of spaces in the sky
Of mute chagrin, my thoughts
Hang like branch-clung hair
To trunks of silence swung,
With the choked soul weighing down
Into thick emptiness.
Christ! end this hanging death,
For endlessness hangs therefrom.

Invisibly – branches break
From invisible trees –
The cloud-woods where we rush,
Our eyes holding so much,
Where we must ride dim ages round
Ere the hands (we dream) can touch,
We ride, we ride, before the morning
The secret roots of the sun to tread,
And suddenly
We are lifted of all we know
And hang from implacable boughs.

'Chagrin' glosses the biblical story of Absalom, favoured son of King David, who rebelled against his father and was consequently punished by God. Fleeing on horseback, he was killed when his long hair caught in overhanging branches. Jon Silkin writes: 'The image of Absalom hanging by the hair articulates the rootlessness of the Diaspora (and English) Jew.' He continues, 'At the moment when all their energies are unwarily exerted ("We ride, we ride"), their appetites and expectations fully roused, suddenly they are lifted of these.'[103]

Here, the 'secret roots' of night lead to suspension from a type of gallows ('hanging death' on 'implacable boughs'), rather than growth and regeneration. Indeed, 'Chagrin' presents a bleak picture of disempowerment: a death in life worthy of Coleridge's 'The Rime of the Ancient Mariner' (1797).[104] Suffering from worse than Moses' stuttering, the alienated narrator becomes like Absalom: 'mute' and 'To trunks of silence swung'. Hanging is mentioned five times and refers to both a gibbet ('this hanging death') and a state of helplessness ('endlessness hangs therefrom'). The speaker is 'caught and hanging still' in despondency ('my thoughts / Hang like branch-clung hair'). The night-time fantasy ('we dream') of escape through 'cloud-woods' leads nowhere but back to diaspora's 'implacable boughs'. In the first two stanzas, the narrator compares himself to Absalom ('my thoughts / Hang'). However, the first person plural which is introduced in the final stanza – 'The cloud-woods where we rush, / Our eyes holding so much' – suggests a collective dilemma. In the context of a biblical narrative, this collective may justifiably be read as Jewish.

If 'Chagrin' articulates the curse of diasporic otherness, 'The Slade and Modern Culture' (1911–12) presents some of its blessings. In these prose fragments, Rosenberg describes erotic suspense and anticipation, 'when our blood hangs suspended at the rustling of a dress ... Our vanity loves to subdue – battle, aggressive ... How we despise those older and duller – we want life, newness, excitement.'[105] Here suspension is related not merely to a suspended time of Jewish diaspora ('our blood hangs suspended'), but also to sexual possibilities ('the rustling of a dress') and the unfulfilled longings of youth ('we want life, newness, excitement'). Suspension is the prelude to battle and empowerment ('Our vanity loves to subdue – battle, aggressive'). This is the rehearsal in imagination for youth's victory over the staid and middle-aged ('How we despise those older and duller'). Youthfulness infuses Jewishness, and suspense becomes giddy hope. Significantly, Rosenberg identifies Jewishness with the future, rather than consigning it to Christianity's theological and historical past. Indeed, it may be no coincidence that Rosenberg collected his favourite poems under the title *Youth* (1915).[106] Youthful optimism generally orientates Rosenberg's Anglo-Jewish verse towards the future.

The change of tone from 'excitement' in 'The Slade and Modern Culture' to desperation in 'Chagrin' is partly explained by the fact that the poem was written after Rosenberg had enlisted and experienced English antisemitism among the troops. Until Rosenberg joined the Bantam Battalion of the 12th Suffolk Regiment in October 1915, the poet had mixed almost exclusively with artists and well-meaning Jews from London. The experience of army antisemitism clearly came as a shock. 'The Jew' (1916) concludes incredulously: 'Then why do they sneer at me?' In his letters, too, Rosenberg noted the strange new conditions: 'my being a Jew makes it bad amongst these wretches'; 'I have a little impudent schoolboy pup for an officer and he has me marked – he has taken a dislike to me I dont know why'.[107] Of course, Rosenberg would not have been unaware of antisemitism prior to enlisting. The Boer War (1899–1902), and the later Marconi and Indian silver scandals (1912–13), fuelled antisemitism both in London and nationally. Rosenberg would have heard 'Whitechapel and the Mile End being referred to as "Jerusalem" or "a second Palestine"', and witnessed antisemitic behaviour. Notoriously, in an area known as 'Jew's Island' in Bethnal Green in June 1903, 'the periodic harassment to which Jews were subjected erupted into open violence, with stone throwing, looting and serious injury'.[108] More civil violence occurred during the First World War, notably in September 1917 when 'street fighting broke out on the fringe of the Jewish East End'.[109]

Rosenberg would also have been sensitive to the language deployed by antisemites. For example, 'rodents, reptiles, insects and germs' were not uncommon synonyms for Jews in pre-First World War antisemitic discourse.[110] Such metaphors are reclaimed and subverted in Rosenberg's poetry, with images of fleas ('The Flea'), lice ('Louse Hunting', 'The Immortals') and rats ('Break of Day in the Trenches') appearing frequently. 'The Flea' (1914),[111] in particular, offers a bonanza of conventional antisemitic images: 'a flea', 'a spider' and 'a rat'. At the poem's close, all have been destroyed by the embattled Londoner:

> O cockney who maketh negatives,
> You negative of negatives.

In overcoming the metaphors of antisemitic discourse, the 'cockney' has secured a victory for anti-antisemitism: a 'negative of negatives'.

Yet another means of subverting anti-Jewish insect imagery is to imagine an entomological metamorphosis. For example, 'I like an insect beautiful wings have gotten' ('What If I Wear Your Beauty' (1914)) suggests the new and transcendent state of a 'butterfly'.[112] Adopting a transcendent otherness ('butterfly') offers both escape from, and resistance to, antisemitism. As we shall see in Chapter 7, Elaine Feinstein's lyrically transcendent poetry can also be considered in this way.

Interestingly, Rosenberg's 'Louse Hunting' (1917)[113] displays empathy with insects, as grotesquely 'gargantuan hooked fingers' proceed to 'smutch supreme littleness'. What should be distasteful turns into a celebration:

> See the merry limbs in hot Highland fling
> Because some wizard vermin
> Charmed from the quiet this revel.

The association of lice with black magic ('wizard vermin') and
Satan ('Soon like a demons' pantomime / The place was raging')
proves as erroneous as the traditional association of Jews with the
Devil in Christendom.[114] These trench insects may irritate and infect,
but they are not essentially evil. If anyone threatens God, it is the
blaspheming soldier 'with oaths / Godhead might shrink at'.
Indeed, the speaker identifies with both the 'we' of the British
soldiers and the 'supreme littleness' of the louse. This is a 'supreme'
moment of Anglo-Jewish hybridity: everyone is envisaged as
simultaneously a victim (of lice) and a 'merry' comrade in 'battled
arms'. Even the 'wizard vermin' prove vital to the atmosphere,
having 'charmed' the soldiers from sleep to 'this revel'. Embattled
diaspora ('battled arms') is staged here as a *danse macabre* ('glee.
Grinning faces', 'The place was raging'), with 'a witty sense of the
soldiers' commonality'.[115]

    Another antisemitic image, the 'rat', appears in what Paul
Fussell calls 'the greatest poem of the war': 'Break of Day in the
Trenches' (1916).[116] Here we meet 'a queer sardonic rat', a 'droll rat'
who 'inwardly grins' at entrenched European nationalisms
engaged in mutual attrition. In 'The Flea', Rosenberg presented: 'A
rat whose droll shape would dart and flit'.[117] Again, in 'Break of Day
in the Trenches', a 'droll' flâneur features as a re-deployed trope of
antisemitic discourse:

> Droll rat, they would shoot you if they knew
> Your cosmopolitan sympathies.

Needless to say, Jews were depicted as wealthy cosmopolitans in
the antisemitic discourse of the day.[118] Here, Rosenberg has the
speaker empathise with the rat's bohemian style:

> A queer sardonic rat,
> As I pull the parapet's poppy
> To stick behind my ear.

A poppy behind the ear suggests a casual insouciance, and perhaps
a saunter with the rodent across the no-man's-land between the

English and the German trenches. However, Rosenberg is English and cannot follow the 'cosmopolitan' rat:

> Now you have touched this English hand
> You will do the same to a German
> Soon, no doubt, if it be your pleasure
> To cross the sleeping green between.

A dialectic is thus established between entrenched Englishness and the highly individualised rat: the 'cosmopolitan' flâneur. Possibly, Rosenberg is reaching for a synthesis to embrace his relationship to English nationalism and diasporic otherness. He had written to Sydney Schiff in 1915 that he held 'no patriotic convictions' and that 'militarism is terrorism'. In similar vein, he informed Marsh: 'I never joined the army from patriotic reasons. Nothing can justify war', and maintained that the army was a 'rat trap affair'.[119] This last phrase – 'rat trap affair' – suggests that Rosenberg extols the 'cosmopolitan' rat's freedom. However, the rat fails to provide a synthesis for the poem's dialectic. The rat remains a rat, without 'men's veins'. Ultimately, 'Break of Day' offers a synthesis in Rosenberg's favoured image of 'roots':

> Poppies whose roots are in men's veins
> Drop, and are ever dropping;
> But mine in my ear is safe –
> Just a little white with the dust.

Jews and Gentiles share the 'roots' of blood, and eventual death ('dust'). Thus, Rosenberg expresses solidarity with all men, learning from the 'cosmopolitan' rat that hands from different nations share the common vulnerability ('Drop, and are ever dropping') of 'men's veins'; and that entrenched nationalism hastens the descent ('Drop') into the 'dust'.

Such a universalistic synthesis in no way detracts from Rosenberg's revolutionary aspirations for socialist-Zionist regeneration. As Michael Berkowitz notes, 'Accompanying the establishment of a modern Jewish nation, Zionist culture envisioned a continuous process of educational and moral regeneration, progressing toward greater freedom of the nation and humankind.' Furthermore, Jewish nationalism was supposed to be different: not 'exclusive and chauvinistic', but leading instead 'to brotherly bonds with the men of other nations'. According to Theodor Herzl, Jewish nationalism was imbued with universalistic notions of 'justice, truth, liberty, progress, humanity, beauty, and Jewish solidarity, in the service of enlightenment'.[120] Indeed, from a position of diasporic otherness, Herzl envisioned Zionist Jews becoming the universal model for all men. Rosenberg's 'The Jew' similarly invokes Jewish values as universal: 'Ten immutable rules, a moon / For mutable lampless men.'

Thus orientated towards a socialist-Zionist future, it is ironic that Rosenberg was killed during the German offensive of spring 1918, when he was just 27 years old.[121]

NOTES

1. This is largely due to the fact that no selection of Rosenberg's poetry was published in Britain between 1972, when *Poems by Isaac Rosenberg*, selected and introduced by Denys Harding (London: Chatto & Windus, 1972), appeared, and 2003, when two selections were published: *Isaac Rosenberg: Selected Poems and Letters* (London: Enitharmon, 2003), edited by Jean Liddiard, and *The Selected Poems of Isaac Rosenberg* (London: Cecil Woolf, 2003), edited by Jean Moorcroft Wilson. The first 'Collected Works' appeared in 1937, and a more recent edition in 1979, Ian Parsons (ed.), *The Collected Works of Isaac Rosenberg* (1979; London: Chatto & Windus, 1984). In 2004, the most scholarly edition to date was published, Vivien Noakes (ed.), *The Poems and Plays of Isaac Rosenberg* (Oxford: Oxford University Press, 2004).
2. Simon Featherstone, 'Isaac Rosenberg, Israel Zangwill and Jewish Culture', in Featherstone (ed.), *War Poetry: An Introductory Reader* (London: Routledge, 1995), p. 77 and pp. 72–89.
3. David Englander (ed.), *A Documentary History of Jewish Immigrants in Britain, 1840–1920* (London: Leicester University Press, 1994), p. 63.
4. Ben Gidley, 'Ghetto Radicalism: The Jewish East End', *New Voices in Jewish Thought* 2 (1999), p. 58.
5. David Feldman, *Englishman and Jews: Social Relations and Political Culture 1840–1914* (London: Yale University Press, 1994), p. 5.
6. Englander (ed.), p. 136.
7. Rosenberg described Pre-Raphaelite art as projecting 'an absolutely new atmosphere that is real in its unreality': 'The Pre-Raphaelite Exhibition' (winter 1911–12), in Parsons (ed.), p. 285.
8. See Michael H. Levenson, *A Genealogy of Modernism: A study of English literary doctrine 1908–1922* (Cambridge: Cambridge University Press, 1984), p. 43. The Imagist T. E. Hulme mooted Whistler as 'a paradigm' of 'the modern poet', and suggested that 'what has "found expression in painting as Impressionism will soon find expression in poetry as free verse"'.
9. Parsons (ed.), p. 238: Rosenberg describes poetry in a letter of 23 July 1916 to Gordon Bottomley as 'understandable and still ungraspable'.
10. See Rosenberg, *Moses* (1916), in Parsons (ed.), p. 151, where the eponymous hero speaks of fashioning the Jewish people into 'a thing, / Ineffable and useable'.
11. See Gilles Deleuze and Félix Guattari, *Kafka: Toward a Minor Literature* (1975; Minneapolis: University of Minnesota Press, 1986), p. 16. Throughout this study, I use the terms 'minor' and 'minor literature' with this definition in mind.
12. 'Editorial', *Jewish Chronicle*, 9 November 1917, in Englander (ed.), p. 306.
13. Parsons (ed.), pp. 55–6, 95.

14. 'At Night', in Parsons (ed.), p. 61.
15. William Blake, 'A Poison Tree', in Alicia Ostriker (ed.), *The Complete Poems of William Blake* (Harmondsworth: Penguin, 1979), pp. 129–30. Rosenberg admired Blake immensely, and believed that in him 'England has turned out one man second to none who has ever lived': Parsons (ed.), p. 198.
16. Parsons (ed.), p. 50.
17. Parsons (ed.), p. 74.
18. See Louis Jacobs, *Concise Companion to the Jewish Religion* (Oxford: Oxford University Press, 1999), p. 51: 'Elijah ... becomes, in later Jewish thought, the herald of the Messiah.'
19. Shelley's 'Ode to the West Wind' (1819) may have been in Rosenberg's mind when he composed 'On Receiving News of the War'. Rosenberg wrote to Miss Wright, the donor of a book of Shelley's poems: 'I owe some of the most wonderful sensations I have ever experienced to that book': Parsons (ed.), p. 188. Shelley's poem invokes the 'Wild Spirit, which art moving everywhere / Destroyer and preserver' and which will naturally lay waste in winter, only. 'Like withered leaves to quicken to a new birth' in spring: see Thomas Hutchinson (ed.), *The Poetical Works of Percy Bysshe Shelley* (London: Oxford University Press, 1908), pp. 573–4.
20. Parsons (ed.), p. 101.
21. Parsons (ed.), pp. 242, 150, 151.
22. See Ezra Pound, *Make It New: Essays by Ezra Pound* (London: Faber, 1934).
23. See Chana Kronfeld, *On the Margins of Modernism: Decentering Literary Dynamics* (London: University of California Press, 1996), pp. 1–17.
24. Parsons (ed.), pp. 69, 204.
25. See Jean Moorcroft Wilson, *Isaac Rosenberg: Poet and Painter* (London: Cecil Woolf, 1975), pp. 138–9: 'Whatever the reasons, it seemed time to leave. He resisted all Minnie's and Miss Molteno's pleas and blandishments'; 'Miss Molteno "assured him that she could sell all his pictures and he would have no financial difficulties"'.
26. Parsons (ed.), p. 204.
27. Parsons (ed.), pp. 215, 151, 230.
28. Jon Silkin discusses Rosenberg 'as a Jew, a working-class man, and a private soldier' in his study of First World War poetry *Out of Battle: The Poetry of the Great War* (Oxford: Oxford University Press, 1972), pp. 262–71.
29. Rosenberg wrote to Edward Marsh in December 1915: 'I am getting on so well that I have been offered a stripe, but I declined.' See Parsons (ed.), p. 226.
30. Rosenberg told Miss Seaton in December 1915: 'I am put down for a Lance-Corporal. The advantage is, though you have a more responsible position, you are less likely to be interfered with by the men, and you become an authority.' See Parsons (ed.), p. 226.
31. Feldman, pp. 164, 215.
32. David Vital, *The Origins of Zionism* (Oxford: Oxford University Press, 1975), p. 251.
33. Vital, p. 327.
34. Michael Berkowitz, *Zionist Culture and West European Jewry Before the First World War* (Cambridge: Cambridge University Press, 1993), p. 100.
35. Berkowitz, p. 94: 'Herzl had written: "the worst that one can say about me ... is that I am a poet".'
36. This dictum forms the motto of Theodor Herzl's utopian novel *Altneuland, Roman* (Leipzig: Hermann Seemann Nachfolger, 1902). See further Sidra DeKoven Ezrahi, *Booking Passage: Exile and Homecoming in the Modern Jewish Imagination* (London: University of California Press, 2000), p. 3.
37. Parsons (ed.), p. 287.
38. Parsons (ed.), p. 242. Interestingly, 'nearly every Zionist regarded [Heine] as the greatest of heroes'. For example: 'The young men of Bar Kochba, the Berlin Jewish gymnastic group, regarded Heine as one of their champions, and maintained that the poet would have admired them for their humanism and cosmopolitanism. After all, they claimed, Heine was a proponent of progress and harmony': see Berkowitz, pp. 94, 108. For an extensive survey of Jewish characters appearing in

Heine's work, see also S. S. Prawer, *Heine's Jewish Comedy: A Study of his Portraits of Jews and Judaism* (Oxford: Clarendon Press, 1983).

39. Parsons (ed.), pp. 2, 115–17. See also Jacobs, p. 154: 'The word Midrash is from the root *darash*, "to enquire", "to investigate". This searching of Scripture has been traced back to the book of Ezra.'

40. Frederick Page (ed.), *Byron: Poetical Works*, third edition (1970; Oxford: Oxford University Press, 1979), pp. 77–84.

41. Despite the fact that Byron jointly published *A Selection of Hebrew Melodies, Ancient and Modern* with Isaac Nathan in 1815, the Romantic poet was by no means immune to the period's prejudices against Jews. See further Michael Scrivener, '"Zion alone is forbidden": Historicizing Anti-Semitism in Byron's *The Age of Bronze*', *Keats–Shelley Journal* 43 (1994), pp. 75–97.

42. Parsons (ed.), pp. 151, 4.

43. For a discussion of Jewish diasporic narrative and potential Zionist closure, see Ezrahi, who finds 'in the poetics of return to Zion, a reification of the symbolic language of exile and closure of its open-ended narrative'. She notes further: 'the logic of narrative (which is exile)': Ezrahi, pp. 35 and 43.

44. Bernard Reich and David H. Goldberg, *Political Dictionary of Israel* (Folkstone: Scarecrow Press, 2000), p. 43.

45. Parsons (ed.), pp. 264, 271, 272.

46. Joseph Cohen, *Journey to the Trenches: The Life of Isaac Rosenberg 1890–1918* (London: Robson Books, 1975), pp. 1–2.

47. Daniel Harris, 'Rosenberg in the Trenches: Imagining King David's World', *Jewish Culture and History* 5:1 (summer 2002), p. 1.

48. Parsons (ed.), pp. 263, 264, 201.

49. Parsons (ed.), p. 267.

50. '*Aliya*' is the Hebrew word for 'immigration of Jews from the Diaspora to the Holy Land': see Bernard Reich and David H. Goldberg, p. 11.

51. Frederick Page (ed.), pp. 82–3.

52. *The New Encyclopaedia Britannica*, fifteenth edition, vol. 1 (Chicago: Encyclopaedia Britannica, 2002), p. 771 dates the Babylonian Exile from the 'conquest of the kingdom of Judah in 598/7 and 587/6' BCE until 538 BCE 'when the Persian conqueror of Babylonia, Cyrus the Great, gave the Jews permission to return to Palestine'.

53. 'On Receiving News of the War' (1914) also envisaged a positive outcome to present destruction: 'O! ancient crimson curse! / Corrode, consume. / Give back this universe / Its pristine bloom.' Further, Rosenberg's lecture 'Art' (1914) embraced the destructive aesthetic of Modernism for a complementary reason: 'Art is now, as it were, a volcano. Eruptions are continual, and immense cities of culture at its foot are shaken and shivered. The roots of a dead universe are torn up by hands, feverish and consuming with an exuberant vitality': see Parsons (ed.), pp. 75, 294. Renewal remained a possibility beyond destruction, as the return from Babylonian exile illustrated, and Zionists resolved to confirm. See further note 19, concerning Shelley's 'Ode to the West Wind'.

54. Jacobs, p. 37.

55. Rosenberg, 'Zion' (1906), in Parsons (ed.), pp. 3–4.

56. Parsons (ed.), p. 272.

57. Berkowitz, pp. 20–1.

58. For a discussion of conventional Zionist poetry following the Balfour Declaration, see Harris, pp. 29–32.

59. Deborah Maccoby, *God Made Blind: Isaac Rosenberg, His Life and Poetry* (London: Symposium Press, 1999), p. 144; Parsons (ed.), p. 144.

60. Maccoby, p. 145. See further Gordon Bottomley (ed.), *Poems by Isaac Rosenberg with a Memoir by Laurence Binyon* (London: Heinemann, 1922), p. 2; Parsons (ed.), p. 182.

61. Rosenberg, 'Rudolph', in Parsons (ed.), p. 281 and pp. 276–83.

62. See Cohen, p. 13: 'David, born on 10 February 1897.'

63. Parsons (ed.), pp. 278, 280, 281.

64. See Rosenberg's letter to Miss Seaton, dated spring 1914, in Parsons (ed.), p. 201.

65. Bryan Cheyette, *Contemporary Jewish Writing in Britain and Ireland: An Anthology*

(London: Peter Halban, 1988), p. lviii: 'The patriarchal representations and received images of an apologetic Anglo-Jewry.'

66. Dennis Silk, 'Isaac Rosenberg (1890–1918)', *Judaism* 14:4 (autumn 1965), p. 464 and pp. 462–74; and Thorlief Boman, *Hebrew Thought Compared with Greek Thought* (Philadelphia: Westminster Press, 1960), p. 27.
67. Cohen, p. 140.
68. Christopher Hassall, *Edward Marsh: Patron of the Arts* (London: Longman, 1959), p. 402.
69. Parsons (ed.), pp. xiv, 143.
70. Henry Ellershaw (ed.), *Keats: Poetry and Prose* (1922; Oxford: Clarendon Press, 1960), pp. 110–11. See further note 73.
71. Rosenberg, Letter to Edward Marsh, dated spring 1915, in Parsons (ed.), p. 210.
72. See, for example, 'The Good Morrow' and 'The Sun Rising', in A. J. Smith (ed.), *John Donne: The Complete English Poems* (Harmondsworth: Penguin, 1971), pp. 60, 80.
73. See Rosenberg, 'Emerson', and a letter to Miss Seaton, dated 15 November 1917, in Parsons (ed.), pp. 288 and 265–6, respectively: 'We do not question Keats or Donne or Blake'; 'London may not be the place for poetry to keep healthy in, but Shakespeare did most of his work there, and Donne, Keats, Milton, Blake – I think nearly all our big poets.'
74. Letters to Edward Marsh, dated December 1913, and Miss Seaton, dated 15 November 1917, in Parsons (ed.), pp. 199–200 and 265–6, respectively.
75. Letter to Miss Wright, dated 16 September 1912, in Parsons (ed.), p. 190.
76. Rosenberg, 'Emerson', in Parsons (ed.), pp. 288–9.
77. Parsons (ed.), pp. 302, 205, 151.
78. Rosenberg, 'Creation', in Parsons (ed.), pp. 50–1.
79. Herzl also yoked the old and new together in his Zionist novel *Altneuland [Old-New Land]* (1902). See also Vital, p. 315: 'There developed a powerful trend to socialism within the general context of Zionism.'
80. Parsons (ed.), pp. 293–4, 296, 300–1.
81. Bryan Cheyette, *Constructions of 'The Jew' in English Literature and Society: Racial Representations, 1875–1945* (Cambridge: Cambridge University Press, 1993), pp. 252, 249.
82. T. S. Eliot, *The Complete Poems and Plays of T. S. Eliot* (1969; London: Faber, 1978), pp. 34–5.
83. Cheyette, *Constructions of 'The Jew'*, p. 252.
84. Cohen, pp. 150–1. See also T. S. Eliot, 'Tradition and the Individual Talent', in *Selected Essays* (1932; London: Faber, 1966), pp. 13–22.
85. Eliot, *Selected Essays*, pp. 15, 16, 21.
86. Eliot, *Selected Essays*, p. 13: 'Every nation, every race, has not only its own creative, but its own critical turn of mind.'
87. Ibid., p. 15.
88. Letter to Edward Marsh, dated 24 July 1914, in Parsons (ed.), p. 205.
89. Parsons (ed.), pp. 151, 238.
90. Exodus 20:4–5, in *The Holy Bible* (Oxford: Oxford University Press, 1862); Jacobs, pp. 39–40.
91. Siegfried Sassoon, *Collected Poems 1908–1956* (1961; London: Faber, 1984), p. 175.
92. Letter to Edward Marsh, dated October–November 1915, in Parsons (ed.), pp. 223–4.
93. Parsons (ed.), pp. 224, 181, 198. In a letter to Miss Seaton dated 1910, Rosenberg stated: 'I always enjoyed Shelley and Keats.' In another letter to Miss Seaton, dated December–January 1912–13, Rosenberg said of Blake: 'England has turned out one man second to none who has ever lived.'
94. Rosenberg, 'Art', in Parsons (ed.), p. 293 and pp. 289–97.
95. Hassall, p. 402. See also Parsons (ed.), p. 205.
96. Cheyette, *Constructions of 'The Jew'*, p. 252: 'Bleistein, like all of Eliot's "jews", is a hybrid creature consisting of an originary "savage" primitivism beneath a cosmopolitan, moneyed modernity.' See also Goldwin Smith, 'The Jewish Question', *The Nineteenth Century* X (1881), pp. 494–515, in Englander (ed.),

pp. 253–61. Within the space of a few pages, Smith states that Jews (in 1881) partake of a 'strange and savage rite' while being members 'of a cosmopolitan race'.

97. Letter to Gordon Bottomley, dated 12 June 1916, in Parsons (ed.), p. 236.
98. Letter to Ruth Löwy, dated October 1912, in Parsons (ed.), pp. 193–4.
99. See further Chapter 3.
100. Letter to Ruth Löwy, dated October 1912, in Parsons (ed.), pp. 193–4.
101. Letter to Miss Seaton, dated spring 1914, in Parsons (ed.), pp. 200–1.
102. Following the Balfour Declaration, the *Jewish Chronicle* of 9 November 1917 announced that the diasporic Jewish state 'of being a hyphenation' might one day be replaced by Jewish nationhood: see Englander (ed.), p. 306.
103. Silkin, *Out of Battle*, pp. 264–5.
104. See 'The Rime of the Ancient Mariner', in Ernest Hartley Coleridge (ed.), *Coleridge: Poetical Works* (1912; Oxford: Oxford University Press, 1980), pp. 186–209. In a letter to Miss Seaton in 1911, Rosenberg stated that Coleridge was one of his major influences. Referring to 'Kubla Kahn', he explained: 'Here feeling is separated from intellect; our senses are not interfered with by what we know of facts': see Parsons (ed.), p. 183.
105. 'The Slade and Modern Culture', in Parsons (ed.), p. 302.
106. See 'Chronological Summary of Rosenberg's Life', in Parsons (ed.), p. xiii: '1915 April: "Youth" printed at Narodiczky's, from type set (?) by Reuben Cohen.'
107. Parsons (ed.), pp. 101, 219, 225.
108. Colin Holmes, *Anti-Semitism in British Society* (London: Edward Arnold, 1979), pp. 68, 79, 17, 16.
109. Englander (ed.), p. 296.
110. Holmes, p. 42.
111. Rosenberg, 'The Flea', in Parsons (ed.), p. 76.
112. Parsons (ed.), pp. 68, 227. Rosenberg wrote to Sidney Schiff, in a letter dated 'late December 1915': 'I feel as if I were casting my coat, I mean, like a snake or butterfly.' See further Chapter 7 in this volume.
113. Rosenberg, 'Louse Hunting', in Parsons (ed.), p. 108.
114. For a wide-ranging analysis of the traditional Christian association of Jews with the Devil, see Joshua Trachtenberg, *The Devil and the Jews* (Jerusalem: The Jewish Publication Society, 1943).
115. Simon Featherstone, 'Isaac Rosenberg, Israel Zangwill and Jewish Culture', in Featherstone (ed.), p. 79 and pp. 72–81.
116. Paul Fussell, *The Great War and Modern Memory* (New York: Oxford University Press, 1975), p. 250; 'Break of Day in the Trenches', in Parsons (ed.), pp. 103–4.
117. Rosenberg, 'The Flea', in Parsons (ed.), p. 76.
118. For example, Goldwin Smith asserted in 'The Jewish Question', *The Nineteenth Century* X (1881), pp. 494–515: '[The Jew is] a member of a cosmopolitan race': see Englander (ed.), p. 259 and pp. 253–61. See further Cheyette, *Constructions of 'The Jew'*, p. 252.
119. Parsons (ed.), pp. 219, 222, 227, 223.
120. Berkowitz, pp. 2, 112, 78.
121. Maccoby, p. 123.

3

Siegfried Sassoon: Rebellion and Nostalgia

Unlike Isaac Rosenberg, Siegfried Sassoon (1886–1967) did not write poetry orientated towards a Jewish future. Rather, he located his Jewishness in the Old Testament past. Indeed, it is clear from Sassoon's First World War poetry and diaries that he related to his own sense of Jewishness as it impacted on him through traces of several prevalent Jewish discourses, such as Old Testament prophecy and an orientalism exoticising the Middle East. Consequently, this chapter considers Sassoon's poems of protest against the First World War in the context of such discourses. Though Sassoon was never a practising Jew, I argue here that he can be relevantly read in a hybrid Anglo-Jewish context. Christian discourses which set Jewish civilisation in the biblical past and Middle East were, after all, particularly useable by an Anglican poet whose paternal Jewish ancestors hailed from Baghdad.[1]

Moreover, I suggest that Sassoon internalised Georgian antisemitism to such an extent that he was keen to distance himself from modern Jewry. Indeed, he deployed traces of antisemitic discourse to describe his private income as 'semitic sovereigns'[2] and to remark on 'awful conversations in [a] Pullman carriage by Jew profiteers'.[3] Yet Sassoon also understood that he was perceived by Gentiles as similarly 'semitic'.[4] As he writes in 'Letter to Robert Graves' (1918):[5]

> Yes, you can touch my Banker when you need him.
> Why keep a Jewish friend unless you bleed him?

Thus, a tension appears in Sassoon's war poetry between 'the dominant Christian and imperialist ideologies of his time',[6] which constructed Jews as Other, and the biblically imagined past of the poet's ancestors, by which he contests such ideologies.

Finally, I discuss Sassoon's post-war prose memoirs as *ex post facto* strategies to harmonise the tensions of his war poetry through 'nostalgic reminiscence'[7] of rebellion, youth and the Old Testament.

THE POETRY OF SIEGFRIED SASSOON

Raised by his mother in the Church of England, Sassoon repeatedly refers to Christ in his poetry. Several of Sassoon's Great War poems have overtly Christian titles, such as 'The Redeemer' (1915–16) (with its reiterated reference to an archetypal 'English' soldier: 'I say that he was Christ'), 'The Prince of Wounds' (1915), 'Christ and the Soldier' (1916) (with its later note that, being a Christian, Sassoon has chosen to become a 'quite unpractising Christian') and 'Golgotha' (1916).[8] Comparable references are conspicuous in Sassoon's diaries. For example:

> In all the noblest passages and the noblest strains of horns and violins [in the music of Elgar] I shut my eyes, seeing on the darkness a shape always the same – in spite of myself – the suffering mortal figure on a cross, but the face is my own.[9]

Here Sassoon empathises with Christianity's noblest Jew (Christ's 'face is my own'), while reassuring himself that such unforced association confirms his Christian status (seeing the cross 'in spite of myself'). The possibility that Sassoon relates to Christ as a fellow 'suffering' Jew is passed over in silence.

By contrast, Sassoon identifies modern Jews with money and juxtaposes them with Christ's spirituality. For example, 'Lieutenant X is a nasty, cheap thing. A cheap-gilt Jew. Why are such Jews born, when the soul of Jesus was so beautiful? *He* saw the flowers and the stars; but they see only greasy banknotes.'[10]

Interestingly, this outburst is followed by a quotation from George Moore's *The Brook Kerith* (1916) about biblical Jews: 'He began to speak to Joseph of God.' The Moore citation indicates that Sassoon does not wish to jettison his Jewish connection with the Old Testament. Indeed, it suggests a certain empathy with Joseph, a boy lost to his father, Jacob, and in diaspora. Similarly, Sassoon's own father, Alfred, died when the poet was a boy.[11] As he writes of his adolescence in *The Weald of Youth* (1942): '[My] actual resemblance was nearer to Joseph in the Old Testament legend.'[12]

Thus, Sassoon appears to espouse a biblically imagined ancestral Jewishness, while distancing himself from contemporary Jews. Further, he resembles Joseph in affiliating with the dominant culture surrounding him. Sassoon identifies with England as the Israelite Joseph did with Egypt.[13]

Sassoon's attitude to music is also racially inflected. In his war diaries, Sassoon dismisses the German-Jewish composer Felix Mendelssohn-Bartholdy as 'futile'. Further, the diaries link the concept of futility with femininity ('the futile chatter of women'), emotion and madness: 'I suppose all this "emotional experience" (futile phrase) is of value. But it leads nowhere now (but to madness).'[14] Thus German-Jewish music is dismissed, together with women and 'emotional experience', as valueless and neurotic ('madness').[15] Of course, rejecting German music during the First World War was a nationalistic desideratum. Nonetheless, for a repressed (non-practising) homosexual with a famous Jewish surname, this three-pronged repudiation – of feminine, German-Jewish and emotional experience – smacks of 'self-hatred'.[16] Interestingly, it also bears traces of a wider racialised discourse about Jewish music. Notoriously, Richard Wagner castigated Jewish composers. Sassoon may have known of Wagner's *Judaism in Music* (1850), which was translated into English in the 1890s.[17] Indeed, his mother had named him Siegfried after a character from the composer's *Der Ring des Nibelungen* tetralogy.[18] *Judaism in Music* categorised Mendelssohn's work as 'a confusion of styles, as a chaotic formalism – cold, indifferent and sterile – without genuine feeling or passion'. The German-Jewish composer Giacomo Meyerbeer was similarly dismissed for his 'trivial, sensational effects'. In Wagner's view, Jews were synonymous with 'the worthlessness [*Nichtswürdigkeit*] of the modern world'.[19] No music escapes this discourse of racial assessment. On a similar note, Sassoon remarks that works by the Austrian-Jewish composer Arnold Schönberg were received in London 'with mystified curiosity and hostility'.[20]

During the Great War, Sassoon deploys traces of this racialised musical discourse to emphasise his affiliation with English nationalism. In his praise of Elgar's music, the poet remarks: 'Elgar always moves me deeply, because his is the melody of an average Englishman (and I suppose I am more or less the same).'[21] National identity is expressed in music. An 'average Englishman' is instinctively moved by the nation's greatest composer, as a foreigner could not be. However, Sassoon's tentative parenthesis – '(and I suppose I am more or less the same)' – hints at an Anglo-Jewish tension between otherness and affiliation *vis-à-vis* such nationalism.

In 1937, Sassoon again alludes to such tension in his famous foreword to *The Collected Works of Isaac Rosenberg*.[22] However, he describes it as 'a fruitful fusion between English and Hebrew culture'. Through traces of a discourse of 'Hebrew' antiquity, Sassoon neutralises Anglo-Jewish tension. He extols what is 'biblical and prophetic' in Rosenberg's verse, and so consigns Rosenberg to the past. This is not Rosenberg's Jewish past of east London and the First World War, but an exoticised 'Hebrew' past. Sassoon praises 'a poignant and nostalgic quality' in Rosenberg's poetry, as if it were already closer to the past than the present when it was written and, therefore, always inhabited an ancient time.

To be sure, such a stance was hardly uncommon among Anglo-Jewish writers. As Linda Zatlin remarks, Victorian Anglo-Jewish novelists tended to 'distance the Jew, showing him not in nineteenth-century England but in Egypt or medieval Spain'.[23] Like Sassoon, Benjamin Disraeli was at pains to emphasise that the past was Hebraic, and the Hebraic was past. A Protestant Jew, Disraeli located Judaism in Protestant memory as the religion of an 'ancient race', and Protestantism in a Jewish trajectory as the religion 'which embalms the memory of my race'.[24] In short, he deployed traces of a discourse which set English Protestantism firmly in the present, and its Judaic roots ineradicably in the past. Politically and culturally, as prime minister and novelist, Disraeli promoted the vision of a conservative and stable England which respected the past, and consequently the Hebraic roots of Christianity. As he wrote in his biography of Lord George Bentinck (1852):

> Since the great revolt of the Celts against the first and second testament, at the close of the last century, France has been alternately in a state of collapse or convulsion. Throughout the awful trials of the last sixty years, England, notwithstanding her deficient and meagre theology, has always remembered Sion.[25]

In this vision of a Protestant England with Hebraic memories, Disraeli posits Catholic France as Other. Whereas England has been blessed with stability for remembering its roots in 'Sion', France has been punished with 'collapse or convulsion' for failing to do so. Thus Disraeli displaces the stigma of Christianity's traditional outcast from the Jew to the French Catholic. Judaism is replaced by continental Catholicism as England's Other.

Interestingly, Sassoon's diaries carry traces of this theologico-nationalist discourse. Posted to France in 1916, Siegfried notes 'a curio-shop full of RC rubbish'.[26] 'RC' was an army abbreviation for Roman Catholic, which was stamped on soldiers' identity discs when appropriate. Sassoon's use of the acronym here may also suggest that nationalistic Britons could unselfconsciously dismiss Roman Catholicism. Its very foreignness (Roman curios in France) seems to justify damning it. Unlike Judaism, Catholicism cannot be allied with English Protestantism. Judaism supplies Protestantism's roots, but Catholicism remains 'rubbish' consigned to the dustbin of theological history.

Similarly, the poem 'Ancestors' (1915)[27] focuses on the influence of a Jewish past[28] on Sassoon's Protestant present:

> Behold these jewelled, merchant Ancestors,
> Foregathered in some chancellery of death;
> Calm, provident, discreet, they stroke their beards
> And move their faces slowly in the gloom,
> And barter monstrous wealth with speech subdued,
> Lustreless eyes and acquiescent lids.
>
> And oft in pauses of their conference
> They listen to the measured breath of night's
> Hushed sweep of wind aloft the swaying trees
> In dimly gesturing gardens; then a voice
> Climbs with clear mortal song half-sad for heaven.
>
> A silent-footed message flits and brings
> The ghostly Sultan from his glimmering halls;
> A shadow at the window, turbaned, vast,
> He leans; and, pondering the sweet influence
> That steals around him in remembered flowers,
> Hears the frail music wind along the slopes,
> Put forth, and fade across the whispering sea.

Though possessing 'monstrous wealth', these 'jewelled' (and *Jewish*) 'merchant Ancestors' are also wise and prophetic ('Calm, provident, discreet, they stroke their beards'). Their speech is 'subdued'; and if one hears *sub-jewed*, one might imagine that part of their discretion is to suppress their Jewishness, to be wise enough to avoid conspicuous, full-voiced Jewish speech.[29] Indeed, these ancestors go further. They avoid full-blooded life. In their 'chancellery of death', they inhabit an incorporeal world where life is 'hushed', 'ghostly' and 'frail'. Even Jewish gesticulation,[30] suggested by 'the swaying trees / In dimly gesturing gardens', is viewed as always already in the past. As Sassoon remarks two decades later, 'It is significant that I have always – and increasingly – seen and felt the present as material for memories – I am as it were *living in the past already'.*[31]

This *is* significant in the light of Sassoon's attachment to the past in his First World War poetry, with its repeated references to ghosts; for example: 'Two Hundred Years After' (1916) ('*he'd* seen soldiers pass along that hill; / "Poor silent things, they were the English dead"'), 'Survivors' (1917) ('They'll soon forget their haunted nights; their cowed / Subjection to the ghosts of friends') and 'Concert Party' (1918) ('Silent, I watch the shadowy mass of soldiers').[32] Similarly, 'Ancestors' boasts a number of ghostly presences:

> A silent-footed message flits and brings
> The ghostly Sultan from his glimmering halls.

Such presences are 'silent' phantoms, like the Jewish past in the poet's Protestant present: 'A shadow at the window', 'remembered flowers', 'night's / Hushed sweep of wind'. Exoticised thus, Sassoon's Jewish forebears are distanced and contained in what Edward Said has termed an 'orientalist' discourse.[33]

Yet 'Ancestors' also relates to Sassoon's racially perceived Jewish 'half'.[34] Indeed, the sinister implication of words such as 'monstrous', 'shadow' and 'whisperings' suggests traces of contemporary antisemitic discourse relating to Jewish conspiracy. For example, Sassoon remarks that the literary editor T. W. H. Crosland invited the poet to dine 'in a grating undertone which produced an impression that the lunch was a sort of conspiratorial assignation'.[35] Similarly in T. S. Eliot's 'Gerontion'[36] (1920), the whispering appears treacherous: 'flowering judas, / To be eaten, to be divided, to be drunk / Among whispers; by Mr Silvero'. Tellingly, 'judas' harks back to the presence of 'the jew' in the poem:

My house is a decayed house,
And the jew squats on the window sill, the owner.

In 'Sweeney Among the Nightingales'[37] (1920), Eliot strikingly dramatises suspicions directed at the Jewish 'Rachel *née* Rabinovitch':

She and the lady in the cape
Are suspect, thought to be in league.

Shadowy, conspiratorial exchanges take place:

The host with someone indistinct
Converses at the door apart.

As Anthony Julius remarks, 'The poem creates suspicion, without delivering certainty.'[38]

Sassoon gives vent to comparable suspicions towards contemporary Jews. En route for Palestine in February 1918, the poet observes 'Jews (of the Battalion here awaiting embarkation)' mounting a show to entertain the troops. In the concert marquee, the few lights make 'a zany-show of leaping shadows and swaying whiteness'. Sassoon records:

A little man jumps into the light, and does some posturing, chin out, with his curved Hebrew beak coming down to the thin-lipped mouth. Another little Jew whispered to me (I was inside the tent by then) 'That's Sid Whelan – the other's his brother Albert' – evidently expecting me to be thrilled. Probably well-known London comedians.[39]

Here, the 'leaping shadows and swaying whiteness' suggest traces of a discourse constructing the racial indeterminacy of Jews, between 'savage' black and 'cosmopolitan' white otherness.[40] Further, Georgian Jews are presented as an eccentric demi-monde ('a zany-show', 'comedians'), far from the dominant culture with which Sassoon affiliates. A 'little Jew' whispers to Sassoon ('evidently expecting me to be thrilled'), perhaps because he considers the man to be Jewish. After all, as John Stuart Roberts remarks, 'a look in the mirror would have revealed the exotic physical characteristics he [Sassoon] shared with his forebears'.[41]

Sassoon condescends towards conspiratorial, whispering 'little' Jews, but he is nevertheless prepared to be 'inside the tent'[42] with them. Imagining himself as a nomadic Hebrew en route to the Holy Land pleases the poet. By contrast, he views working-class London Jews as wholly Other.

To be sure, Sassoon's characterisation of London Jews is preceded and largely determined by a decades-old discourse of urban degeneration. As Daniel Pick observes, articles with titles such as 'Degeneration amongst Londoners' had appeared in the medical journal *The Lancet* since the 1880s.[43] Further, both liberalism and Toryism 'intersected in their common idealisation of Nature, their dream of rural regeneration and their rejection of the supposed rootlessness of the city'.[44] Thus Sassoon's profession of ignorance concerning 'probably well-known London comedians' may also be a strategy for distancing himself from urban (and Jewish) 'rootlessness'. Affiliating with the rural and the rooted, Sassoon's self-definition precludes both urban and Jewish degeneration.

Certainly, contemporaneous discourses about the Jewish East End categorised it as a degenerate place. As Juliet Steyn remarks:

> T. H. Huxley compared East Londoners with primitive tribes, writing that 'the Polynesian savage in his most primitive condition' was not 'so savage, so unclean, so irreclaimable as the tenant of a tenement in an East London slum'.[45]

Further, degeneracy and criminal behaviour were spoken of together. For example, the *Encyclopaedia Britannica* (1910–11) noted: 'The high incidence of physical, mental, moral anomalies in the criminal, is "due partly to degeneration, partly to atavism. The criminal is a special type of the human race, standing midway between the lunatic and the savage".'[46] Thus early twentieth-century sociological and medical discourse linked degeneration and criminality with East End Jews.

Similarly, Modernist art was tarred with the brush of Jewish and foreign degeneracy.[47] As Sassoon notes in 1921, after attending a London concert with his homosexual lover Gabriel Atkin: 'G represents green chartreuse and Epstein sculpture. Mother is GF Watts[48] and holy communion. They can't be mixed.'[49] Apparently, the poet judges Modernist art, homosexuality and Jewishness ('Epstein'[50]) acceptable within London's degenerate – and decadent

– atmosphere ('green chartreuse'), but incompatible with Christian England ('Mother is GF Watts and holy communion'). Sassoon's supposition that Jewishness and Englishness 'can't be mixed' leaves him abandoned to an existential Anglo-Jewish tension. It also suggests the uses to which a sense of *'living in the past already'* might be put in evading such 'continuous active tension'.[51]

'Ancient History'[52] (1918), for instance, constructs Jewishness in a biblical past:

> Adam, a brown old vulture in the rain,
> Shivered below his wind-whipped olive-trees;
> Huddling sharp chin on scarred and scraggy knees,
> He moaned and mumbled to his darkening brain;
> *'He was the grandest of them all – was Cain!*
> 'A lion laired in the hills, that none could tire;
> 'Swift as a stag; a stallion of the plain,
> 'Hungry and fierce with deeds of huge desire.'
>
> Grimly he thought of Abel, soft and fair –
> A lover with disaster in his face,
> And scarlet blossom twisted in bright hair.
> 'Afraid to fight; was murder more disgrace? ...
> *'God always hated Cain'*... He bowed his head –
> The gaunt wild man whose lovely sons were dead.

The sonnet depicts Cain as an Hebraic hero: *'He was the grandest of them all.'* Like the soldier-poet Sassoon, Cain is a killer who is not 'Afraid to fight'. His virility ('deeds of huge desire') is as natural as his strength ('A lion') and grace ('Swift as a stag; a stallion of the plain'). Significantly, Sassoon's Cain exists within the past of what is already the Old Testament of 'Ancient History': he is 'dead'. Perhaps for this reason, Sassoon feels comfortable affiliating with his Jewish power. By contrast, Abel is effeminate and, implicitly, homosexual: 'Abel, soft and fair – / A lover with disaster in his face, / And scarlet blossom twisted in bright hair.'

Sassoon's association of sexual 'disaster' with Abel suggests that he cannot idealise his own queerness through nostalgia. Gay sexuality is both a contemporary and biblical 'disgrace'. Consequently, Sassoon turns to Cain as a role model, since the latter's Hebrew strength killed the 'soft' homosexuality which Sassoon perceives as 'lovely' but an irredeemable 'disaster'.

'Ancient History' sets Old Testament virility in the landscape of the 'Judean hills'.[53] Similarly, 'The Fathers'[54] (1917) relates ancestral sexual prowess to the Middle East:

> Snug at the club two fathers sat,
> Gross, goggle-eyed, and full of chat.
> One of them said: 'My eldest lad
> Writes cheery letters from Bagdad.
> But Arthur's getting all the fun
> At Arras with his nine-inch gun.'
>
> 'Yes,' wheezed the other, 'that's the luck!
> My boy's quite broken-hearted, stuck
> In England training all this year.
> Still, if there's truth in what we hear,
> The Huns intend to ask for more
>   Before they bolt across the Rhine.'
> I watched them toddle through the door –
>   Those impotent old friends of mine.

Sassoon's reference to 'Bagdad' may have autobiographical significance,[55] implying that a martial and virile past was once enjoyed by the poet's Middle Eastern ancestors. The 'eldest lad' in 'Bagdad' is associated here with 'Arthur's' phallic 'nine-inch gun' placed 'at Arras', with its homoerotic promise of 'fun'. By contrast, the narrator remains as 'impotent' as his 'friends' in Georgian England. Thus, the poem satirises the rhetoric of English 'fathers' who neither fight nor fornicate, but leave those activities to their faraway sons ('lad', 'boy's'). War and sexuality are located among young soldiers and, by autobiographical implication, in Sassoon's Jewish ancestral past ('Bagdad').

Several studies have already appeared detailing the homo-eroticism of Sassoon's First World War poetry.[56] Though we are primarily concerned with the impact of the poet's Jewishness on his Great War verse, Sassoon's queerness is also pertinent here. Certainly, Sassoon socialised within a gay circle which included Oscar Wilde's friend Robbie Ross and the musicologist Edward Dent. It was probably Dent who introduced Sassoon to the novelist E. M. Forster and Cambridge University librarian Theo Bartholomew, fellow members of a group of gay intellectuals.[57] Clearly, Sassoon found support among gay men.[58] Unlike Jews, to whom his diaries referred with opprobrium as quite Other to English Christian gentlemen, gays offered the idealism of sexually repressed camaraderie within nationally acceptable parameters. As Paul Fussell notes, the First World War sanctioned affections for 'beautiful suffering lads' in language which was 'more overt than ever before'.[59]

Moreover, Sassoon may be said to affiliate with what Alan Sinfield terms gay 'ethnicity'. Sinfield contends that 'gay men have understood themselves on the model of ethnicity'.[60] In Sinfield's sense, Sassoon's chosen wartime 'ethnicity' was non-practising homosexuality. Such gay 'ethnicity' differed from its Jewish counterpart during the First World War, since British gay men remained part of the dominant nationalist culture despite their difference. So long as their homosexuality was 'silenced, invisible, discreet',[61] they would not be stigmatised as Other.

Sassoon voices an idealised affiliation with 'soldier boys'[62] in several poems.[63] The narrator of 'Sick Leave' (1917),[64] for example, dreams of dead combatants asking:

> 'When are you going out to them again?
> Are they not still your brothers through our blood?'

These lines articulate affiliation with dead soldiers through the metaphor of ethnicity ('brothers through our blood'). However, the blood brothers evoked are ghosts:

> Out of the gloom they gather about my bed.
> They whisper in my heart; their thoughts are mine.

Indeed, 'the gloom' here recalls the spectral atmosphere of 'Ancestors',[65] where Jewish family phantoms similarly 'move their faces slowly in the gloom'. Imagining homoeroticism as ethnicity, Sassoon sets his 'brothers' in the past alongside the 'Hebrew'[66] family of 'Ancestors'. Such distancing of both queerness and Jewishness *'in the past already'*[67] suggests suppression of minority otherness in the present.

In 'The Poet as Hero' (1916),[68] Sassoon again refers to dead soldiers. However, here he evokes the Old Testament to protest against 'the dominant Christian and imperialist ideologies of his time':[69]

You've heard me, scornful, harsh, and discontented,
Mocking and loathing War: you've asked me why
Of my old, silly sweetness I've repented –
My ecstasies changed to an ugly cry.

You are aware that once I sought the Grail,
Riding in armour bright, serene and strong;
And it was told that through my infant wail
There rose immortal semblances of song.

But now I've said good-bye to Galahad,
And am no more the knight of dreams and show;
For lust and senseless hatred make me glad,
And my killed friends are with me where I go.
Wound for red wound I burn to smite their wrongs;
And there is absolution in my songs.

What appear to be 'ugly' adjectives in the poem's opening lines ('scornful, harsh, and discontented, / Mocking and loathing') are righteously deployed against the dominant culture's false ideals. Myths of Christian knights, such as 'Galahad', are demystified and revealed as lies ('the knight of dreams and show'). Christianity and Victorian images of medieval combat ('the Grail, / Riding in armour') are presented as no more than an 'infant wail' in the face of trench warfare ('killed friends'). Indeed, 'The Poet as Hero' translates what the dominant Christian culture considers negative Old Testament vengeance[70] into positive moral energy: 'Wound for red wound I burn to smite their wrongs.' Such vengeance becomes one with the prophetic 'hatred' that makes the narrator 'glad' because it is righteous. Framed as Other to Christian and chivalric 'dreams and show', Old Testament language articulates Judaic justice. Through traces of a discourse relating to the Hebrew Bible, Sassoon finds the means to challenge dominant ideologies concerning war.

It is possible that the relative spontaneity of life during the First World War facilitated Sassoon's radical use of the Old Testament in the service of contemporary protest. As Sassoon writes in *Memoirs of a Fox-Hunting Man*:

We had averaged four miles a day, and it was now after ten; a dark, still night, with a little rain at times. Men, transport horses, officers' chargers, limbers, and field-kitchens (known as 'the cookers') were unloaded. All this took two hours. We had some tea ... If I could taste that tea out of the dixies now I should write it all very much as it was. Living spontaneity would be revived by that tea, the taste of which cannot be recovered by any effort of memory.[71]

Such 'living spontaneity' may have helped Sassoon to fulfil his ambition to burst through 'intellectual and emotional suppression' and write 'a tremendous poem full of prophetic sublimity'.[72] Freer from 'suppression' in the French trenches than in England, Sassoon produced verse which deployed the language of the Old Testament as a tool for rebellion in the present.

Indeed, Sassoon's satirical poems protest against continuation of the war precisely by challenging 'Christian and imperialist ideologies'. For example, 'They' (1916)[73] suggests that crusader rhetoric is rooted in hostility to non-Christians and Middle Eastern peoples. Because of his traumatic experiences in the trenches and the fact that his patrilineal ancestors were Mesopotamian Jews, the poet rejects the ideology of a nationalist, racial and religious war as inadequate to his specific, alienated situation:

> The Bishop tells us: 'When the boys come back
> They will not be the same; for they'll have fought
> In a just cause: they lead the last attack
> On Anti-Christ: their comrades' blood has bought
> New right to breed an honourable race,
> They have challenged Death and dared him face to face.'
>
> 'We're none of us the same!' the boys reply.
> 'For George lost both his legs; and Bill's stone blind;
> 'Poor Jim's shot through the lungs and like to die;
> 'And Bert's gone syphilitic; you'll not find
> 'A chap that's served that hasn't found *some* change.'
> And the Bishop said: 'The ways of God are strange!'

The 'us' addressed here is presumed by 'the Bishop' to be affiliated religiously, racially ('an honourable race') and nationally ('they'll have fought / In a just cause') in a crusade against 'Anti-Christ'.[74] Indeed, 'They' echoes contemporary First World War sermons. For example, the Bishop of London informed his congregation at

Westminster Abbey in 1915 that they were, 'banded in a great crusade – we cannot deny it – to kill Germans: to kill them, not for the sake of killing, but to save the world'.[75]

As the military campaign to conquer Jerusalem gained pace with the first battle of Gaza in March 1917, such crusader rhetoric became more common.[76] However, neither the ideology nor the history of Christian crusades inspired Sassoon. As the second stanza of 'They' individualises the soldiers, so it reveals Church rhetoric to be comically inadequate to the savage reality of the war. Indeed, 'We're none of us the same!' insists on an 'ungraspable'[77] self which the delimiting rhetoric of race, nation and religion is unable to express. Like Rosenberg, Sassoon refuses rhetorical boundaries to identity in his war poems. The 'us' Sassoon champions is universal, rather than nationalist and Christian.

Interestingly, Sassoon refers to 'They' as 'my "syphilitic" poem'.[78] He is, of course, alluding to the phrase 'Bert's gone syphilitic'. This reference to venereal disease was considered a daring use of 'non-poetic language'[79] at the time, and consequently attracted critical attention to the poem. In October 1917, Sassoon wrote to Robert Graves, 'The *Nation* quoted my "syphilitic" poem in an article on "Venus and Mars" last Saturday.'[80] Clearly, the *Nation* associated Sassoon with a satirical anti-war poem which mentioned disease. Further, that disease was related to Jews in 'a detailed medical literature' of the time.[81] As Sander Gilman argues, 'the view of the Jew as syphilitic was not limited to the anti-Semitic fringe'. Indeed, 'the Jew in European science and popular thought was closely related to the spread and incidence of syphilis'.[82] Rupert Brooke, for instance, famous for his nationalistic First World War poem 'The Soldier' (1914),[83] expressed a conventional antisemitic linkage of Jews with syphilis when he wrote to James Strachey in 1912: 'She'll be ripe for anybody. But not for you, dear Boy. Some rather small & shiny man, probably syphilitic & certainly a Jew.'[84]

Further, Jews were not considered sick simply for being 'syphilitic'. Gilman notes that 'Jews [– perceived] as the essential "moderns" – were at special risk as hysterics'.[85] Thus, when Sassoon was admitted to a 'convalescent home for neurasthenics at Craiglockhart' on 19 July 1917, the popular stereotype became useable. On 30 July Sassoon's war statement, in which he protested against the continuation of the fighting, was read in Parliament by the pacifist MP H. B. Lees-Smith, and subsequently reported in the press. It was generally perceived as unpatriotic, and popular broadsheets such as the *Daily Chronicle* 'concentrated on Sassoon's family background'; that is, a 'potted history of the Sassoon clan'. His mother's Gentile ancestry was largely ignored, as was the fact 'that a prominent member of that clan, Sir Philip Sassoon, was on the staff of the British Army in France'. Traces of antisemitic discourse were deployed to explain Sassoon's behaviour. Although awarded the Military Cross 'for conspicuous gallantry' in May 1916, Sassoon was readily associated with neurotic, syphilitic, unpatriotic – in short, Jewish – behaviour.[86]

Thus, it appears significant that Sassoon presents himself in fictionalised autobiographies as calm and physically fit. In *The Weald of Youth*, for example, Sassoon maintains that 'Reynardism' is beneficial to his 'character and constitution'.[87] Sport and physical activity signify affiliation with England. As Juliet Steyn notes: 'Healthy bodies were perceived as a contribution to the well-being of the nation and a sign of patriotism.'[88] Indeed, somatically expressed patriotism serves to distance Sassoon from Jewish otherness, which he proceeds to project onto degenerate 'London' Jews and 'Jew profiteers'.[89] Sport helps Sassoon keep fears of Jewish degeneration at bay. He notes in his First World War diaries: 'From what I've seen of him [Bunny Tattersall, whose leg had just been amputated], he seemed the sort that needs sport and activity to keep him from going wrong. *Now* he will probably end with DT like his father.'[90]

Significantly, sport has stopped Bunny 'going wrong' like his 'father'. Henceforth, he faces a future of *delirium tremens* ('DT'). Sassoon's belief that Bunny will probably follow his father's descent into degenerate alcoholism echoes contemporary scientific thought on the subject. According to Daniel Pick, alcoholism was considered to be 'not only a cause but also an effect in a chain of degeneration. The individual might be born with a kind of inherited profligacy.'[91]

Sassoon may well be reflecting on himself and his own (Jewish) father in this diary entry. On 28 April 1918, he tellingly confesses: 'Reading through these notes of the past two months, I find, as usual, that they represent my self.'[92] Feasibly, Sassoon advocates morally beneficial 'sport and activity' in order not to go 'wrong' like his father Alfred, a Jew he could readily associate with syphilitic degeneration due to Alfred's supposed dalliance with the French-Jewish actress Sarah Bernhardt, herself commonly represented as syphilitic.[93]

Concerns about congenital Jewish syphilis and degeneracy are pertinent. For example, Sassoon records soldiers who go 'into the dark city to look for harlots', and juxtaposes such behaviour with his own: 'Alone in my room; looking out of a balconied window at the town, with few lights, and the moon and silver drifts of cloud going eastward; and the railway station looming romantic as old Baghdad.'[94]

Here, Sassoon evokes a sanitised Jewish ancestry ('romantic as old Baghdad'). Rather than associating Jewishness with syphilis, the poet sets it in a chaste ('moon') and 'romantic' past. Significantly, the present is similarly sexless. Since this gay Anglo-Jew is 'alone', he is clearly not engaged in potentially syphilitic sex.

By contrast, Sassoon links syphilis with Gentiles in dominant social positions. For example, he wonders: 'When will someone write the true life of Lord Kitchener, Britain's syphilitic hero?' Sassoon's diary records a claim that the former Chief of Staff in South Africa 'imported fifteen well-known harlots from London to Pretoria' during the Boer War.[95] By accusing an iconic authority in the British army of infecting officers, Sassoon transfers accusations of (congenital Jewish) syphilis back to the British establishment. In doing so, he is defending himself against such accusations by de-Judaising the discourse of venereal disease, and exorcising fears of (congenital Jewish) degeneracy.

Naturally enough, Sassoon affiliates with a masculine Jewish past associated with his dead father. Considering that past, he seeks support from older men whom he often imagines as ancient Hebrews. Following Max Beerbohm's death, for example, Sassoon describes him as 'spectacled, skull-capped, and long-white-bearded', and a 'veteran exile' who entertained 'with ironic recordings of the contemporary scene'.[96] Other father figures include Robbie Ross ('seventeen years my senior')[97] and Thomas Hardy, the latter venerated as a 'grim, wise'[98] patriarch. Thus Sassoon portrays Beerbohm, Ross and Hardy as different versions of a biblically imagined Jewish father.

Further, Sassoon's decision to protest against continuation of the First World War owes something to this paternal affiliation. In a diary entry for May 1917, Sassoon decides to 'make some protest against the War'. He notes on the same page: 'Hardy is merely "an unpleasant writer", as my own mother would say.'[99] Apparently, Sassoon's affiliation with Hardy as a biblically prophetic father figure spurs him to protest in a 'grim, wise' frame of mind, while he condemns his mother's dismissal of the man as 'merely "an unpleasant writer"'. Indeed, Sassoon depicts his mother as wholly Other to both himself and this 'unpleasant' father figure.

Moreover, it is in the context of a discussion about the Church of England that Sassoon decides to make his protest.[100] Evidently, Sassoon associates his mother with both the Anglican Church and its support for the First World War. Theresa Thornycroft was, indeed, a 'High Church'[101] patriot. Sassoon's 'mother's militarism, which he compared to that of Churchill, made it very difficult for him to get on with her'.[102] Consequently, Sassoon's paternal affiliation helps the poet to protest simultaneously against a Church-supported war and his Christian mother.

Certainly, in poems such as 'Glory of Women' and 'Their Frailty' (both 1917),[103] Sassoon focuses his ire on Christian women. The former verse reprises the theme of misplaced chivalric credence evident in 'The Poet as Hero':

> You love us when we're heroes, home on leave,
> Or wounded in a mentionable place.
> You worship decorations; you believe
> That chivalry redeems the war's disgrace.
> You make us shells. You listen with delight,
> By tales of dirt and danger fondly thrilled.
> You crown our distant ardours while we fight,
> And mourn our laurelled memories when we're killed.
> You can't believe that British troops 'retire'
> When hell's last horror breaks them, and they run,
> Trampling the terrible corpses – blind with blood.
>   O German mother dreaming by the fire,
> While you are knitting socks to send your son
> His face is trodden deeper in the mud.

Here, responsibility for the continuation of trench warfare is attributed to 'women'. Christian women 'believe / That chivalry redeems'; presumably, through suffering ('When hell's last horror breaks them, and they run, / Trampling the terrible corpses – blind with blood'). Significantly, the sonnet concludes with a 'mother dreaming' of the sort of decent war ('knitting socks') which does not exist. Indeed, the reference to a 'German mother' universalises the shameful gullibility of all nationalistic, Christian mothers ('You can't believe', 'the war's disgrace').

Similarly, 'Their Frailty' targets mothers as culpably implicated in the war's perpetuation. The poem's final stanzas read:

> He's back in France. She loathes the listless strain
>   And peril of his plight,
> Beseeching Heaven to send him home again,
>   She prays for peace each night.
>
> Husbands and sons and lovers; everywhere
>   They die; War bleeds us white.
> Mothers and wives and sweethearts, – they don't care
>   So long as He's all right.

In this instance, 'Mothers' are shown to be concerned solely with the safety of their particular son ('send him home', 'So long as He's all right'). Such selfishness ('they don't care') leads only to more war ('everywhere / They die; War bleeds us white'). Together, 'Their Frailty' and 'Glory of Women' suggest that women's passive nationalism, domesticated Christianity ('Beseeching Heaven to send him home') and selfish concern for only one man – 'He's' rather than 'They' – lend support to the war. Moreover, 'Their Frailty' hints that heterosexual love ('wives and sweethearts, – they don't care') is similarly Other to the all-male heroism of the trenches ('the doomed and prisoned men'). In a protest against women[104] (such as his mother), the Church and First World War nationalism, Sassoon's sympathies appear to be with 'soldier boys'[105] and Old Testament father figures.

At Craiglockhart War Hospital, from July to November 1917, Sassoon continued to draw inspiration from Old Testament texts. Alluding to Psalm 114, he informed Ottoline Morrell: 'The Pentland hills are glorious. I leap on their ridges like a young ram';[106] and to Robbie Ross, he cited Job 39:25: 'I play golf every day and say "Ha ha," among the captains. But in the dusk of day I whet my trusty Waterman and slay them with my songs.'[107]

However, Sassoon's ardour for the Old Testament did not lead him to Zionism. On 11 December, General Allenby entered Jerusalem as its British conqueror.[108] A fortnight later, Sassoon referred to the foreign secretary who gave his name to the declaration committing the British government to support for a Jewish national home: 'Eddie Marsh writes that A. J. Balfour is much interested in my new poems.'[109] Coincidentally or otherwise, within one month Sassoon learnt that he was being sent to Palestine. Possibly, the War Office was shipping this troublesome protester to the embryonic Jewish State in order to marginalise and quieten him.

Once in Palestine, Sassoon's sense of his Old Testament inheritance became more pronounced. In March 1918, he writes of feeling 'like a budding prophet' in 'an Old Testament environment', and describes Palestine as 'a heavenly place'. Decamping in April, he notes: 'It is positive agony to leave these Palestine hills in all their beauty and glory. Here I sit in a flapping tent, close to the main road. The wind is strong, and sand blows everywhere. Nearest tree God knows how far off.'[110]

Sassoon seems to picture himself as an 'Old Testament', nomadic Jew, close to 'God' and 'in a flapping tent'. His sonnet 'In Palestine' (1918)[111] paints a more contemporary picture:

> On the thyme-scented hills
> In the morning and freshness of day
> I heard the voices of rills
> Quickly going their way.
> Warm from the west was the breeze;
> There were wandering bees in the clover;
> Grey were the olive trees;
> And a flight of finches went over.
> On the rock-strewn hills I heard
> The anger of guns that shook
> Echoes along the glen.
> In my heart was the song of a bird,
> And the sorrowless tale of the brook,
> And scorn for the deeds of men.

The last line of the octave – 'And a flight of finches went over' – suggests a movement towards a new place, or perhaps a *going over* to contemporary Palestinian affiliation. This movement can be read as Zionistic: an ingathering of 'wandering' Jews from the West to the East ('Warm from the west was the breeze'). However, the sonnet's final line deploys traces of prophetic discourse ('And scorn for the deeds of men') which retrenches Jewish affiliation within an Old Testament past. Sassoon loved the landscape of 'Judaea', not as a Zionist who would go 'over' to Jewish nationalism, but as a spectator of 'Old Testament pictures'[112] who was accustomed to '*living in the past already'*.[113] Palestine's landscape appealed to Sassoon precisely because he envisaged it, too, as living in past times.

Further, Sassoon's prose volumes of 'nostalgic reminiscence'[114] written after the First World War – *Memoirs of a Fox-Hunting Man* (1928), *Memoirs of an Infantry Officer* (1930), *Sherston's Progress* (1936), *The Old Century* (1938), *The Weald of Youth* (1942) and *Siegfried's Journey* (1945) – transpose this sense of a fixed and ancient Jewish past, rooted in the Bible and a biblical landscape, to English history and an English landscape. For example, *The Old Century* evokes the Kent countryside through the figure of Abraham:

> The ploughed land slopes upward. Marching across it, the sower in his sackcloth apron scoops and scatters the seed from a wooden trug on his left arm, providing my mother with a simple picture, for he has only the brown field and the blue sky behind him. A grand hale-looking man he is, like someone out of the Bible – Abraham, perhaps.[115]

The Old Testament ('Bible – Abraham') determines Sassoon's perceptions of the English scene. Indeed, *The Old Century* features Sassoon's nanny, Mrs Mitchell, as 'a sort of nursery Jehovah': 'She was the Old Testament, and my mother was the New Testament. Much as we loved Mamsy, her personal influence was less powerful than Mrs Mitchell's.'[116] Substituting for Sassoon's dead father, Mrs Mitchell emphasises Hebraism at home ('a sort of nursery Jehovah').

Anglicisation of the Old Testament is evident, too, in such colloquial phrases as 'the exodus' and 'England's green and pleasant land', which Sassoon deploys in *Memoirs of a Fox-Hunting Man*:

> It had not occurred to me that a hole in a fence through which fifty horses have blundered is much the same as an open gate, so far as the exodus of a farmer's cattle is concerned. However, this problem of trespassing by courtesy has existed as long as fox-hunting, and it is not likely to be solved until both the red-coated fraternity and the red-furred carnivorous mammal which they pursue have disappeared from England's green and pleasant land.[117]

Although a common term, 'the exodus' also evokes the Old Testament story of the Jews' establishment of a divinely sanctioned homeland in Canaan.[118] Similarly, 'England's green and pleasant land' refers to Parry's wartime choral song 'Jerusalem' (1916)[119] – based on a poem by Blake – which superimposes Israel's biblical destiny onto England. Together, the phrases discreetly hint at a transposition of Hebraic myth to imperial Britain.

Sassoon was not alone in making such a manoeuvre. The poet inherited a national discourse in which Protestant Britons were wont to speak of themselves as 'a chosen people', and of Britain as 'nothing less than another and a better Israel'.[120] This practice of 'superimposing the language of the Bible on their countrymen's progress' was common among English Puritans as far back as the seventeenth century.[121] For example, Milton wrote in 'Areopagitica' (1644): 'Why else was this nation chosen before any other, that out of her, as out of Sion, should be proclaimed and sounded forth the first tiding and trumpet of reformation to all Europe?'[122]

Tradition sanctioned a Hebrew typology in England. Indeed, followers of nineteenth-century 'British Israelism' identified the British as direct descendants of the lost tribes of Israel.[123] 'For most Victorians', Linda Colley suggests:

> the massive overseas empire which was the fruit of so much successful warfare represented final and conclusive proof of Great Britain's providential destiny. God had entrusted Britons with empire, they believed, so as to further the worldwide spread of the Gospel and as a testimony to their status as a Protestant Israel.[124]

Rudyard Kipling's 'Recessional' (1897) hammers home the point that Britons are God's people, heir to the Jews' special status:

> If drunk with sight of power, we loose
> Wild tongues that have not thee in awe
> Such boasting as the Gentiles use
> Or lesser breeds without the Law –
> Lord God of Hosts, be with us yet,
> Lest we forget – lest we forget![125]

A. F. Walls remarks: 'It took some knowledge of biblical exegesis to pick up the full implications of "Gentiles", "lesser breeds", and "without the Law".' Walls continues: 'Kipling's idea of chosenness involved the application to Britain of a series of images of old

Israel.'[126] Pertinently, Sassoon writes of attending a lecture in 1935 where Kipling spoke 'like a prophet' in comparing 'modern European nations' to 'Old Testament tribes'. Kipling was deploying traces of a time-sanctioned discourse in order to imagine England's imperial future. Sassoon does the same to construct in 'nostalgic'[127] reminiscences an England *'living in the past'*[128] it shares with the Old Testament.

Sassoon did not explicitly acknowledge his Jewishness until he converted to Catholicism at the age of 70. He told Dame Felicitas Corrigan: 'I sometimes surmise that my eastern ancestry is stronger in me than the Thornycrofts. The daemon in me is Jewish.'[129] By associating creativity ('the daemon') with Jewishness, Sassoon is again echoing Kipling. The latter confides in his autobiography, *Something of Myself* (1936):

> My Daemon was with me in the *Jungle Books*, *Kim*, and both Puck books, and good care I took to walk delicately, lest he should withdraw ... *Note here*. When your Daemon is in charge, do not try to think consciously. Drift, wait, and obey.[130]

Something of Myself continues with reflections on Kipling's fountain pen: 'In later years I clung to a slim, smooth, black treasure (Jael was her office name) which I picked up in Jerusalem.'[131]

Kipling's 'black treasure', like Sassoon's 'daemon', has a Jewish provenance ('Jerusalem'). The feminisation of the pen, which Kipling 'picked up' in British Mandate Palestine in 1929, by no means deprives it of power. In Kipling's deployment of antisemitic discourse, Jael symbolizes the Jews. Sensual and seemingly weak ('slim, smooth') – like the Jerusalem pen – Jael was the Old Testament wife of Heber the Kenite who won notoriety by driving a tent-peg through the head of the sleeping Sisera.[132] Thus, the pen may signify hidden power, as well as wealth ('treasure'), beneath a 'black' (with connotations of Jewish non-whiteness[133]) surface.

Jael's blackness also reflects the fundamental ambiguity of 'daemon', a term that since the fourteenth century has borne concurrent inspirational and malignant meanings in English. Kipling clings to a Jewish murderer ('Jael'), effectively a daemon who is both 'an attendant, ministering, or indwelling spirit; a genius' *and* 'an evil spirit; a malignant being of superhuman nature; a devil'.[134] Significantly, Gentile Kipling externalises his 'Daemon' in 'Jael' (the vowels of the words serve to emphasise their synonymity in this context), whereas Sassoon locates his Jewish 'daemon in me'. However, the linguistic double entendre which both writers employ suggests a similar ambivalence towards Jewry as both creative and evil. Thus Sassoon's 'daemon' implies both affiliation with creative Jewish 'ancestry' and negative feelings towards contemporary Jewry.

Interestingly, Sassoon's autobiographical prose often evokes the writer as a contemporary Jewish Other. I am 'a bit of a chameleon', he notes in 1930: 'I adapt my style.'[135] Reflecting on his youthful hunting days, Sassoon remarks, 'While going about with him [the Master of the Atherstone Hunt] I was conscious of being little more than an imitative appurtenance.'[136] Such expressions of unease in England are reminiscent of what Rosenberg calls 'a super-selfconsciousness, a desire not to frustrate expectation'.[137] Eventually, Sassoon's efforts to please lead to a wail of discontent in *The Weald of Youth*: 'Why must I always be adapting my manners – and even my style of speaking – to different sets of people?'[138] By striving for clear social boundaries ('manners', 'style of speaking') within which to feel at ease, Sassoon only confirms his mutability with 'different sets of people'. 'I wanted to be strongly connected with the hunting organism,' he writes, 'a clearly defined world.'[139] Yet Sassoon's attempts to affiliate with the 'clearly defined world' of the hunt merely exaggerate his apprehension of parasitic Jewish otherness *vis-à-vis* 'the hunting organism'. By implication, such otherness extends to his relationship with the national 'organism' imagined in early twentieth-century England.

Significantly, Sassoon also refers to framed pictures. 'Ideal regions of classic achievement' provide boundaries for his uncategorisable ('chameleon') half-Jewish identity. Like a painter in the tradition of 'Italian humanism', Sassoon delimits Jewishness as 'Old Testament pictures'.[140] Such 'pictures' neutralise contemporary Anglo-Jewish tensions by framing Jewishness in a distant Hebraic past.

Indeed, Sassoon's prose memoirs present youth, rebellion and Hebraism as complementary stages of development from the past:

> The inexorable rules of slow-motion reminiscence must be obeyed; the mirror must be kept polished, each pictured episode carefully composed, and all youth's gesticulating volubility and convulsiveness taken for granted or toned down to a harmonious retrospect.[141]

I suggest three closely related readings of the above passage. First: Sassoon's mature ('composed') prose nostalgia ('slow-motion', 'harmonious retrospect') redeems his war poems' youthful spontaneity ('volubility and convulsiveness'). Second: Sassoon's authoritative memoirs ('the inexorable rules' of which 'must be obeyed') bring the rebelliousness evident in his war poems under control. Third: 'harmonious' Christian power is achieved in England by similarly assimilating ('taken for granted or toned down') Old Testament Jewry ('gesticulating volubility and convulsiveness'), and regarding it in 'retrospect' as national and theological history.

Certainly, Sassoon's six volumes of autobiography re-affirm 'the dominant Christian and imperialist ideologies of his time'[142] by linking youth, rebellion and the Old Testament in 'a harmonious retrospect'. Conversely, his 'discontented'[143] Great War protest poems tap into Old Testament discourse precisely to contest such delimiting nationalist perspectives.

NOTES

1. Jean Moorcroft Wilson, *Siegfried Sassoon, The Making of a War Poet* (1998; London: Duckworth, 1999), pp. 29, 8.
2. Letter from Siegfried Sassoon to Robert Graves, undated but *c*.1923: Wilson, *Siegfried Sassoon, The Making of a War Poet*, p. 217.
3. Diary entry for 19 December 1917, in Rupert Hart-Davis (ed.), *Siegfried Sassoon Diaries 1915–1918* (London: Faber, 1983), p. 197.
4. For example, T. S. Eliot writes in 1917 about a 'youth named Siegfried Sassoon (semitic) and his stuff is better politics than poetry': Valerie Eliot (ed.), *The Letters of T. S. Eliot: 1898–1922* (London: Faber, 1988), p. 82.
5. Rupert Hart-Davis (ed.), *Siegfried Sassoon: The War Poems* (London: Faber, 1983), p. 131.
6. Adrian Caesar, *Taking it Like a Man: Suffering, Sexuality and the War Poets* (Manchester: Manchester University Press, 1993), p. 63 and pp. 60–114: '[Sassoon was imbued] with the dominant Christian and imperialist ideologies of his time.'
7. Letter of 1 November 1939, in Rupert Hart-Davis (ed.), *Siegfried Sassoon: Letters to Max Beerbohm, with a few answers* (London: Faber, 1986), p. 81.
8. Hart-Davis (ed.), *Siegfried Sassoon: The War Poems*, pp. 16–17, 19, 24, 45–7.
9. Diary entry for 23 January 1917, in Hart-Davis (ed.), *Siegfried Sassoon Diaries 1915–1918*, p. 124.
10. Diary entry for 22 January 1917, in Hart-Davis (ed.), *Siegfried Sassoon Diaries 1915–1918*, p. 123.
11. Wilson, *Siegfried Sassoon, The Making of a War Poet*, p. 49.
12. Siegfried Sassoon, *The Weald of Youth* (London: Faber, 1942), pp. 262–3.
13. See Genesis 37–50, in *The Holy Bible* (Oxford: Oxford University Press, 1862).
14. Diary entries of 22 December 1916, 15 January 1917 and 22 February 1917, in Hart-Davis (ed.), *Siegfried Sassoon Diaries 1915–1918*, pp. 104, 118–19 and 133.
15. See Sander Gilman, *Jewish Self-Hatred: Anti-Semitism and the Hidden Language of the Jews* (Baltimore, MD: Johns Hopkins University Press, 1986), p. 292, where Gilman notes the widespread early twentieth-century opinion that 'neurasthenia, the

American disease, the disease of modern life, is also the disease of the Jews, modern people incarnate'.

16. Gilman, *Jewish Self-Hatred*, p. 247: 'In his aphorisms [Otto] Weininger observes that "the hatred of the woman is always an unsuccessfully overcome hate of one's own sexuality". The analogy [of the Jew] did not occur to him.'

17. Paul Lawrence Rose, *Wagner: Race and Revolution* (London: Faber, 1992), pp. 4, 193: '*Richard Wagner's Prose Works*, trans. W. A. Ellis, 8 vols, London, 1892–9'.

18. Wilson, *Siegfried Sassoon, The Making of a War Poet*, p. 29.

19. Rose, pp. 82, 45.

20. Sassoon, *The Weald of Youth*, p. 239.

21. Diary entry for 23 January 1917, in Hart-Davis (ed.), *Siegfried Sassoon Diaries 1915–1918*, p. 124.

22. Siegfried Sassoon, 'Foreword', in Ian Parsons (ed.), *The Collected Works of Isaac Rosenberg* (1979; London: Chatto & Windus, 1984), p. ix.

23. Linda Gertner Zatlin, *The Nineteenth-Century Anglo-Jewish Novel* (Boston, MD: Twayne, 1981), p. 30.

24. Michael Ragussis, *Figures of Conversion* (London: Duke University Press, 1995), p. 197.

25. Ragussis, p. 232.

26. Diary entry for 20 May 1916, in Hart-Davis (ed.), *Siegfried Sassoon Diaries 1915–1918*, p. 62.

27. Siegfried Sassoon, *Collected Poems 1908–1956* (1961; London: Faber, 1984), pp. 46–7.

28. See Sassoon, *The Weald of Youth*, pp. 250–1. Siegfried wrote of his great-grandfather, David Sassoon: 'I had found it difficult to connect myself with an ancestor who couldn't speak English and dressed like a Biblical patriarch.'

29. See Patrick Campbell, *Siegfried Sassoon: A Study of the War Poetry* (Jefferson: McFarland, 1999), p. 18: 'Sassoon was at pains to suppress – as he suppressed so much else – his Jewish background.'

30. Sassoon was advised by a friend that his own hands 'were somewhat over-illustrative': see Siegfried Sassoon, *Siegfried's Journey* (London: Faber, 1945), p. 32.

31. Wilson, *Siegfried Sassoon, The Making of a War Poet*, p. 526.

32. Hart-Davis (ed.), *Siegfried Sassoon*, pp. 55, 97 and 120.

33. Edward Said, *Orientalism* (1978; London: Penguin, 1991), p. 73.

34. See D. Felicitas Corrigan, *Siegfried Sassoon: Poet's Pilgrimage* (London: Gollancz, 1973), p. 21: 'You have got it *right* about my Jewish blood,' Sassoon wrote to the author in the last year of his life.

35. Sassoon, *The Weald of Youth*, p. 173. Interestingly, Crosland was an outspoken antisemite. As Colin Holmes notes in *Anti-Semitism and British Society 1876–1939* (London: Edward Arnold, 1979), p. 217: 'There was, in addition [to "carefully worded" antisemitism], a viciousness in T. W. H. Crosland's *The Fine Hebrew Gentleman* [*c*.1922], revealed in its reference to "nasal protuberance", "shent per shent", "Yids" and "bithness".' Possibly, Sassoon reciprocally deploys traces of antisemitic discourse here against one of its more venomous purveyors.

36. T. S. Eliot, *The Complete Poems and Plays of T. S. Eliot* (1969; London: Faber, 1978), pp. 37–9.

37. Eliot, *The Complete Poems*, pp. 56–7.

38. Anthony Julius, *T. S. Eliot, Anti-Semitism, and Literary Form* (Cambridge: Cambridge University Press, 1995), p. 83.

39. Diary entry for 22 February 1918, in Hart-Davis (ed.), *Siegfried Sassoon Diaries 1915–1918*, p. 216.

40. See Bryan Cheyette, 'Neither Black Nor White: The Figure of "the Jew" in Imperial British Literature', in Linda Nochlin and Tamar Garb (eds), *The Jew in the Text* (London: Thames and Hudson, 1995), pp. 31–41. See further my discussion of John Rodker's 'The Descent into Hell' (1914), 'The Fair' (1914) and 'Dead Queens' (1917) in Chapter 4.

41. John Stuart Roberts, *Siegfried Sassoon* (London: Richard Cohen Books, 1999), p. 1.

42. See Sassoon, *The Weald of Youth*, p. 22: 'It was one of these [sentences in C. M. Doughty's *Travels in Arabia Deserta*] that I had taken as the motto of my *Verses* [*Sonnets and Verses* (1909)]. "In the first evening hour there is some merrymake of

drum-beating and soft fluting, and Arcadian sweetness of the Persians singing in the tents about us; in others they chant together some piece of their devotion." The connexion between these words and my *Verses* will have been, I take it, that my supposed Persian ancestry qualified me to claim that I was singing in my tent.'

43.   Daniel Pick, *Faces of Degeneration: A European Disorder, c.1848–c.1918* (Cambridge: Cambridge University Press, 1989), p. 174. See also Zygmunt Bauman, *Modernity and Ambivalence* (Cambridge: Polity Press, 1991), p. 33: 'Concepts like "tabid and wilted stock" (coined by Whethams in 1911), "degenerate stock", "submen", "low-grade types" and "biologically unfit" became staple figures of intelligent debate, while the tremendously influential Karl Pearson sounded in 1909 the alarm that shook the reading and debating public: "the survival of the unfit is a marked characteristic of modern town life".'

44.   Pick, *Faces of Degeneration*, p. 213.

45.   Juliet Steyn, *The Jew: Assumptions of Identity* (London: Cassell, 1999), p. 83.

46.   Pick, *Faces of Degeneration*, p. 189.

47.   Steyn, p. 99, 108: 'Some critics [of a Whitechapel Art Gallery exhibition in 1914], seemingly blinded by fear, even went so far as to explicitly connect Cubism and Futurism with Jewish artists. Modern art was associated with foreign or malign influences.'

48.   Watts was a Victorian painter of allegorical 'pictures based on high-minded generalities or abstractions': see Peter and Linda Murray, *The Penguin Dictionary of Art and Artists*, fourth edition (1959; Harmondsworth, Penguin, 1978), p. 477. He was also a friend of Sassoon's mother, and his picture 'Love and Death' features in *Memoirs of a Fox-Hunting Man* (1928): 'My own silent face looked queerly at me out of the mirror. And there was the familiar photograph of "Love and Death", by Watts, with its secret meaning which I could never quite formulate in a thought': see Siegfried Sassoon, *The Complete Memoirs of George Sherston* (1937; London: Faber, 1972), p. 48. Note the uneasy juxtaposition of the domestically 'familiar photograph' with Sherston/Sassoon's (homosexual) face which 'looked queerly' 'out of the mirror'.

49.   Diary entry for 28 June 1921, in Rupert Hart-Davis (ed.), *Siegfried Sassoon Diaries 1920–1922* (London: Faber, 1981), p. 72.

50.   Jacob Epstein (1880–1959) was 'an American-born Jew of Polish descent': see Richard Cork, *Jacob Epstein* (London: Tate Gallery Publishing, 1999), p. 8.

51.   The phrase is Jon Silkin's. See his *The Life of Metrical and Free Verse in Twentieth-Century Poetry* (Basingstoke: Macmillan, 1997), p. 61: 'The meaning of unity is not singleness and homogeneity, but heterogeneous elements momentarily unified in interaction. A state of continuous active tension.'

52.   Sassoon, *Collected Poems 1908–1956*, p. 109.

53.   Wilson, *Siegfried Sassoon, The Making of a War Poet*, p. 507.

54.   Hart-Davis (ed.), *Siegfried Sassoon: The War Poems*, p. 93.

55.   Wilson, *Siegfried Sassoon, The Making of a War Poet*, pp. 8, 11.

56.   See, in particular, Caesar, pp. 60–114 and Paul Fussell, *The Great War and Modern Memory* (1975; New York: Oxford University Press, 1977), pp. 90–105, 270–309.

57.   Wilson, *Siegfried Sassoon, The Making of a War Poet*, pp. 200–5, 254.

58.   Ibid., pp. 204–5: 'In practical terms Ross was part of a group of influential men who could exert influence in the literary world for Sassoon when the need arose. At least part of Sassoon's success as a war poet would be due to the efforts of this band of admirers and supporters. Sassoon himself was to acknowledge Ross's prime role in the process by dedicating his second volume of war poetry "To Robbie Ross".'

59.   Fussell, p. 282.

60.   Alan Sinfield, 'Diaspora and hybridity: queer identities and the ethnicity model', *Textual Practice* 10:2 (1996), pp. 271–93.

61.   Sinfield, p. 286.

62.   Fussell, p. 270.

63.   See, for example, 'Banishment' (1917) ('They smote my heart to pity, built my pride. / Shoulder to aching shoulder, side by side'), 'Reward' (1918) ('O brothers in my striving') and 'Night on the Convoy' (1918) ('We are going home ...

victims ... three thousand souls'), in Hart-Davis (ed.), *Siegfried Sassoon: The War Poems*, pp. 108, 121–2.

64. Hart-Davis (ed.), *Siegfried Sassoon: The War Poems*, p. 94.
65. Sassoon, *Collected Poems*, pp. 46–7.
66. See Sassoon, 'Foreword', in Parsons (ed.), p. ix.
67. Wilson, *Siegfried Sassoon, The Making of a War Poet*, p. 526.
68. Hart-Davis (ed.), *Siegfried Sassoon: The War Poems*, p. 61.
69. Caesar, p. 63.
70. Sassoon knew the Old Testament solely within its Christian context. '[His nanny] entertained Siegfried with numerous stories from the Old Testament. He was familiar with most of them, since [his mother] Theresa made sure that her sons received an adequate Christian upbringing': see Wilson, *Siegfried Sassoon, The Making of a War Poet*, p. 54.
71. Sassoon, *The Complete Memoirs of George Sherston*, p. 252.
72. Sassoon, *The Weald of Youth*, p. 192.
73. Hart-Davis (ed.), *Siegfried Sassoon: The War Poems*, p. 57.
74. Arthur Foley Winnington-Ingram, Bishop of London, is satirised here. See S. C. Carpenter, *Winnington-Ingram: The Biography of Arthur Foley Winnington-Ingram, Bishop of London 1901–1939* (London: Hodder and Stoughton, 1949), pp. 281, 287, respectively: 'He [Winnington-Ingram] was no pacifist.' In 1915, Winnington-Ingram stressed the importance of a 'National Church'.
75. Alan Wilkinson, *The Church of England and the First World War* (London: SPCK, 1978), p. 217.
76. See Archibald p. Wavell, *The Palestine Campaigns* (1928; London: Constable, 1940), pp. 67–82.
77. Rosenberg, Letter to Gordon Bottomley, dated 23 July 1916, in Parsons (ed.), p. 238.
78. Diary entry for 4 October 1917, in Hart-Davis (ed.), *Siegfried Sassoon Diaries 1915–1918*, p. 188.
79. Campbell, p. 26.
80. Diary entry for 4 October 1917, in Hart-Davis (ed.), *Siegfried Sassoon Diaries 1915–1918*, p. 188.
81. Sander Gilman, *The Jew's Body* (London: Routledge, 1991), p. 93.
82. Gilman, *The Jew's Body*, pp. 125, 96.
83. Rupert Brooke, *1914 and Other Poems* (1915; London: Penguin, 1999), p. 7.
84. Keith Hale (ed.), *Friends and Apostles: The Correspondence of Rupert Brooke and James Strachey, 1905–1914* (London: Yale University Press, 1998), p. 247.
85. Gilman, *The Jew's Body*, p. 78.
86. Wilson, *Siegfried Sassoon, The Making of a War Poet*, pp. 384–5, 260.
87. Sassoon, *The Weald of Youth*, p. 193.
88. Steyn, p. 28.
89. Hart-Davis (ed.), *Siegfried Sassoon Diaries 1915–1918*, pp. 216, 197. See also Gilman, *Jewish Self-Hatred*, pp. 213, 270.
90. Diary entry for 9 May 1918, in Hart-Davis (ed.), *Siegfried Sassoon Diaries 1915–1918*, p. 246.
91. Pick, *Faces of Degeneration*, p. 195.
92. Diary entry for 28 April 1918, in Hart-Davis (ed.), *Siegfried Sassoon Diaries 1915–1918*, p. 240.
93. See Roberts, p. 6. For the common association of Sarah Bernhardt with Jewish syphilis, see Sander Gilman, 'Salome, Syphilis, Sarah Bernhardt, and the Modern Jewess', in *The Jew in the Text*, pp. 97–120.
94. Diary entry for 30 March 1917, in Hart-Davis (ed.), *Siegfried Sassoon Diaries 1915–1918*, p. 146.
95. Diary entry for 9 May 1918, in Hart-Davis (ed.), *Siegfried Sassoon Diaries 1915–1918*, p. 247.
96. Siegfried Sassoon, 'A Tribute to Sir Max Beerbohm', in Hart-Davis (ed.), *Siegfried Sassoon: Letters to Max Beerbohm*, pp. 104–9. Interestingly, Max Beerbohm's half-brother, the actor Herbert Beerbohm Tree, played the malign Jew of George du Maurier's imagination, Svengali, on stage in the 1890s, and in a film version of 1914: see Daniel Pick, *Svengali's Web: The Alien Enchanter in Modern Culture*

(London: Yale University Press, 2000), pp. 153–60.

97. Siegfried Sassoon, *Siegfried's Journey 1916–1920* (London: Faber, 1945), p. 6.

98. See Terry Eagleton, *Exiles and Emigrés: Studies in Modern Literature* (London: Chatto & Windus, 1970), pp. 17–18: 'Hardy ... came from a culture in severe tension with English society, a remote and declining sector far removed from the metropolis.' Sassoon's empathy with the older author may also relate to a shared sense of 'tension' experienced within his own country.

99. Diary entry for 21 May 1917, in Hart-Davis (ed.), *Siegfried Sassoon Diaries 1915–1918*, p. 171.

100. See diary entry for 21 May 1917, in Hart-Davis (ed.), *Siegfried Sassoon Diaries 1915–1918*, p. 171: 'Lady Brassey and I discuss religion. Agree that C. of E. "is a bit *passé*"... Hardy is merely "an unpleasant writer", as my own mother would say ... I'd better go back to the First Battalion as soon as possible, unless I can make some protest against the War.'

101. Wilson, *Siegfried Sassoon, The Making of a War Poet*, p. 23.

102. Ibid., pp. 514–15.

103. Hart-Davis (ed.), *Siegfried Sassoon: The War Poems*, pp. 100–1.

104. Sassoon's misogyny was qualified by praise for women with male characteristics. For example, he writes of Mrs [Edmund] Gosse: 'Like all the best women, she had an element of masculinity in her. The bigness of her nature was visible in the cast of her features, which were noble without being perfect in their proportions': see Sassoon, *The Weald of Youth*, p. 90.

105. Fussell, p. 270.

106. Letter of 30 July 1917 to Ottoline Morrell, in Hart-Davis (ed.), *Siegfried Sassoon Diaries 1915–1918*, p. 183. See also Psalm 114, *The Holy Bible*: 'When Israel went out of Egypt, the house of Jacob from a people of strange language; Judah was his sanctuary, *and* Israel his dominion. The sea saw *it*, and fled: Jordan was driven back. The mountains skipped like rams, *and* the little hills like lambs.'

107. Letter of 17 September 1917 to Robbie Ross, in Hart-Davis (ed.), *Siegfried Sassoon Diaries 1915–1918*, p. 186.

108. Wilson, *Siegfried Sassoon, The Making of a War Poet*, p. 449.

109. Diary entry for 25 December 1917, in Hart-Davis (ed.), *Siegfried Sassoon Diaries 1915–1918*, p. 198.

110. Hart-Davis (ed.), *Siegfried Sassoon Diaries 1915–1918*, pp. 223, 228, 234.

111. Wilson, *Siegfried Sassoon, The Making of a War Poet*, p. 452. 'In Palestine' is reprinted in neither Sassoon's own arrangement of *Collected Poems* nor Hart-Davis's edition of *The War Poems*.

112. Hart-Davis (ed.), *Siegfried Sassoon Diaries 1915–1918*, pp. 233, 221.

113. 'Unpublished papers in the hands of a private collector': see Wilson, *Siegfried Sassoon, The Making of a War Poet*, pp. 526, 582.

114. Hart-Davis (ed.), *Siegfried Sassoon: Letters to Max Beerbohm*, p. 81.

115. Siegfried Sassoon, *The Old Century and seven more years* (London: Faber, 1938), p. 13.

116. Sassoon, *The Old Century*, p. 23.

117. Sassoon, *The Complete Memoirs of George Sherston*, p. 93.

118. See Exodus in *The Holy Bible*.

119. See *Reader's Digest Universal Dictionary* (1987; London: Reader's Digest, 1995), p. 1127: '[Parry's] works include the oratorios *Judith*, *Job* (1892), and *King Saul* (1894), and the choral song *Jerusalem* (1916).' Parry takes his lyrics from Blake's *Milton* (1808): see Alicia Ostriker (ed.), *The Complete Poems of William Blake* (Harmondsworth: Penguin, 1977), p. 514: 'I will not cease from Mental Fight, / Nor shall my Sword sleep in my hand / Till we have built Jerusalem / In England's green and pleasant Land.'

120. A. F. Walls, 'Carrying the White Man's Burden: Some British Views of National Vocation in the Imperial Era', in William R. Hutchison and Hartmut Lehmann (eds), *Many are Chosen: Divine Election and Western Nationalism* (Minneapolis: Fortress Press, 1994), pp. 28, 30 and pp. 29–56.

121. Hutchison and Lehmann (eds), p. 30.

122. John Milton, 'Areopagitica', in K. M. Burton (ed.), *Milton's Prose Writings* (1958;

London: Everyman, 1974), p. 176.
123. The Association of British Israelites was founded in the 1870s. See John Wilson, 'British Israelism: The Ideological Restraints on Sect Organisation', in Bryan R. Wilson (ed.), *Patterns of Sectarianism: Organisation and Ideology in Social and Religious Movements* (London: Heinemann, 1967), pp. 345–76.
124. Linda Colley, *Britons: Forging the Nation 1707–1837* (London: Yale University Press, 1992), pp. 368–9.
125. Rudyard Kipling, *The Complete Verse* (1996; London: Kyle Cathie, 1998), p. 266.
126. Hutchison and Lehmann (eds), pp. 34, 36.
127. Letters of 17 May 1935 and 1 November 1939, in Hart-Davis (ed.), *Siegfried Sassoon: Letters to Max Beerbohm*, pp. 24, 81.
128. Wilson, *Siegfried Sassoon, The Making of a War Poet*, p. 526.
129. Roberts, *Siegfried Sassoon*, p. 317; Corrigan, p. 17. In a letter to Dame Felicitas Corrigan, 'Sassoon explained that another factor on his road to faith was the experience of visiting churches in Italy while staying with Max Beerbohm. He recalled climbing the steep path behind Beerbohm's house at Rapallo to a hill-top church, and also visiting "a lovely little old one – S. Pantaleone – on the headland along the Spezzia road – and both produced a wistful awareness of devotion which I longed to share. I *knew* that they were different to Heytesbury church (in which I have never attended service!)"': Joseph Pearce, *Literary Converts: Spiritual Inspiration in an Age of Unbelief* (London: HarperCollins, 1999), p. 320 and pp. 319–22. Pearce cites Corrigan, pp. 182–3. Confirming his contemporary otherness in England ('I *knew* that they were different to Heytesbury church (in which I have never attended service!)') was clearly more important to Sassoon than overcoming an earlier distaste for Catholicism (see note 26 above). Indeed, Sassoon's conversion to Catholicism was an assertion of his sense of otherness ('different') *vis-à-vis* the Anglicans among whom he lived in Heytesbury.
130. Rudyard Kipling, *Something of Myself* (1936; London: Penguin, 1992), p. 157.
131. Kipling, *Something of Myself*, p. 169.
132. See Judges 4:8–22 and 5:24–27, in *The Holy Bible*.
133. See note 40 above.
134. *The Oxford English Dictionary*, second edition, vol. IV (1989; Oxford: Clarendon Press, 2001), p. 445.
135. Letter of 11 April 1930, in Hart-Davis (ed.), *Siegfried Sassoon: Letters to Max Beerbohm*, p. 11.
136. Sassoon, *The Weald of Youth*, p. 157.
137. See Rosenberg, 'Rudolph' (1911), in Parsons (ed.), p. 281.
138. Sassoon, *The Weald of Youth*, p. 214.
139. Sassoon, *The Complete Memoirs of George Sherston*, p. 187.
140. Sassoon, *The Weald of Youth*, pp. 182, 16. See also Hart-Davis (ed.), *Siegfried Sassoon Diaries 1915–1918*, p. 221.
141. Sassoon, *The Weald of Youth*, p. 140.
142. Caesar, p. 63.
143. See 'The Poet as Hero' (1916), in Hart-Davis (ed.), *Siegfried Sassoon: The War Poems*, p. 61.

4

John Rodker: Minority Modernist

The poetry of John Rodker tends to be read as a generic variant of canonical Modernist verse. Andrew Crozier, for example, notes that 'Rodker's career shadowed [Ezra] Pound's'.[1] To date, no biography or collection of critical essays addresses this Anglo-Jewish Modernist.[2] Rodker remains a largely neglected poet, perceived as little more than a shadow thrown by the dominant figures of Ezra Pound and T. S. Eliot. Since his *Collected Poems 1912–1925* (1930), just one selection of Rodker's poetry has appeared: *Poems & Adolphe 1920* (1996).[3]

By contrast, I want to approach Rodker as a *minority Modernist* at work in specific Anglo-Jewish social circumstances. Like Isaac Rosenberg, Rodker was the son of Yiddish-speaking Jewish immigrants who spent his early years in London's East End ghetto,[4] with its 'cultural energies, at once assimilative and counter-assertively independent'.[5] In this milieu, Rodker struck up a friendship with Rosenberg, and other first-generation Anglo-Jewish poets and artists. As Joseph Leftwich relates: 'My own group was [Samuel] Winsten, Rodker, and Rosenberg. But we often joined with others, [David] Bomberg and [Mark] Gertler, [Jack] Isaacs and [Lazarus] Aaronson.'[6]

This 'brilliant' Whitechapel group[7] asserted an identity 'in defiance of official Anglo-Jewry'[8] and the 'British conservatism'[9] which it espoused. Like Rosenberg, Rodker was acutely aware that he was among 'the "foreign" Jews' in England.[10] Thus, the recurrent affirmations of 'foreign-ness'[11] and 'revolutionary'[12] arts in Rodker's oeuvre appear to have their roots in the Jewish East End. Indeed, I want to suggest that Rodker affiliated with Modernism in order to promulgate such Otherness as a universal condition.

THE POETRY OF JOHN RODKER

Rodker worked with the canonical practitioners of Modernism: T. S. Eliot, Ezra Pound, Wyndham Lewis and James Joyce. Unfortunately, his activities as a publisher – notably of Eliot's *Ara Vos Prec* (1919), Pound's *Hugh Selwyn Mauberley* (1920)[13] and Joyce's *Ulysses* (1922)[14] – have tended to overshadow his performance as a poet in the eyes of past and present critics. All too often, Rodker is dismissed as a Jewish middle-man. As Adam Phillips remarks: 'Rodker's writing needs to be rescued' and his reputation as Modernism's 'minor accomplice and failed businessman' reassessed.[15]

Rodker's Jewishness is relevant here. That is to say, his reputation among his peers was permeated by perceptions of Jews between 1914, when *Poems*, Rodker's first collection, appeared, and 1930, when *Collected Poems* was published. Certainly, it is no revelation to read of this generation's 'supercilious and spiteful variety of antisemitism that was *de rigueur* for members of the upper and upper-middle classes such as Pound's wife, Dorothy Shakespear and Wyndham Lewis'.[16]

Such antisemitism is apparent, for example, in the following letter from Lewis to Pound:

> I found Rodker a most poisonous little bugger on Saturday, repellently hoarse (this may be a form of jealousy) & with abominable teeth, not to mention his manners. I am sure you cant say anything too bad about him. He told me he had written a lot of filthy sexual verse, which, if he sends it, I shall hang in the W.C. He described it as Verlainesque, damn his dirty little eyes. Well, well.
>
> Sturge Moore turned up, & we had Bomberg to entertain us, on Saturday.[17]

Though Rodker's Jewishness is not explicitly identified in this passage, I suggest that Lewis seems provoked to atavistically medieval slanders against the 'poisonous', together with modern disgust ('repellently') towards 'dirty', Jews. The letter's concluding allusion to 'Bomberg to entertain us' conveys a countervailing tolerance of amusing Jews, as it contemptuously relegates the Anglo-Jewish painter David Bomberg to the status of an eccentric clown. Nevertheless, Rodker's Ovid Press went ahead and published Lewis's *Fifteen Drawings* in 1922.[18]

It is notable, too, that Rodker's edition of Eliot's *Ara Vos Prec* contains both 'Burbank with a Beidecker: Bleistein with a Cigar' and 'Gerontion', two of Eliot's less subtly antisemitic poems.[19] Evidently, Rodker affiliated with a Modernism, the most prominent practitioners of which (excepting Joyce)[20] were implicated in reproducing and refining tropes of antisemitic discourse.

To be sure, Eliot had not yet written 'reasons of race and religion combine to make any large number of free-thinking Jews undesirable'[21] when he was corresponding with Rodker; nor had Pound penned the following lines from Canto LII (1940):

> Remarked Ben: better keep out the jews
>   Or yr/ grand children will curse you
> jews, real jews, chazims, and *neschek*
> also super-neschek or the international racket.[22]

Rodker's relationship with Modernism was at its most commitedly intense between 1914 and 1930, before social and literary antisemitism developed into the fascist politics of Pound and his sympathisers.

Indeed, Rodker's commitment to Modernism was, arguably, a commitment to a *minority art* which displaced his *minority Jewishness* onto a group of mainly exiled intellectuals in London and Paris. He was 'London Editor of the Little Review' when the American journal was declaring on its cover: 'A Magazine of the Arts: Making No Compromise with the Public Taste.'[23] If affiliation with 'the Arts' entailed jettisoning 'public' popularity, so be it. Rodker affiliated with a more discerning (non-racial) minority. Further, Rodker's commitment to publishing works by present and future antisemites emphasises the intensity of his asymmetrical affiliation with them. During the 1910s and 1920s, Rodker's poems also appeared in Eliot's *Egoist*, Harriet Monroe's *Poetry*, and Lewis's *The Tyro*, as well as several other journals.[24]

Importantly, Pound's antisemitism did not prevent him supporting Rodker as one of the protégés on whom his talent-finding reputation (and income) was based. Pound also supported Rosenberg, for similar reasons. Indeed, it was while he was working for *The Little Review* that Pound recommended Rodker to its editor, Margaret Anderson. 'Rodker is too good not to be printed now and again,' Pound urged. 'One must keep a chap like that "one of us". He will do something.'[25] Rodker was being shepherded into

the Modernist coterie ('one of us'). His affiliations were recipro-
cated in the form of Pound's patronage.

A month later, Pound was again reassuring a sceptical Anderson
of Rodker's worth:

> Rodker has convinced me, at last, that he 'has it in him.' And
> one must have les jeunes. Rodker ought to be up to regulation
> in a few years' time.
> He will go further than Richard Aldington, though I don't
> expect anyone to believe that statement for some time. He has
> more invention, more guts. His father did not have a library
> full of classics, but he will learn.
> They are neither of them STUPID, blockheaded as F——[26]

Pound places Rodker, in contradistinction to Aldington, outside the
classical tradition: 'His father did not have a library full of classics.'
One is reminded of Pound's remark that Rosenberg was 'horribly
rough but then "Stepney East" ... we ought to have a real burglar ...
ma che!'[27] Implicit in Pound's contrast of Rodker with Aldington and
'classics' is the Arnoldian opposition between the Hellenic
('classics') and Hebraic. Perhaps empathetically, Pound champions
the outsider with 'more invention, more guts' against the classically
trained Englishmen Aldington and 'STUPID, blockheaded ... F'.
Aldington himself attacks Rodker within a more explicit Hellenic-
Hebraic paradigm when reviewing *Poems* (1914); while in a later
review of *Hymns* (1920), he strongly supports 'F' – 'Mr. Flint' –
against Rodker.[28]

Aldington's 1914 review of *Poems* introduces 'Mr. Rodker as a
Slav'.[29] 'Slav' can conceivably be read: Jew. Nancy Cunard, for
example, describes Rodker as 'half-Polish', and proceeds to speculate
whether this racial 'fact' explains why he was 'so introspective,
sometimes brooding and self-critical to the point of self-torture?'[30]
Neither she nor Aldington mention Rodker's Jewishness. Indeed,
Rodker himself avoids the word Jew in both fiction and verse (but not
criticism), yet notes that when in France a 'higgler, taking us for Poles,
complained of the foreign labour coming into the country'.[31] Less
speculatively, within Aldington's polarised paradigm 'Slav' is
Hebraised as the opposite of 'Hellenic'. Aldington explains:

> Now, I think everyone who has read my articles here [in
> Harriet Monroe's *Poetry*], will know of my sympathies with

the tradition of Greek poetry. I find that tradition in Miss [Amy] Lowell's work, for her tradition is French, which is Latin, which is Greek (with a difference). I have no doubt that – so uncritical are the times – if her work and Mr. Rodker's fall into the hands of the same reviewer they will be treated as belonging to the same school. As I have indicated, they are at the antipodes. Miss Lowell's work has at least a strong tendency towards the 'hard edges' and precision, which are so dear to the Hellenic tradition. She is logical and common-sensical, where Mr. Rodker is illogical and nonsensical.[32]

Aldington sets 'Greek' Lowell and 'illogical and nonsensical' Rodker at 'antipodes' to one another. Clearly, Aldington affiliates both with Amy Lowell as a fellow *Imagiste* and with 'Hellenic' classicism as a Modernist desideratum. In 1912 Pound had championed Aldington as 'one of the "Imagistes", a group of ardent Hellenists'.[33] Subsequently, Aldington appeared alongside Lowell in Pound's anthology *Des Imagistes* (1914).[34] Moreover, when Pound repudiated *Imagisme* later that year, he derided it as 'Amygism' in reference to Lowell's recently assumed chairmanship of the movement.[35] Thus, Aldington's review may be read as defending Lowell and 'Hellenic' *Imagisme*, while simultaneously attacking Rodker as its Other.

Certainly, Rosenberg suffered similar aesthetic condemnation at the hands of Edward Marsh, who urged that the Anglo-Jewish poet 'renounce the lawless and grotesque manner in which he usually writes, and pay a little attention to form and tradition'.[36] Both Aldington and Marsh were thinking of a 'tradition ... which is Latin, which is Greek', alongside a complementary preference for '"hard edges"' and unambiguous referents ('precision'). It was this Latin/Greek tradition which pressured Rosenberg to plead with Marsh: 'Don't say they're obscure ... I think myself the poem is very clear.'[37] It is with this same tradition in mind that Aldington damns Rodker with faint praise:

Indeed, though I personally detest his kind of art ... yet I shall be extremely sorry if Mr. Rodker does not get the money and support that he wants for his theatrical experiments. He is perfectly justified in demanding the right to experiment, at least; and however un-Latin he may be, I hereby promise to come to his first night and to buy my seat ...[38]

Speaking as a liberal Englishman ('personally'), Aldington detests Rodker's foreign 'kind of art'. Only when the critic situates 'un-Latin' Rodker within the stereotype of a Jewish entrepreneur ('the money and support that he wants'), rather than a foreign poet ('a Slav indirectly and perfectly unconsciously acted on by Prussian theories of art') for whom he has 'no use', can he accommodate the Anglo-Jew to his own English liberalism: 'I hereby promise to come to his first night and to buy my seat.' Further, Aldington's contractual language ('I hereby promise ... to buy') is tactfully chosen for the Jewish businessman to understand without rancour.

Aldington's antisemitic understanding of what constitutes the polar opposite of 'Hellenic' poetry is extended to his perception of the undesirability of Rodker's poetry in a 1920 review of *Hymns*. Here again, a structural dichotomy is deployed; this time, between healthy English honesty and diseased Jewish mendacity. Aldington writes:

> I find Mr. Rodker's *Hymns* the exact opposite of Mr. Flint's book. Where the one is all candor, simplicity, naturalness and health, the other is affectation, insincerity, falseness and disease. I can find little in Mr. Rodker's hymns which is not the expression of a vain and morbid sensibility ... Numerous remarks scattered through these pages are possibly intended to cater to the amateur of furtive pornography; they can serve no other purpose.[39]

As we have seen, Rosenberg and Sassoon were similarly implicated in a nationalist discourse of 'health'. Specifically, Rosenberg's Jewish patron Mrs Cohen threatened to withdraw her support for the poet-painter unless he adopted a more 'healthy style of work'.[40] Again, Sassoon was concerned to promote a healthy image of himself in a succession of autobiographical works, from *Memoirs of a Fox-Hunting Man* (1928) to *The Weald of Youth* (1942). Sassoon's self-representations as a sportsman served to distance the poet from the common association of Jews with syphilis. Such a binary discourse around English 'health' and Jewish 'disease' helpfully illuminates Aldington's 1920 review of *Hymns*.

Clearly, Aldington is accusing Rodker 'of furtive pornography', while being at pains to insinuate that he is also immoral:

> There was once a man who said, '*En art tout est faux qui n'est pas beau*' – a strong though noble dogmatism. Mr. Rodker is

not of the opinion of M. France; he would say, '*En art tout est faux qui n'est pas sale.*' It is the fashion of the day.

Thus, Aldington deploys traces of antisemitic discourse to describe Rodker as a dirty ('*sale*') Jew (with a spitefulness reminiscent of Lewis's 'dirty little eyes')[41] who touts dishonest trivia ('*faux*', 'fashion'), rather than writing 'noble' English verse. Evidently, Rodker affiliated with a Modernist milieu where he was welcomed or despised as Other, and where antisemitism was very much at home.

Rodker's affiliations were with art, and the objet d'art, 'Making No Compromise with the Public Taste'.[42] Consequently, he was keen to deflect and transpose accusations of Jewish triviality ('fashion'). To do so, Rodker resorted to a strategy also deployed by Sassoon: namely, trivialisation of women instead of Jews. For example, Rodker's verse-play *The Dutch Dolls* (1917) features 'she who watches / from trivial curtains / my footfalls onto eternity'. Here 'mere women' are 'trivial', domestic ('curtains') creatures, while the male narrator steps into 'eternity'.[43] Similarly, the narrator of Rodker's anonymous autobiography, *Memoirs of Other Fronts* (1932), envisages 'her again; the luxurious and domestic, the banal, the frivolous'.[44]

Since Rodker affiliated with an artistic rather than racial minority, he also rejected a particularist Jewish orientation. Significantly, the only Yiddish word to appear in his published poetry is 'Schlemihl' (fool). Further, the Jewish 'Schlemihl' of 'Wild West Remittance Man' (1919)[45] is associated with the feminine, the domestic and, by implication, the trivial: 'Schlemihl no mother weeps for / doomed for a certain term.' The particularised (male) Jew is one who does not leave his trivial (female) home ('mother'), thus resigning himself to a traditional Jewish fate ('doomed'):

> Body linings peel
> from the deep core
> in siroccos of Alkali
> england ... thy drawing rooms ...
> sundays ... mahogany ...
> the fire leaps!
>
> Rye whiskey!
> shuffle of counters ...

revolvers, marked cards.
A million tons of locust-sirocco
blasts and grinds.

And the cayuse snorts by
hey-up ... hey up ...
shots ... the loud greeting.

He turns to the counters ...
rustling paper ... marked cards;
gravely the whisker droops
his eyes are cold.

Such a 'Schlemihl' is ground down ('grinds'). His life is one of commercial ('Remittance Man') surfaces ('counters', 'the bondstreet exterior'). Comedy ('hey-up ... hey up ...') fails to redeem him, and merely leaves 'his eyes ... cold'. Moreover, the 'Schlemihl' appears conspicuously Other ('loud'), like a ('Wild West') American, among the reserved English ('drawing rooms ... / sundays ... mahogany').

However, the 'Schlemihl' is not simply trivial. His otherness emerges from a 'deep core', not to mention a Judaic ('thy') observance of Sabbath on Saturdays rather than England's 'sundays'. The 'siroccos of Alkali' may allude to the Arizona Desert;[46] but they also call to mind the sandstorms of an Old Testament desert through which the Children of Israel wander in exile. Thus, Rodker ambivalently presents Jewishness as both trivial and 'deep', embarrassingly 'loud' *and* free from the claustrophobic reserve of 'england ... thy drawing rooms', domestically constricting *and* biblically exilic.

Rodker refers to a 'Schlemihl' just once again, in his review of *Poèmes Juifs* (*Jewish Poems*) (1920) by André Spire.[47] He paraphrases Spire:

The jew [*sic*] lies like a rye grain buried in fat and bursting wheat ears. For a time as he sees how completely he has swallowed the habits of the wheat ear, its exquisite intonations, its passion to get outside itself in a wild pursuit of objets-d'arts, he may even persuade himself that he is 'one of them'. Yet always he must see himself eventually nameless, an eternal Schlemihl.

In Rodker's only explicit consideration of Jewish poetry, he identifies Jewishness with raw life ('so real, so jewishly [*sic*] real'), rather than the cultivation of art ('you will find these poems artless'). Having thus differentiated Jewishness and art, Rodker affiliates with the latter. Art offers universal otherness: 'to get outside itself in a wild pursuit of objets-d'arts'. By contrast, affiliation with a particularised Jewishness ('like a rye grain') leads only to marginalisation through public indifference ('eventually nameless').

Still, Rodker is not completely dismissive of Spire. He notes the Franco-Jew's 'capacity for feeling; for suffering which would have done credit to Walt Whitman'. Though rejecting Spire's Jewish particularism ('Schlemihl'), Rodker appears to admire his Jewish universalism ('eternal'). After all, Modernist poetry also aspired to be a universal communicator, like 'Whitman', of 'feeling' and 'suffering'. Here is Rodker's positive perspective on Jewishness. Like Rosenberg, Rodker affiliates with a Jewish and Whitmanesque universalism.[48]

Further, both Anglo-Jewish Modernists look to America for an *extraterritorial* English: a 'Wild West' language beyond England's national, racial and religious particularisms ('england ... thy drawing rooms ... / sundays ... mahogany ...'[49]). Like Rosenberg again, Rodker finds in Whitman's American poetry a means to challenge the parochial notion of a monocultural English literature. As Chana Kronfeld remarks of Modernism and its Jewish practitioners:[50]

> Works that have come to be associated with one period, trend, or movement not only are located in discontinuous or at least partially incompatible points in time but are also situated in *disparate* social and geographic spaces [*my italics*].

Rodker is acutely aware of such '*disparate* social and geographic spaces'. In his critical essay *The Future of Futurism* (1927), the poet is at pains to discuss *foreign* Jews in English arts. Rodker introduces his polemic by identifying Futurism with the American-Jewish sculptor Jacob Epstein: 'Of Futurism so much has been said in the past fifteen years that, with a country very much divided on the subject of Mr Epstein's Rima, some belated definition seems necessary.' He continues by speculating 'that mathematical pre-occupation has lately touched all the arts in some degree. In music

Schoenberg ... and in Literature Miss Stein'.[51] Thus, Rodker identifies music, literature and the visual arts of Futurism through *foreign* (German and American) Jewish practitioners. Indeed, Rodker is not so much affiliating with Jewishness here as with *foreignness*; the sense of foreignness which Leftwich describes as felt in common by the '"foreign" Jews'[52] of London's East End during the First World War. He is affiliating with Jews in so far as they are also *foreigners* and outsiders (unacceptable to 'the academies'[53]).

Significantly, Rodker's autobiography *Memoirs of Other Fronts* has no declared author. To be sure, 'impersonality' is a key tenet of Modernism, advocated especially by Eliot and Pound.[54] However, *Memoirs of Other Fronts* suggests further an anonymity forced upon the author by ethnic circumstances:

> In Paris I feel English, in London a foreigner. There are a lot of men like that, but it is only now, well on in life, I realise how much of a foreigner I am, how much of one I always was. And even if I still wished to avoid acknowledging it, I could not any longer get away from the testimony of my face and form. It is as though the very fibres that composed me, tired at last of the incessant struggle with the thing I longed to be, at last in intense consciousness of what it was I strove to suppress, stressed only that side of me, piling on me in two decades the atavisms of centuries, releasing me at last from the harsh bonds of ideal behaviour, propriety, that adolescence forced upon me and which finally too much circumscribed me. Is it not strange that just when our antagonism to the family, race, the claims of the future is [at] its most violent, the mind enthrals itself to ideals which hardly half a century's struggle will throw off, a life-long handicap which hides the form but where the spirit, too close to the thing it struggles with, ends by identifying itself with it and confesses the liaison. So at the time of this story I looked what I wanted to look. Instinctively my life fell among strangers and if I met others it was to what was foreign in them I turned. How else should I have noticed them?[55]

As it were, the narrator religiously 'confesses' to currently affiliating with ('identifying', 'close', 'liaison') 'the family, race, the claims of the future'. Beyond these, he is 'always' Other ('a foreigner', 'among strangers'). Possibly, this is also a confession that the narrator formerly wished to pass ('I looked what I wanted to look') as a non-Jew. Now, by contrast, he feels uncomfortable with the 'incessant struggle' and psychosomatic repression of passing ('suppress', 'the harsh bonds of ideal behaviour'). 'Tired', he relaxes his physical 'fibres', and acknowledges 'the testimony of my face and form'. Finally, maturity reconciles him to the Jewish 'family, race', and 'atavisms of centuries'.

Like Siegfried Sassoon's autobiographical narrators, Rodker's recalls an 'adolescence' of 'circumscribed' conformity to English mores ('in London', 'propriety'). However, Rodker Judaises maturity ('the atavisms of centuries', 'well on in life') and consigns delimiting affiliations ('the harsh bonds of ideal behaviour') to the past; whereas Sassoon Judaises 'youth's gesticulating volubility', and depicts his 'toned down' maturity as post-Jewish.[56] In middle age, Rodker embraces an unbounded ('releasing me at last', 'half a century's struggle will throw off') Jewish universalism ('a foreigner I am'). Conversely, Sassoon narrates Jewishness as a stage of national and psychosomatic ('gesticulating') history.

Being an artistic 'revolutionary',[57] the narrator of *Memoirs of Other Fronts* has his eyes fixed on the future: 'Always, always I had wanted time to fly quickly, to be cut out, myself, by force of longing, to be suddenly months ahead, to be there, to know at last what life had for me, above all get out of "here and now".'[58] Much as Sassoon flees contemporary Anglo-Jewish tensions through the nostalgia of his autobiographical prose, so Rodker's narrator rushes to 'get out of "here and now"' into a stress-free future ('to know at last what life had for me'). Sassoon flees Jewish otherness by affiliating with an idealised Old Testament and English past; whereas Rodker looks to a Modernist future to universalise such otherness.

Perhaps it is no coincidence that Rodker the 'revolutionary' is dismissive of evolutionary theory. In *The Future of Futurism*, he pours scorn on English literature's penchant for 'the psychology of Apes'.[59] The poet 'violently react[s] from a pre-occupation' with such simian psychology, rejecting Darwin's 'butcher's shop' theory of the survival of the fittest 'Apes', together with evolutionary indifference towards the survival of the stranger.[60]

Possibly, simian traits are condemned so forcefully because they suggest assimilation to English traditions and mores displayed by (according to Leftwich) 'official Anglo-Jewry'. In Rodker's prose poem 'Monkeys' (1917),[61] for example, conformist behaviour is pointedly portrayed in a 'large Ape house': 'She was very pleased with him. He was affectionate, yet well-bred and undemonstrative, and the hairy arm tickled her face pleasantly. She sat very still as with a lover.' By contrast, Rodker, Rosenberg and Leftwich espouse rebellion against establishment Anglo-Jewry's policy of aping ('Apes') English Gentiles. These poets opt for 'the self-assertion of the "foreign" Jews'.[62] They prefer Jewish otherness to what Sassoon terms 'chameleon'[63] imitation.

Rodker presents such otherness through a variety of strategies. Gilles Deleuze and Félix Guattari ask how a minority writer can 'become a nomad and an immigrant and a gypsy in relation to one's own language?'[64] Rodker articulates such a *'deterritorialization'*[65] of language through the depiction of, precisely, nomads, immigrants and Gypsies. His novel *Adolphe 1920* (1929), for example, presents in its opening paragraph 'a bugle, in a far land heard before. A tent. A child skips, a trumpet to its mouth; a Moor'.[66] Immediately, a certain orientalist ('Moor', 'in a far land') and nomadic ('tent') atmosphere is established. The 'child skips' like the rams of Psalm 114; the same rams to which Sassoon alludes in a letter of 1917 to Ottoline Morrell.[67] ('Rams', incidentally, appear again in Rodker's 'Lamps' (1920): 'Charging rams hide men.')[68] Contextually, the 'far land heard before' is suggestive of an ancient, orientalised Israel, and the horn ('bugle', 'trumpet') of the ceremonial *shofar*, 'a ram's-horn trumpet used in Jewish religious services and in biblical times as a war-trumpet'.[69]

Gypsies and circus-travellers figure in both *Adolphe 1920* and Rodker's poems. In 'The Fair' (1914), for example:

> The gypsy girl eyes me and her scorn
> crushes my old identity upon me,
> then while I take the balls
> I am in the dim Basrah bazaar

Forced to assume his 'old identity', the narrator imaginatively heads East to the 'Basrah bazaar'. In 'Acrobats' (1914), the eastern associations of a circus are more geographically precise:

> When they had finished all their tricks,
> blindfolded – leaping, somersaulting, forming pyramids –

> They crossed the stage in little jerky rushings,
> bodies very pink across the footlights
> bottoms prominent and shoulders held well forward,
> legs detached and stiff, like those of dolls –
> and again leaping, somersaulting; made more pyramids
> and caught each other from great heights
> and all blindfolded –
> How we clapped them.
>
> They took the call calmly,
> placid and unsmiling like horrible pink dolls.
>
> Suddenly I saw their bellies breathing fiercely.

Here the gymnasts are 'forming pyramids'. One is reminded of 'Under the Trees VI' (1916)[70] which deterritorialises an English tree to present it as an Egyptian pyramid: 'Under you, green pyramid, / what King with gold-glued face is hid?' Of course, Egypt is not Israel. However, it is recorded in the Old Testament Book of Exodus as a place of exile and slavery for the Jews who built the pyramids. Rosenberg deploys this very narrative in his verse-play *Moses*. In 'Under the Trees VI', the narrator asks: 'Do you wave your leaves at his whim / like his slave waved fan for him?' Feasibly, that 'slave' might be an ancient Hebrew. Indeed, Rodker resembles Rosenberg in borrowing from the Old Testament for *minority Modernist* purposes.

Moreover, references to an orientalised Egypt are evident beyond Rodker's poems in the very presentation of his work. As Nancy Cunard notes:

> The covers [of *Collected Poems*] are striking compositions, photographic designs by Len Lye, which look as if they had been modelled in wax, with a graceful, semi-Egyptian influence. The initial lettering of the poems, designed by Edward Wadsworth, is the same as that used for *The Seven Pillars of Wisdom*, by Lawrence of Arabia.[71]

In the early 1920s, Rodker 'founded his publishing house, the Casanova Society, which produced very fine work, such as ... a set of *The Arabian Nights*, put into beautiful English by William Powys Mathers'.[72] In 'Who thinks of Pensaers now?' (*c*.1925), the poem's persona speaks of how he 'admired his egyptology'.[73]

To be sure, the placing of semitic references in the ancient past accords with widespread Modernist practice. For example, in the *The Waste Land* (1922) T. S. Eliot alludes to a 'Jew' in the context of 'Phlebas the Phoenician'.[74] As Bryan Cheyette notes, 'the Phoenicians ... were a mercantile, Hebrew-speaking people who were commonly perceived as ancient equivalents of the contemporary Jewish bourgeoisie'.[75] These 'ancient' semites inhabited 'a narrow strip of land on the coast of Syria, to the north-west of Palestine'.[76] Thus, Rodker conforms to Modernist anthropology[77] when he evokes 'ancient' semitic civilizations in the Middle East.

Interestingly, Rodker's 'pyramids' are the site for 'dolls'[78] who perform what he terms elsewhere a theatre of primitive and pure emotion:

> No two senses may be concentrated without one losing somewhat in intensity. A sonata cannot be criticised and heard intensely at the same moment ... The only form of drama which evades these mistakes is that made by 'Marionettes'. That is, conventionalised figures which do not draw attention to their idiosyncrasies; placed in a neutral environment which does not detract from the evocation of pure emotion.[79]

In this manifesto on 'The Theatre' (1914), Rodker emphasises 'intensity', artificiality ("Marionettes") and 'a neutral environment' which is both non-sectarian ('figures which do not draw attention to their idiosyncrasies') and universal ('pure emotion'). He moves away from the particular environment of England, and from national or ethnic 'idiosyncrasies', to *deterritorialise* his theatre. In this, he resembles the Irish poet W. B. Yeats who deployed the similarly minimalist rituals of Japanese Noh drama to escape the constrictions of England's parochial, naturalist theatre.[80] According to Ernest Fenollosa, the first translator of Noh plays into English: 'All elements – costume, motion, verse and music [are] ... elevated to the plane of universality by the intensity and purity of treatment.'[81] Rodker deploys traces of just such a universalising discourse to champion primitive emotions in 'The Theatre', under the sub-heading 'The Evocation of Race Memories':

> I want to take a theatre in London, using for the plays either human marionettes of the Dutch-doll type or naked humans,

or to clothe them in a sort of cylindrical garment. The plays will be the completion of a cycle dealing with the primitive emotions, of which Fear is one, these being I think the simplest for the evocation of race memories.

Though 'race memories' may be read as synonymous with universalist 'primitive emotions', the phrase also has a specific bearing on Rodker's situation as a 'London' Jew. After all, the child of parents who fled the Russian pogroms after 1880 would understand such atavistic and contemporary 'Fear'. Within a Modernist context, however, Rodker's particularist Jewish 'race' is presented as simply ('simplest') something shared and 'human'. 'Marionettes', as Rodker says, 'do not draw attention to their idiosyncrasies', Jewish or otherwise.

Rodker's directions for a theatre of mannequins appear together as prose poems under the title *Theatre Muet* (1917).[82] The first scenario, 'Fear', was published separately in 1914 alongside 'The Theatre' manifesto in *The Egoist*. Here 'Pierrot and Columbine' were introduced, pantomime figures which weave in and out of the series.[83] They re-emerge in Rodker's verse-drama *The Dutch Dolls*. Such marionettes are both familiar and anonymous, in social space and isolated, embodying what Rodker describes elsewhere as 'isolation, ... fear of personal dying, ... love of the stranger'.[84] While evoking 'race memories', they are also marked by their pantomime costumes as artificial, as 'marionettes' resembling a 'Wax Dummy in [a] Shop Window' (1918) or the 'Aunt Sallys' of 'Hymn to Cold' (1916) and 'The Fair'.

Of course, 'Aunt Sallys' are dummies at which to throw or shoot things in fairgrounds. Rodker writes in 'The Fair': 'But the shooting gallery does not draw me / not the Aunt Sallys.'[85] Such dummies are targets of (staged and, therefore, safe) animosity. However, in 'Hymn to Cold'[86] Rodker relates such dummies to Old Testament suffering:

O cold – cold cold – maddening cold.
Blood
thou dost freeze in a moment to
Ice.
We stand – Lot's wives –
the snow piles a mound over us –
sleet shoots at the Aunt Sallys.

Under the title of a biblical 'hymn', in a vocabulary evoking the King James Bible ('O', 'thou dost'), Rodker alludes to the Old Testament tale of Lot's wife. Genesis 19:17 states that God warned Lot and his family not to look back when they were fleeing the destruction of Sodom and Gomorrah.[87] When Lot's wife disobeyed, she was turned into a pillar of salt.[88] 'Hymn to Cold' wittily mingles the white 'piles' of English snow and Hebrew salt. Such trans-historical mingling further relates the narrator's collective 'we' to the Hebrew past: in recollecting that past, 'we stand' like 'Lot's wives' looking back on Sodom and Gomorrah, and thus 'freeze' to snow/salt. This freezing of motion leaves the collective 'we' like dummies, or 'Aunt Sallys'. Similarly, Rosenberg's 'Through These Pale Cold Days' (1918)[89] juxtaposes biblical imagery with the frozen ('blond still') contemporaneity of England. However, Rosenberg looks forward to a Zionist reconstitution of Jewish nationhood, whereas Rodker appears to associate Jewish particularism with past victimhood. Indeed, the Judaised 'Aunt Sallys' are also present victims, as the 'sleet shoots at' them. Nevertheless, the poem's 'we' are only victimized in so far as they look back, like 'Lot's wives', from the present to the past. Although 'the gypsy girl' in 'The Fair'[90] 'crushes my old identity upon me', the narrator of that poem refuses to be a dummy, victim or Aunt Sally. 'Not the Aunt Sallys', he decides. Rather, his focus is resolutely fixed on the present where he dances 'ragtime on the sward' in a celebration of modern otherness.

Rodker stages a present which is relatively free of victimization. To be sure, such a present is painstakingly shown to be artificial and theatrical. In 'The Acrobats', for example, the performers 'crossed the stage in little jerky rushings, / bodies very pink across the footlights'. In 'Theatre' (1920),[91] only 'a façade' of performance brings something 'very peaceful / and probably like heaven'. Like the gypsy in 'The Fair', who 'crushes' the narrator with his 'old identity', in 'Theatre' 'sound – / Fills the horizon to crush us / with a noise like tearing silk'. Theatricality is a precarious, 'thin' construct which can be torn apart ('like tearing silk') by the violence with which life crushes 'old' Jewish identity upon 'us'.

The American-Jewish poet Maxwell Bodenheim notes in a review of Rodker's *Poems* how the Anglo-Jew discerns English manners to be theatrical: 'We have him here, a youth half-afraid of the life-tangle about, half satirically sad, and at times bewildered or disdainful of the elaborately acting people about him.'[92] I suggest that Rodker acculturates to England's 'elaborately acting people' by imagining diasporic life as inherently theatrical. In 'The Acrobats',[93] for example, a minority assemblage of people has to perform on 'stage' before an English audience. Only when the act concludes and the semitically signified 'pyramids' of 'pink dolls' are dismantled, does the narrator note how 'Suddenly I saw their bellies breathing fiercely.' For a moment, the acrobats appear free of their socially circumscribed role-play before the surrounding English audience.

Further, the fact that Rodker refers to the acrobats as 'they' and the audience as 'we' suggests his ambivalently apprehended position between minority Jewishness and majority Englishness. Similarly, in his article 'The Theatre in Whitechapel' (1913),[94] Rodker compares the 'virility' of Whitechapel's 'perfect theatre' with 'the emasculation of *our own* [Anglophone] drama' [*my italics*]. Writing a eulogistic article on East End Yiddish theatre, Rodker nevertheless emphasises that he is outside the Whitechapel ghetto. He distances himself from 'these [Yiddishphone] audiences' in order to connect with a majority Anglophone readership. Since it is clear that Rodker understands Yiddish, ultimately he presents himself as occupying a 'foreign'[95] space between the Jewish ghetto and his English readers: between affiliation and otherness to both.

Rodker's poems detail the theatrical and fundamentally artificial quality of modern life alongside myriad 'breathing' animal life forms. Poems which construct a mechanical worldview include 'Dancer' (1918) ('the machine clanks'), 'The Pub' (1914) ('The automatic piano plays and plays') and 'Nude with a Wrist-watch' (1916) ('The watch ticks on her wrist / Her life is naked – its meaning gone').[96] Concurrently, the poet depicts a host of animals which escape such assemblages by slipping through the cogs of (socio-cultural) machines. Worms ('Married', 'Out of the Water'), frogs ('I'd have loved you as you deserved had we been frogs', 'Frogs') and fish ('The Flying Banvards', 'To a Renault in the Country') are just some of the slippery creatures which abound in Rodker's verse.[97] Similarly, rats and vermin refuse mechanical organisation, 'scuttling' away ('Wax Dummy in Shop Window') to leave only 'a rodent strain of verdigris' ('To Any Idol').[98]

To be sure, insects and rats also appear in the poetry of Isaac Rosenberg.[99] However, it is Rodker's slippery creatures – frogs, fish and worms – and their relationship to a mechanical and staged world which I want to examine here. Indeed, it is the very slipperiness of such animals that, I suggest, bestows them with significance, since it implies what Gilles Deleuze terms the quality of 'speed', or slipping 'between'.[100] Such a quality is key for Rodker, who locates his Anglo-Jewish identity as Other, 'among strangers'.

Consider Rodker's role as a conscientious objector during the First World War. In *Memoirs of Other Fronts*, he writes:

> I was alone [as a CO], and it is painful, almost impossible to pit your will against a crowd's, when you – and all your instincts – fear it will, and want it to fall on you, trample you into nothing.
>
> No, it is not easy, it is very difficult to set yourself (even if you have to slide out) against the will of a nation, of a camp.[101]

During the war, 'Basil'[102] refuses to fight; rather, he places himself between friend and foe. He decides to 'slide out' of conflict. Otherness is his life; but it cannot be maintained through confrontation. It can only be sustained, as it were, in opposition to opposition: in pacifism. In opposition *tout court*, the Other faces the 'crowd's' will without hope, expecting, then desperately desiring ('want it to fall on you'), the end ('nothing') of an 'impossible' battle.

To be sure, 'slide' also carries negative connotations of disreputable behaviour, of choosing not 'to see it as much through as I could'. It is an onomatopoeically slippery signifier, commonly twinned with 'slip' or 'slip away'. (The COs who choose not to stay in prison, but instead to do work of national importance, feel: 'They themselves had evaded the issues. They had slipped round the corner.'[103])

In prison, the narrator notes how 'you go on reading and the slide that screens the judas in your door slips back in place and you hear the warder's slippers shuffling to the cell next door'.[104] The term 'judas' calls to mind Judas's betrayal of Jesus, and is linked semantically with the 'slide' that 'slips' in the door. As we have seen, T. S. Eliot refers to 'flowering judas' with a similar lower-case 'j' in 'Gerontion' (1920), thus associating it with the 'jew' of that poem.[105] In *The Apes of God* (1930), Wyndham Lewis evokes Rodker (through the character 'Ratner') as 'the Judas without the kiss (for no fairly intelligent Christ would ever trust him)'.[106] Apparently, antisemitic Modernists followed traditional Christian homiletics in presenting Judas as the paradigmatic Jewish traitor. Here, Rodker de-Christianises and universalises the term and condition of 'judas'.

'Among soldiers' in prison, the narrator remains institutionally affiliated; by contrast, it is the warder who is seen as the potential Judas peering through the 'judas', the stranger who spies on neighbours ('the cell next door'), the outsider 'with slippers shuffling' (approaching furtively as neither friend nor foe) from 'slide' to 'slide'. There is an ambivalence here, for the potentially treacherous warder is also a free man, Other to the prisoners. He is a modern Everyman, the ambivalently apprehended stranger who 'slips' and slides (in 'slippers') between significations. The warder is a universalised successor of Christianity's paradigmatic Jewish traitor, but he is also what the narrator ardently desires to be: free in his slippery otherness to do as he pleases.

Significantly, the narrator is 'reading' while the warder 'slips back' the 'slide' over the 'judas'. This is no coincidence, for 'reading' is as slippery and ambivalently apprehended a process as living the thrilling, yet insecure freedom of modern otherness. In this regard, 'reading' also resembles writing, which slides between the 'solid' and the 'liquid',[107] and is at its best (as Rosenberg writes of poetry) 'understandable and still ungraspable',[108] celebrating the slippery ('ungraspable') otherness of language in the face of attempts to make it conform to one graspable explication.

Interestingly, Christian groups – including the 'British Israelites'[109] – are parodied in *Memoirs* for construing the governor of 'Dartmoor' Prison as 'a Pontius Pilate' oppressing the 'saved'. In fact, such groups awaiting 'the day of doom' are no more 'saved' than the governor is anti-Christ. The entire narrative of the 'Last Trump' is 'a great deception'; language has slipped, Judas-like, away from Christian certainties and declared again only its own otherness.[110]

Freedom is otherness for the narrator. When he is released from prison on 'work of National Importance', Basil revels in freedom by purchasing chocolate:

> I ate some chocolate. I had felt wonderfully rich to be able to buy something, but it had a cold slimy richness altogether different from the grateful warmth of the boiling ship's cocoa that would have been coming round at about this hour … Above all I wanted to be shut tight in the small cell, in warm gas light, with my book, all of me aware that soon it would be

time for the eight o'clock bed-time bell. I felt lonely and afraid.[111]

The chocolate outside prison has a 'cold slimy richness'. Such sliminess evokes the otherness of freedom (as, indeed, does the chocolate's 'cold' atomisation of the purchaser according to economic power ('richness')). Freedom's 'slimy' indeterminacy leaves the narrator feeling, on the one hand, 'wonderfully rich', and on the other, 'lonely and afraid'. Fear of freedom spurs his affiliation with prison's barrack-like regimentation: the quasi-naval camaraderie of 'ship's cocoa' and rules reminiscent of a boys' boarding school ('soon it would be time for the eight o'clock bed-time bell'). To be a free man means to be a 'slimy' Other; whereas a boy is bound to an unquestioned routine marked by the 'bed-time bell'. Back on a train, Basil notes that 'the steam-clotted windows began to shut me in, warmly, reassuringly. I forgot that I was free'.[112] Once the slippery, slimy otherness of freedom is 'clotted', freedom's flux is replaced by amnesia ('I forgot that I was free'). The train replaces slippery freedom with its own mechanical agenda.

Rodker's language implies that slipping, sliding and the slimy are ways out of machines, and mechanical socio-cultural structures, into the freedom of otherness. Zygmunt Bauman relates precisely the 'slimy' to modern perceptions of Jews:

> The Jews, already construed as 'slimy' in religious and class dimensions, were more than any other category vulnerable to the impact of the new tensions and contradictions which the social upheavals of the modernizing revolution could not fail to generate.[113]

According to Bauman, Jews inevitably crossed national, 'religious and class' boundaries in 'modernizing' countries such as England. Consequently, 'the conceptual Jew' was constructed 'as *visqueux* (in Sartrean terms), slimy (in Mary Douglas's terms) – an image construed as compromising and defying the order of things.'[114]

One reading of Rodker's autobiography and poems might understand them as de-Judaising such antisemitic constructions of Jewish sliminess. Ezra Pound, for example, spoke of 'Jew slime'[115] while T. S. Eliot characterised a 'Semite' in 'Burbank with a Beidecker: Bleistein with a Cigar' as 'protozoic slime'.[116] Such 'viscosity' which 'blurs the boundary between things'[117] appears frequently in Rodker's verse; for example, in 'Pregnant' (1915) ('the slimes of fear'), 'War Museum – Royal College of Surgeons' (*c.*1923) ('fruit / rotting in verdigris'), 'Hymn to Love' (1920) ('mucous surfaces') and 'Out of the Water' (1923) ('mush / jelly that sweats').[118] Rodker, I suggest, deploys traces of antisemitic discourse to universalise the 'slimy', and Jewish, freedom of slipping between taxonomical definitions.

Similarly, Rodker's sense of slipping between categories applies to skin colour, and the implications of skin colour within British imperial literature and society. In Chapter 3, we saw how Siegfried Sassoon reproduced traces of a discourse which situated Jewishness ambivalently between black and white peoples. I argued there that such a discourse constructed Jews as 'neither black nor white', but disturbingly uncategorisable.[119] At this point, I want to add that Rodker also negotiates an ungraspable Jewish position between black colonial subject and white imperial master.

Reviewing Rodker's *Poems*, Richard Aldington singles out the following lines for his disapproval: 'White perfection / Black and immobile' ('The Descent into Hell' (1914)).[120] For an *Imagiste* who favoured the '"hard edges" and precision' of 'Greek poetry', such lines were nothing save 'vagueness and useless reaction to primitivism, all woody [*sic*] edges ... careless of aesthetic effect'.[121] How on earth could black be white, or (worse) vice versa?

'The Descent into Hell' further features such ambivalent sentiments as 'From the light / Woven into the dark / Part ... and not part', 'Part and not part / I am' and 'Woven into the dark / I ... and yet / Not I'. Thus, the reader is left to wonder to what extent the poet is part of the 'dark', and what the relationship between 'White perfection' and 'Black' might be. Apparently, black and white interrelate in a hybrid form which mirrors the poem's uncategorisable persona: 'White perfection / Black and immobile / Fills me ... '

In 'The Fair'[122], the 'gypsy girl' is 'daughter of moon and heath / and black and magic sires'. Her 'black' nomadic ancestry ('moon and heath', 'daughter') is in sharp distinction to the 'pallid', 'Pale faces' of the 'white' crowd. As the narrator dances 'ragtime on the sward', the 'fungus of white faces / envied us and gibbered'. It appears that the poem's persona affiliates with the 'black' gypsy through his Jewish ancestry ('my old identity'), while simultaneously relating to the 'white' crowd through the slimy metaphor of 'pallid fungus'. Sliding between 'black' and 'white', he slips away from (Aldington's) '"hard edges"' of precisely categorisable colour.

Further, 'The Fair' depicts a black American 'ragtime' 'dance' on English turf ('sward'). To be sure, 'ragtime' is black music; but it relates also to the poem's abbreviated term 'a new rag'. That many East London Jews were involved in the commonly denominated 'rag trade'[123] at this time may associate Anglo-Jews with the blackness of 'ragtime' here.

'Sward' suggests 'swart'. The latter word appears in the context of the Hebrew Bible in 'Dead Queens' (1917):[124] 'Lilith laughs at the old Adam, / Caught serpent-wise by the swart eastern woman.' Here Eve is depicted as both black ('swart') and 'eastern'. By contrast, Lilith is placed in the company of (western) Celtic and French figures of 'high romance / Lilith, Iseult and Guinevere'. While Lilith and Eve are both Old Testament figures,[125] the former is identified with white western culture (the women whose 'cheeks grow pale') and the latter with the black and 'eastern'.

Significantly, Adam is described as 'old', as in Sassoon's 'Ancient History' (1918) (where Adam, tellingly, is neither black nor white, but 'a brown old vulture in the rain').[126] In 'Dead Queens', also, Adam represents an outmoded, Judaic system of belief. Indeed, he resembles the 'Schlemihl' of 'Wild West Remittance Man' in so far as he is affiliated to Jewish particularism with 'the swart eastern woman'. 'Lilith laughs' at him with a 'scorn' similar to that displayed by the 'gypsy girl' of 'The Fair' towards the narrator's 'old identity'. However, Rodker differs from Sassoon in not consigning 'swart eastern' Jewishness – the marriage of Adam and Eve – to the nostalgic, irretrievable past. Rather, the legacy of the Old Testament is very much alive in the poem's tense present:

> Lilith laughs at the old Adam,
> Caught serpent-wise by the swart eastern woman
> God gave him to his sorrow!
> Her sorrows are his sorrow,
> Her thoughts his thoughts;
> For she has bound him to her
> With the strong toils of pity –
> His heart would burst to break them.

Here the legacy of Eden is contemporary 'sorrow'. Such sorrow is related to the 'toils of pity' with which Eve today binds men to women ('him to her'). Thus, one basis for Rodker's misogyny is his association of 'sorrow' with biblically sanctioned marriage. Still, Rodker's ambivalent position towards such 'God'-given matrimonial 'toils' is made plain in the poem's final line: 'His heart would burst to break them'. Rodker's Adam is 'bound' to his 'swart eastern woman' by ambivalent desire: the 'toils' of his 'heart'. Indeed, 'Dead Queens' suggests that Anglo-Jewish identity is similarly situated ambivalently between black colonial subjugation ('Caught', 'bound him', 'toils') and white imperial rule ('Queens'), between entrapment ('bound') and voluntary affiliation ('heart'). Moreover, this Anglo-Jewish tension between otherness and affiliation is dramatised in the context of sexual relationships with women.

Certainly, Rodker focuses on the bodies of women as sites of Modernist significance. 'Nude with Wrist-watch',[127] for example, concerns sex and psychology, rather than landscape and history:

> The watch ticks on her wrist.
> Will, must, can't but tick on –
> And how she writhe or twist
> or furbish; her life's gone.
>
> The watch ticks on her wrist,
> where she lies on the bed,
> measures each moment, kissing, kissed:
> Each moment, by what passion fed.
>
> The watch ticks on her wrist.
> Her life is naked – its meaning gone –
> Her watch in a last tryst
> with Time, Space and Decay, ticks on.

Interestingly, 'Each moment, by what passion fed' recalls lines from Shelley's 'Ozymandias' (1817):[128]

> Tell that its sculptor well those passions read
> Which yet survive, stamp'd on these lifeless things,
> The hand that mock'd them and the heart that fed.

'Ozymandias' is a sonnet about ruins in a 'desert', which concludes with the bleak line: 'The lone and level sands stretch far away.'

Rodker's poem ends on a similar note: 'Time, Space and Decay, ticks on.' Indeed, I want to suggest that Rodker transposes Shelley's meditation on ruins from desert 'sands' to a modern woman's body. Rodker's scene of inexorable 'Decay' takes as its locus a sexualised nude ('writhe or twist', 'kissing, kissed'), rather than an 'antique'[129] civilisation. Possibly, 'Nude with Wrist-watch' suggests psychological resolutions of present dilemmas. Unlike Rosenberg, Rodker does not look to the Zionist reclamation of Palestinian 'desert' to resolve contemporary Anglo-Jewish tensions.

Similarly, James Joyce's *Ulysses* (1922) transposes thoughts of Palestine to the site of a woman's body:

> A barren land, bare waste. Vulcanic lake, the dead sea: no fish, weedless, sunk deep in the earth ... It lay there now. Now it could bear no more. Dead: an old woman's: the grey sunken cunt of the world.[130]

Rodker admired Joyce's work in progress, *Ulysses*, years before his Egoist Press published the second and third editions of the book. Thus, it may be no coincidence that for both Rodker and Joyce's fictional Jew, Leopold Bloom, the psychological reverberations of 'cunt' are of more relevance than Zionism. Rodker depicts sex as a *psychological* return to the Jews' Promised Land. In 'Hymn to Heat' (1920),[131] for example, the poet compares his lover's body to the Judaic 'Ark',[132] in a context of 'yearning':

> O eternally insatiate.
> O yearning ones.
>
> Under her caressing fingers,
> Desire wells up in you.
> You swell ... strive nearer,
> O Proud Erection!
> She is a magnet
> and Ark of life.

Here traditional diasporic 'yearning' for a return to Jerusalem, incorporated into the Passover Haggadah,[133] is displaced to a yearning for 'her caressing fingers'. Rather than seek Judaic consummation in the re-erection of Solomon's Second Temple,[134] Rodker's persona finds satisfaction, *tout court*, in the 'Erection' of his penis. The eternal ('eternally') is sexualised ('insatiate') as man's unceasing 'Desire'. On the one hand, here is serious Freudian psychology;[135] and, on the other, 'a mocking or an ironizing' of such seriousness, suggestive of what Adam Phillips identifies as Rodker's 'acutely self-conscious' personae.[136] Read either way, the poem avoids engagement with English and Zionist landscapes and histories.

Further, Rodker situates his verse in a space of similar foreignness. His prefatory 'Note' to *Collected Poems 1912–1925*[137] explains:

> One thing this collection makes me realize very clearly is how much influenced I was by the French Poetry of 1850–1910. That was because I first came to poetry through that language (the foreign-ness already evocative and moving; which with its content satisfied my particular demand for what poetry ought to be). But until this had happened I was closed to English poetry, so that perhaps later it was too late to write poetry that would be nearer the traditions of the language I was using.

Rodker locates his poetry between French ('what poetry ought to be') and English ('the language I was using') traditions. What attracted him to French, Rodker states, was 'the foreign-ness already evocative and moving'. As an Anglo-Jew who felt 'in London a foreigner',[138] Rodker is likely to have identified with such 'foreign-ness'. Thus, he situates his poetry between French and English 'traditions', and as Other to both.

Rodker's note continues: 'When I wrote poetry I was, as it were, hanging in the void, and these poems are my efforts to establish contact.' In other words, the verse is Rodker's medium for affiliation ('to establish contact') with an English readership from a position of inbetweenness ('hanging in the void'). Rosenberg's 'Chagrin' (1915–16) similarly depicts the 'void' experienced by a first-generation Anglo-Jew as 'emptiness'.[139] Rodker also, I suggest, attempts a 'revolutionary'[140] challenge to the dominant, monocultural English tradition which dismisses or ignores minority literature. As he says, the 'main function' of some of the poems 'when they were written, was to shock'.[141]

Significantly, this 'void' where Rodker claims he was 'hanging' finds explicit articulation throughout his oeuvre. In 'London Night' (1914), for example, 'Still the void turns ... '; and in 'To a Renault in

the Country' (1927), 'rain / flies in the void' above 'the shining
abyss of tar'. Similarly, the prose-poem 'The Lunatic' (1915) features
'a wide French window, which looks on to a terrace overhanging
the edge of the world'; and 'The Dutch Dolls' (1915) evokes 'poor
fools, on the world's edge'.[142] In particular, 'The Flying Banvards'
(c.1925)[143] merits closer examination in relation to Rodker's Anglo-
Jewish 'void'. Here is a poem which relates religion and semitic
geography to otherness, suspension and 'the still / Void':

> How like a fish this woman in mid-air
> Floats ere she whirls, teeth clenched upon a wire;
> Taut body a new moon. Her hands respire
> Like tadpole gills or hovering wings. Fair
> Angel rapt and mute, quiring round what flare
> Of Godhead, unsinged ever? while your shrill
> Climbing hosannas strike out from the still
> Void, sultriness as from Aghreb, rare
> Sphere. The whiles your impotent male friends try
> From springy asphodel to jump to sky,
> But roughly tumble, fall with a cheap jest.
> Alas! your wet secret raptures scattered
> You come to earth ... now I see your battered
> Face and ruined breast.

The familiar figure of a circus performer (consider, for example,
'The Acrobats'[144]) initially appears in deterritorialised mode,
suspended 'in mid-air'. She 'Floats', apparently 'hovering' above
the 'earth'. She is 'like a fish' out of water, far from her home
environment, in a form of diaspora. However, 'in mid-air' she
seems like an 'Angel'; and Rodker proceeds to depict the trappings
of religion ('Godhead, unsinged ever', Hebrew 'hosannas'[145])
against a sceptical, secular backdrop of 'still / Void'. The trapeze
artist may seem like an 'Angel', but there is no Yahweh ('Godhead')
to acknowledge her reality as such here.

The poem progresses with its sole geographical reference: to the
'Aghreb' (better known as the Maghreb) in North Africa.
Deterritorialisation from England – significantly to a semitic (Arab)
area evocative of semitic (Jewish) geography in the ancient Middle
East – is again evident. Meanwhile, on Hellenised ground ('springy
asphodel'[146]) the religious and geographical dreams of diaspora 'fall
with a cheap jest'. Hebraic 'secret raptures' are 'scattered' and

mocked. Nothing is left of ancient Jewish geography, religion and history save dispiriting ruins ('ruined breast').

Elsewhere, the past is similarly evoked as ruins. In 'Under the Trees' (1916),[147] for example, the narrator sits 'quiet':

> I sit. And all the débris of ten thousand years
> snows me under.
> Godlike,
> inert,
> bleak and friable,
> porous like black earth,
> I sit –
> where quietly
> pitters the ruin of ten thousand years.

Looking back on past 'ruin', the narrator resembles Lot's wife (in the Old Testament and 'The Fair'[148]): 'All is become metallic – / Salt bitter.' Appearing white ('snows me under'), the speaker nevertheless feels 'porous like black earth' as he recollects history. Like Yahweh ('Godlike'), he appears passive ('inert') before the site of such destruction ('the ruin of ten thousand years'). Here is a persona 'hanging in the void',[149] sensing a 'black' ancestry in the 'black earth', while internalising the slimy state of existing between black-and-white categories as 'porous', 'friable' 'mould'. Moreover, he empathises with the 'diffuse', a salty scattering like that of diasporic Jews since 'the ruin'.

Sidra DeKoven Ezrahi suggests that lamentation for 'a world in ruins to be preserved [in words] until such time as it could be reclaimed'[150] is common to pre-Holocaust Jewish poets. According to Ezrahi, this literary tradition emerges from diaspora, with 'Jewish culture as a *minority* culture, whose paradigmatic experience is exile'.[151] To be sure, Rodker takes his poetry to ancient ruins. Nonetheless, I contend that Rodker seeks to live in a modernity free from the Zionist pressure of reclaiming a Jewish past he identifies as 'unutterably mournful' ('Interior' (1917)). It is no coincidence that Rodker informed Pound he had 'no history to speak of'.[152]

However, modernity intensifies antisemitism:

> Bilge
> of sneers, insults
> kindnesses and obligations;

evil:
by me and to me –
squelches inside me.

No purge expels it,
it swinks in the hulk
like a ball of
plaster-of-paris
in a rat.

I can't keep going long
with that inside me.

In 'Hymn to Friends and Enemies: Atlas, twentieth century' (1916),[153] Rodker deploys the common antisemitic image of the 'rat' precisely to address responses to himself as a Jew in early twentieth-century England. As we have seen, Rosenberg also depicted rats, most notably in 'Break of Day in the Trenches' (1916). Disturbingly, this 'rat' is compared to the poem's persona himself ('inside me', 'in a rat'). Inside him, specifically, is something 'like a ball of / plaster-of-paris': a cast of a 'ball'. To be sure, the poet moulded himself in the 'plaster-of-paris' cast of a Parisian bohemian.[154] Inside the 'rat' is also something foreign, something French. The 'rat' itself is associated with strangers, since it resembles the 'hulk' of a ship in which rats are sometimes unwelcome occupants. 'Sneers, insults' and 'evil' follow the immigrant arriving by ship to England, the stranger, the would-be-Parisian 'rat'.

The poem's persona is also costive, full of 'Bilge' which 'squelches inside' and cannot be purged. Apparently, his sphincter is as tight as this short, terse verse: 'I can't keep going long / with that inside me.' Indeed, this persona resembles the narrator of part III of *Memoirs of Other Fronts* whose refusal to trust his former lover Muriel means he 'would not loosen', and stays 'hanging on hard, oh wanting to let go!' This (autobiographical) narrator thinks 'with secret pleasure of purges, violent drugs to swallow, to undermine and violently blast all out of me'.[155] He is seriously constipated, unable to relax and 'to let go'.

Rodker's evocation of constipation, and the discomfort caused by excessive anal retention, demands further investigation; particularly in view of the poet's commitment to Freudian psychoanalysis. Despite the fact that his *Collected Poems 1912–1925*, covering the verse output of a full fourteen years, contains an unassuming, even minimal, twenty-eight poems, Rodker remarks in the prefatory note: 'Some of these poems, which partly I should have liked to omit, do seem to me successful in their 'genre', and so they are included, excessive as, at this date, they seem. I think this much apology is needed – but only this much.'[156]

Apparently, several ('some') of the few poems chosen by Rodker are 'excessive'. Further, the poet apologises for not omitting such poems ('this much apology is needed'), while making sure he does not embarrass himself by apologising excessively ('but only this much'). All of this embarrassment is in the context of a 'fastidiously elegant' collection; the only 'Hours Press' book 'not to have been printed in France'. In this special instance, Rodker personally supervised the book's production in England.[157]

In effect, Rodker is apologising here to an English readership for his lack of poetic continence: a failure to 'omit' the 'excessive'. Like Rosenberg asking Miss Seaton to 'forgive this little excursion into the forbidden lands of egotism',[158] Rodker is embarrassed into apology. His tone, too, chimes with a species of Anglo-Jewish apologetics[159] in which Jewishness *per se* is somehow perceived to be 'excessive' in England. Regardless of the minimalism and elegance of the *Collected Poems*, its very provenance appears to damn it.

Considered together, it seems to me that 'Hymn to Friends and Enemies', *Memoirs of Other Fronts* and the prefatory note to *Collected Poems 1912–1925* articulate a tight, anally fixated control over potentially 'excessive' Jewish behaviour in English literature and society. Conversely, I want to suggest that Rodker's *deterritorialised* poetry gestures towards universalistic freedom from such constraints.

In its universalism, Rodker's verse is both Modernist and Hebraic. The very title of Rodker's collection *Hymns* (1920) implies an Hebraic counterpoint to the Hellenic leanings of Anglo-American Modernism. Certainly, Rodker's Job-like[160] 'Hymn of Hymns' (1916)[161] damns the biblical universe, but it also engages with its universality:

> God damn
> the prurulent pestilent wind,
> and the pullulating sea.
> The eternal infinite, cosmical, blue,

deep, unfathomed, boundless, free,
racing, wild, mysterious sea –
its argus-eyed, winged and lanthorned dwellers.
And you   Walt.

As in his review of André Spire's *Poèmes Juifs*, here too Rodker associates 'Walt' Whitman with Jewish universalism ('God', 'eternal infinite'). Further, such universalism complements the 'boundless' Anglo-Jewish otherness which Rodker is at pains to present in his poetry and elsewhere. This is not the classical universalism of 'Greek ... tradition', with the '"hard edges" and precision' demanded by Richard Aldington and T. S. Eliot.[162] Rather, it is a *deterritorialised* humanism ('Walt'), with an emphasis on 'love of the stranger'.[163]

Jon Silkin resembles both John Rodker and Isaac Rosenberg in looking to the Hebrew Bible and American poets for an 'ineffable but useable'[164] Anglo-Jewish universalism. In Chapter 5, I argue that Silkin produces a minority Modernist poetry like his Anglo-Jewish predecessors. Moreover, Silkin writes explicitly on Anglo-Jewish landscapes and history from a post-Holocaust perspective.

NOTES

1.   Andrew Crozier (ed.), *John Rodker: Poems & Adolphe 1920* (Manchester: Carcanet, 1996), p. xvi.
2.   At the time of writing (summer 2004), Professor Tom Staley of the University of Texas at Austin is preparing a biography.
3.   See John Rodker, *Collected Poems 1912–1925* (Paris: The Hours Press, 1930). See also Crozier (ed.), *John Rodker: Poems & Adolphe 1920*.
4.   See Ben Gidley, 'Ghetto Radicalism: The Jewish East End', *New Voices in Jewish Thought* 2 (1999), pp. 50–69.
5.   Crozier (ed.), p. vii. See also Joseph Leftwich, who corroborates such self-assertiveness in '"Jewish" London Fifty Years Ago', in *1915–1965 Fifty Years Achievement in the Arts* (London: Ben Uri Art Society, 1966), pp. 12–16: 'It was a time [1915] of Yiddish ferment in the East End, the self-assertion of the "foreign" Jews.'
6.   Leftwich, p. 14.
7.   See Jack Isaacs, 'Mr. John Rodker: Literature in the Twenties', *The Times*, 11 October 1955, p. 11.
8.   Leftwich, p. 14.
9.   Crozier (ed.), *Poems & Adolphe 1920*, p. vii.
10. Leftwich, p. 14.
11. Rodker, *Collected Poems 1912–1925*, p. vii.
12. John Rodker, *The Future of Futurism* (London: Kegan Paul, Trench, Trubner, 1927), p. 8.
13. See Nancy Cunard, *These Were The Hours: Memoirs of My Hours Press, Réanville and Paris 1928–1931* (Carbondale: Southern Illinois University Press, 1969), p. 142: 'He had learned printing and publishing years before at his Ovid Press, in London, which he had founded "to bring before the public work that was considered

advanced". Its first book was T. S. Eliot's *Ara Vos Prec*, of which 264 copies were brought out in a fine and very individual format, on beautiful paper with initials and colophon by E. A. Wadsworth. Eliot's poems appeared in December 1919; the following April Ezra Pound's *Hugh Selwyn Mauberley* was published.'

14.   See the obituary to Rodker in *Publishers' Weekly: The American Book Trade Journal* 168:21 (19 November 1955), p. 2127: 'He was the English publisher of the second and third editions of James Joyce's "Ulysses".'

15.   Adam Phillips, 'Unofficial Modernist: John Rodker', *The Jewish Quarterly* (winter 1998/1999), pp. 69–71.

16.   Wendy Stallard Flory, 'Pound and antisemitism', in Ira B. Nadel (ed.), *The Cambridge Companion to Ezra Pound* (Cambridge: Cambridge University Press, 1999), pp. 284–300.

17.   'Letter from Lewis to Pound, before July 1915', in Timothy Materer (ed.), *Pound/Lewis: The Letters of Ezra Pound and Wyndham Lewis* (London: Faber, 1985), p. 13. Lewis depicts Rodker, transformed into 'Julius Ratner', in his novel *The Apes of God* (London: Arthur Press, 1930). As Ian Patterson notes in '"The Plan Behind the Plan": Russians, Jews and Mythologies of Change: The Case of Mary Butts', in Bryan Cheyette and Laura Marcus (eds), *Modernity, Culture and 'the Jew'* (Cambridge: Polity Press, 1998), pp. 126–40, Lewis's descriptions of Ratner deploy the 'familiar stereotypes of antisemitism: impersonation, inauthenticity, deviousness, dirtiness, business acumen, sexual appetite'.

18.   Materer (ed.), p. 135.

19.   See 'Letter from Eliot to Rodker, 9 July 1917', in Valerie Eliot (ed.), *The Letters of T. S. Eliot: vol. 1, 1898–1922* (London: Faber, 1988), p. 312: 'I hope the book may be more nearly what you had in mind. I think you have all the newer poems: beside the [Leonard] Woolf volume there is a French poem in *L. Review* ("Dans le Restaurant"), "Bleistein" and "Sweeney Erect", "Cooking Egg" – of which I enclose revised version *with* quotations – and this new one, "Gerontion".' See also Bryan Cheyette, *Constructions of 'The Jew' in English Literature and Society: Racial Representations, 1875–1945* (Cambridge: Cambridge University Press, 1993), pp. 234–67 and Anthony Julius, *T. S. Eliot, Anti-Semitism, and Literary Form* (Cambridge: Cambridge University Press, 1995), pp. 41–110.

20.   See, for example, 'Letter from Joyce to Carlo Linati, 21 September 1920, Paris', in Richard Ellmann (ed.), *Selected Letters of James Joyce* (London: Faber, 1975), p. 270: 'Scriva al Rodker che Le farà avere gli altri esemplari [of *Ulysses*] … È l'epopea di due razze (Israele–Irlanda) e nel melemimo tempo il ciclo del corpo umano ed anche una storiella di una giornata (vita).' ['Write to Rodker and ask him to let you have the other copies [of *Ulysses*] … It is the epic of two races (Israel–Ireland) and at the same time the cycle of the human body as well as a little story of a day (life).'] See further Cheyette, *Constructions of 'The Jew'*, pp. 206–34.

21.   T. S. Eliot, *After Strange Gods* (London: Faber, 1934), p. 19.

22.   Ezra Pound, *The Cantos of Ezra Pound* (London: Faber, 1987), p. 257. 'Ben' is Benjamin Franklin; '*neschek*' is Hebrew for 'usury': see Nadel (ed.), p. 293.

23.   See Margaret Anderson, 'Editorial Note', *The Little Review* 6:2 (June 1919), p. i: 'Ezra Pound has abdicated and gone to Persia. John Rodker is now the London Editor of the Little Review.' See further Thomas L. Scott, Melvin J. Friedman and Jackson R. Bryer (eds), *Pound/The Little Review: The Letters of Ezra Pound to Margaret Anderson* (New York: New Directions, 1988), p. 262: 'John Rodker's name as editor last appears in the January–March 1921 issue.'

24.   See Crozier (ed.), p. 187.

25.   'Letter from Pound to Anderson, 10 August 1917', in Scott, Friedman and Bryer (eds), p. 109.

26.   'Letter to Anderson, September 1917', in D. D. Page (ed.), *The Letters of Ezra Pound, 1907–1941* (London: Faber, 1951), p. 179.

27.   Unpublished letter from Pound to Harriet Monroe, August 1915 , cited in Joseph Cohen, *Journey to the Trenches: The Life of Isaac Rosenberg 1890–1918* (London: Robson Books, 1975), p. 121. In *The Apes of God*, pp. 143–4, Wyndham Lewis describes Ratner similarly as one 'whose ambition led him to burgle all the books of Western romance'.

28. Richard Aldington, 'Flint and Rodker', *Poetry: A Magazine of Verse* 17:1 (October 1920), pp. 44–8.
29. Richard Aldington, 'Two Poets', *The Egoist* 1:22 (16 November 1914), pp. 422–3.
30. Cunard, p. 141.
31. John Rodker, *Memoirs of Other Fronts* (London: Putnam, 1932), p. 62.
32. Aldington, 'Two Poets', *The Egoist* 1:22, p. 423.
33. Ezra Pound, 'Notes and Announcements', *Poetry* 1:2 (November 1912), p. 65. See also Charles Doyle, *Richard Aldington: A Biography* (Basingstoke: Macmillan, 1989), p. 17.
34. Doyle, pp. 22, 28.
35. Doyle, p. 29. See also Richard Eugene Smith, *Richard Aldington* (Boston: Twayne, 1977), p. 22.
36. Christopher Hassall, *Edward Marsh: Patron of the Arts* (London: Longman, 1959), p. 402.
37. Letter to Edward Marsh, dated spring 1915, in Ian Parsons (ed.), *The Collected Works of Isaac Rosenberg* (1979; London: Chatto & Windus, 1984), p. 210.
38. Aldington, 'Two Poets', *The Egoist* 1:22, p. 422.
39. Aldington, 'Flint and Rodker', *Poetry* 17:1, p. 47.
40. Letter from Rosenberg to Ruth Löwy, dated October 1912, in Parsons (ed.), pp. 193–4.
41. 'Letter from Lewis to Pound, before July 1915', in Materer (ed.), p. 13.
42. Anderson, 'Editorial Note', *The Little Review* 6:2, p. i.
43. Crozier (ed.), pp. 37, 43.
44. Rodker, *Memoirs of Other Fronts*, p. 191.
45. Crozier (ed.), pp. 86–7.
46. See *The New Shorter Oxford English Dictionary*, fourth edition, vol. I (Oxford: Oxford University Press, 1993), p. 52: 'The limitless alkali of the Arizona plains.'
47. John Rodker, 'Other Books', *The Little Review* 7:3 (September–December 1920), pp. 64–5.
48. See 'Emerson' (1913), in Parsons (ed.), pp. 288–9: '[Emerson's] freedom, his daring, his inspiration, in Whitman's hands became a roadway right through humanity.'
49. Crozier (ed.), pp. 86–7.
50. Chana Kronfeld, *On the Margins of Modernism: Decentering Literary Dynamics* (London: University of California Press, 1996), p. 47.
51. Rodker, *The Future of Futurism*, pp. 5, 8.
52. Leftwich, p. 14.
53. Rodker, *The Future of Futurism*, p. 8.
54. See Maud Ellmann, *The Poetics of Impersonality: T. S. Eliot and Ezra Pound* (Brighton: The Harvester Press, 1987), p. 2.
55. Rodker, *Memoirs of Other Fronts*, p. 16.
56. See Siegfried Sassoon, *The Weald of Youth* (London: Faber, 1942), p. 140.
57. See Rodker, *The Future of Futurism*, p. 8, (London: Faber, 1942) for a summary of Modernism's 'artistic activities called revolutionary by the academies'.
58. Rodker, *Memoirs of Other Fronts*, p. 161.
59. Rodker, *The Future of Futurism*, p. 60.
60. See further John Rodker, 'W. H. Hudson', *The Little Review* 7:1 (May–June 1920), pp. 18–28.
61. Crozier (ed.), pp. 60–1.
62. Leftwich, p. 14.
63. Letter of 11 April 1930, in Rupert Hart-Davis (ed.), *Siegfried Sassoon: Letters to Max Beerbohm, with a few answers* (London: Faber, 1986), p. 11.
64. Gilles Deleuze and Félix Guattari, *Kafka: Toward a Minor Literature* (1975; Minneapolis: University of Minnesota Press, 1986), p. 19. For a more detailed discussion of 'deterritorialisation', see Chapter 1.
65. Deleuze and Guattari, p. 16.
66. Crozier (ed.), p. 133.
67. See Psalm 114, in *The Holy Bible* (Oxford: Oxford University Press, 1862). See also Rupert Hart-Davis (ed.), *Siegfried Sassoon Diaries 1915–1918* (London: Faber, 1983), p. 183.

68.   Crozier (ed.), p. 82.
69.   *The New Shorter Oxford English Dictionary*, fourth edition, vol. II, p. 2833.
70.   See 'The Fair', 'The Acrobats' and 'Under the Trees', in Crozier (ed.), pp.98–100, 106–7.
71.   Cunard, p. 143.
72.   Cunard, p. 142.
73.   Crozier (ed.), p. 128.
74.   T. S. Eliot, *The Complete Poems and Plays of T. S. Eliot* (1969; London: Faber, 1978), p. 71.
75.   Cheyette, *Constructions of 'The Jew'*, p. 259.
76.   *The Oxford English Dictionary*, second edition, vol. XI (1989; Oxford: Clarendon Press, 2001), p. 695.
77.   For further examples of anthropology in Modernism, see Michael H. Levenson, *A Genealogy of Modernism: A Study of English Literary Doctrine 1908–1922* (Cambridge: Cambridge University Press, 1984), pp. 72, 195.
78.   Crozier (ed.), p. 100.
79.   Rodker, 'The Theatre', *The Egoist* 1:21 (November 1914), pp. 414–15.
80.   Interestingly, 'it was Ezra Pound who introduced Yeats to Noh drama': see Christopher Innes, 'Modernism in Drama', in Michael Levenson (ed.), *The Cambridge Companion to Modernism* (Cambridge: Cambridge University Press, 1999), p. 135 and pp. 130–56.
81.   Levenson (ed.), *The Cambridge Companion to Modernism*, p. 135.
82.   John Rodker, 'Theatre Muet', *The Little Review* 4:4 (August 1917), pp. 12–15.
83.   Crozier (ed.), p. 25.
84.   John Rodker, 'Twenty Years After', in Julian Bell (ed.), *We Did Not Fight: 1914–18 Experiences of War Resisters* (London: Cobden-Sanderson, 1935), p. 290 and pp. 283–91.
85.   Crozier (ed.), p. 99.
86.   Crozier (ed.), pp. 73–5.
87.   See Genesis 19:17, in *The Holy Bible*: 'He said, Escape for thy life; look not behind thee, neither stay thou in all the plain; escape to the mountain, lest thou be consumed.'
88.   Genesis 19:26, in *The Holy Bible*: 'But his wife looked back from behind him, and she became a pillar of salt.'
89.   Parsons (ed.), p. 117.
90.   Crozier (ed.), pp. 98–100.
91.   Crozier (ed.), pp. 100, 123.
92.   Maxwell Bodenheim, 'Poems by John Rodker', *Others* 2:4 (April 1916), pp. 212–13.
93.   Crozier (ed.), p. 100.
94.   John Rodker, 'The Theatre in Whitechapel', *Poetry and Drama* 1:1 (March 1913), pp. 43–4.
95.   Rodker, *Memoirs of Other Fronts*, p. 16.
96.   Crozier (ed.), pp. 59, 15–16, 104.
97.   Crozier (ed.), pp. 126–7, 79, 115, 127–8.
98.   Crozier (ed.), pp. 85, 103.
99.   See, for example, 'The Flea' (1914) and 'Break of Day in the Trenches' (1916), in Parsons (ed.), pp. 76, 103–4.
100. See Gilles Deleuze and Claire Parnet, *Dialogues* (Paris: Flammarion, Collection Dialogues, 1977), pp. 40–1.
101. Rodker, *Memoirs of Other Fronts*, pp. 16, 117, 120.
102. Rodker, *Memoirs of Other Fronts*, p. 98.
103. Rodker, *Memoirs of Other Fronts*, pp. 132, 165.
104. Rodker, *Memoirs of Other Fronts*, p. 138.
105. T. S. Eliot, *The Complete Poems and Plays*, pp. 37–9.
106. Lewis, pp. 143–4.
107. See Rodker, *Memoirs of Other Fronts*, p. 122: 'And when I sat down to work in the morning the words came steadily out, solid enough and liquid enough, hour after hour, and they and I were one and we worked together, neither of us pulling on or holding back the other[,] and it was perfect.'

108. Parsons (ed.), p. 151.
109. For more on British Israelism, which may have influenced Siegfried Sassoon, see Chapter 3, note 123.
110. Rodker, *Memoirs of Other Fronts*, pp. 190, 171, 172.
111. Rodker, *Memoirs of Other Fronts*, pp. 148, 150–1.
112. Rodker, *Memoirs of Other Fronts*, p. 152.
113. Zygmunt Bauman, *Modernity and the Holocaust* (1989; Cambridge: Polity Press, 1991), p. 45.
114. Bauman, *Modernity and the Holocaust*, p. 39.
115. Leonard W. Doob (ed.), *Ezra Pound Speaking* (Westport: Greenwood Press, 1978), p. 219. See further Maud Ellmann, 'The Imaginary Jew: T. S. Eliot and Ezra Pound', in Bryan Cheyette (ed.), *Between 'Race' and Culture: Representations of 'the Jew' in English and American Literature* (Stanford, CA: Stanford University Press, 1996), p. 99 and pp. 84–101. Ellmann discusses Pound's association of usury with 'semitic ooze'.
116. Eliot, *The Complete Poems and Plays*, pp. 40–1.
117. Bauman, *Modernity and the Holocaust*, pp. 40, 50.
118. Crozier (ed.), pp. 80, 125, 71–2, 126–7.
119. Bryan Cheyette, 'Neither Black Nor White: The Figure of "the Jew" in Imperial British Literature', in Linda Nochlin and Tamar Garb (eds), *The Jew in the Text* (London: Thames and Hudson, 1995), pp. 31–41.
120. See Aldington, 'Two Poets', *The Egoist* 1:22, p. 422: 'I personally detest his kind of art, and have no use for a man who can write lines like: "white perfection, black and immobile".' See further John Rodker, *Poems* ('To be had of the Author, 1 Osborn Street, Whitechapel', 1914), pp. 29–31.
121. Aldington, 'Two Poets', *The Egoist* 1:22, p. 423. Possibly, 'woody edges' is a misprint for 'woolly edges'.
122. Crozier (ed.), pp. 98–100.
123. The 'rag trade' remains, colloquially, 'the business of designing, making, and selling clothes': see *The New Shorter Oxford English Dictionary*, fourth edition, vol. II, p. 2464. See further Anne J. Kershen, 'Trade Unionism amongst the Jewish Tailoring Workers of London and Leeds, 1872–1915', in David Cesarani (ed.), *The Making of Modern Anglo-Jewry* (Oxford: Basil Blackwell, 1990), pp. 34–52: 'During the years covered by this essay [1872–1915] the clothing trade dominated the Jewish trade union movement. This is not surprising when it is remembered that tailoring was the occupation most favoured by the Eastern European immigrant.'
124. Crozier (ed.), pp. 93–4.
125. 'In the Hebrew scriptures, there is only one clear reference to Lilith. *Isaiah* 34:14, describing the devastation of Edom, maintains that Lilith shall be at rest in the desert, among wild animals, screech owls, and satyrs': see Mircea Eliade (ed.), *The Encyclopedia of Religion*, vol. 8 (New York: Macmillan, 1987), p. 554.
126. Siegfried Sassoon, *Collected Poems 1908–1956* (1961; London: Faber, 1984), p. 109.
127. Crozier (ed.), p. 104.
128. Thomas Hutchinson (ed.), *The Poetical Works of Percy Bysshe Shelley* (London: Oxford University Press, 1908), p. 546.
129. Ibid.
130. James Joyce, *Ulysses* (1922; London: Penguin, 2000), p. 73.
131. Crozier (ed.), pp. 72–3.
132. Rodker may be referring to the Ark which held the two tablets of stone on which the Decalogue was originally inscribed (see Exodus 25:10–22, in *The Holy Bible*), or the Ark which is consequently placed in every synagogue containing the Scrolls of the Torah. Of course, since he speaks of a repository of 'Life', he may also be alluding to Noah's Ark.
133. See *Passover Haggadah*, trans. Rabbi Nathan Goldberg (1949; New York: Ktav Publishing House, 1966), pp. 42–3: 'Have compassion, O Eternal our God, upon us, upon Israel Your people, upon Jerusalem Your city … Rebuild Jerusalem, Your holy city, speedily in our days. Bring us there, and cheer us with her rebuilding … NEXT YEAR IN JERUSALEM.'
134. See *Passover Haggadah*, p. 44: 'God is First, Great and Renowned! / May He soon

rebuild His Temple. / Speedily, speedily, / In our days, soon.'

135.   To be sure, Rodker was intensely serious about Freudian psychology. As Marie Bonaparte relates in her 'Obituary: John Rodker 1894–1955', *The International Journal of Psychoanalysis* 37:2–3 (March–June 1956), pp. 199–201: 'In 1939 he founded the Imago Publishing Company ... Hitler, after his entry into Vienna in 1938, confiscated the whole stock of Freud's Internationaler Psychoanalytischer Verlag and condemned all his works to the flames. John Rodker offered to republish them, and it is thus to him that we owe the impressive new edition of the *Gesammelte Werke*.' Bonaparte also mentions that she first met Rodker 'in 1939, in London, in the house of Freud'.

136.   Phillips, 'Unofficial Modernist: John Rodker', *Jewish Quarterly*, pp. 71, 70.

137.   Rodker, *Collected Poems 1912–1925*, p. vii.

138.   Rodker, *Memoirs of Other Fronts*, p. 16.

139.   Parsons (ed.), p. 95.

140.   Rodker, *The Future of Futurism*, p. 8.

141.   Rodker, *Collected Poems 1912–1925*, p. vii.

142.   Crozier (ed.), pp. 17, 128, 26, 40.

143.   Crozier (ed.), p. 127.

144.   Crozier (ed.), p. 100.

145.   The Hebrew word 'Hosanna' means, 'Save now, I beseech thee, O Lord'. See Psalms 118:25, in *The Holy Bible*: 'Save now, I beseech thee, O Lord: O Lord, I beseech thee, send now prosperity.' See further Louis Jacobs, *Concise Companion to the Jewish Religion* (Oxford: Oxford University Press, 1999), p. 94.

146.   See *The New Shorter Oxford English Dictionary*, fourth edition, vol. I, p. 128: 'Gk. *asphodelos* ... An immortal flower, said to cover the Elysian fields.'

147.   Crozier (ed.), p. 83.

148.   Crozier (ed.), pp. 98–100.

149.   Rodker, *Collected Poems 1912–1925*, p. vii.

150.   Sidra DeKoven Ezrahi, *Booking Passage: Exile and Homecoming in the Modern Jewish Imagination* (London: University of California Press, 2000), p. 15.

151.   Ezrahi, p. 240.

152.   See Crozier (ed.), p. 28. See also Ezra Pound, 'Foreword to the Choric School', *Others* 1:4 (October 1915), p. 53 and pp. 53–4: 'He [Rodker] tells me likewise that he has no history to speak of.'

153.   Rodker, *Collected Poems 1912–1925*, p. 14.

154.   See, for example, Isaacs, 'Rodker: Literature in the Twenties': 'He belonged to the period of true Bohemianism ... I am happy to recall him ... in Paris.'

155.   Rodker, *Memoirs of Other Fronts*, pp. 250, 236.

156.   Rodker, *Collected Poems 1912–1925*, p. vii.

157.   Cunard, p. 143.

158.   Parsons (ed.), p. 201.

159.   See Bryan Cheyette, *Contemporary Jewish Writing in Britain and Ireland: An Anthology* (London: Peter Halban, 1988), p. lviii, where Cheyette discerns: 'The patriarchal representations and received images of an apologetic Anglo-Jewry.'

160.   See Rodker, 'A CO's Biography' (1918), in Crozier (ed.), pp. 115–22: 'He read Job and the Song of Solomon.' See further The Book of Job 1:1 – 42:17 in *The Holy Bible*.

161.   Crozier (ed.), pp. 77–8.

162.   Aldington, 'Two Poets', *The Egoist* 1:22. See also T. S. Eliot, 'Tradition and the Individual Talent', in *Selected Essays* (1932; London: Faber, 1966), p. 16 and pp. 13–22, where Eliot invokes 'the rock drawing of the Magdalenian draughtsmen'.

163.   Bell (ed.), p. 290.

164.   See Rosenberg, *Moses* (1916), in Parsons (ed.), p. 151.

5

Jon Silkin: Post-Holocaust Universalist

Despite the fact that Jon Silkin wrote explicitly Anglo-Jewish poetry, he is rarely read as an Anglo-Jewish poet. Rather, critics tend to consider him as a committed radical, northern and ecological poet.[1] Commonly, Silkin is discussed as part of the poetry scene in post-war Leeds alongside Geoffrey Hill, Tony Harrison and other northern writers.[2]

When Silkin's poetry is recognised for its particular Jewish concerns it tends to be marginalised as non-English. For example, 'Jews without Arabs' (1989) is Silkin's sole poem to feature in Peter Forbes' anthology *Scanning the Century: The Penguin Book of the Twentieth Century in Poetry* (1999).[3] Through this choice, Forbes neatly de-Anglicises and delimits Silkin's Jewishness in a section of his anthology entitled 'Lost Tribes: The Middle East 1948–'.[4]

By contrast, I want to demonstrate how much of Silkin's Anglo-Jewish poetry is explicitly *territorialised* in English landscapes. Further, Silkin engages with a specific Anglo-Jewish history in order to suggest its universal resonances relating to victims, martyrs and resistance.

Silkin is a Jewish universalist. He promulgates 'humanism and … a cosmopolitanism, cautioned, as it were, by English and Jewish specifics'.[5] Moreover, he explicitly follows Isaac Rosenberg in mining the Hebrew Bible for non-Judaic purposes and dramatising the tensions of Anglo-Jewish life through *minority Modernist* verse. In the wake of the Holocaust, I suggest, Silkin's poetry argues for political affiliation with universal morality in the struggle against fascism and antisemitism. It also takes a stand against victimhood and divisive parochialism in England and Israel. Considered in this combative context, it is perhaps no surprise that Silkin named his campaigning literary journal *Stand*.[6]

THE POETRY OF JON SILKIN

The Peaceable Kingdom (1954) was Silkin's first commercially published volume of verse.[7] It takes as its epigraph Isaiah 11:6–8:

> The wolf also shall dwell with the lamb, and the leopard shall lie down with the kid; and the calf and the young lion and the fatling together; and a little child shall lead them. And the cow and the bear shall feed; their young ones shall lie down together: and the lion shall eat straw like the ox. And the suckling child shall play on the hole of the asp, and the weaned child shall put his hand on the cockatrice'[s] den.[8]

The King James Bible glosses these Old Testament verses christocentrically as '*Christ's peaceable kingdom*'.[9] However, Silkin's reference is Judaic. As he argued during an interview, 'Why could not one have Isaiah as a recognition mark for the Jews? Although I think I can tell you why: because the Church has collared Isaiah for itself. It claims it prophesied the coming of Christ.'[10]

The Judaic context of Isaiah's vision is made clear in *The Peaceable Kingdom*'s opening poem, 'Prologue', as the animals enter Noah's Ark:

> The animals in my poems go into the ark
> There are two scrolls on the doors as they go.[11]

The 'two scrolls on the doors' feasibly constitute a *mezuzah*, which is affixed to the door-post (Hebrew: '*mezuzah*') of religious Jews' homes, and contains two sections of Deuteronomy 6:4–9 and 11:13–21.[12]

There is also an American significance to the volume's title. As Silkin explains, '*The Peaceable Kingdom* is the name of one of something like a hundred paintings by the [American] Quaker Primitive artist Edward Hicks, who took his vision from Isaiah.'[13] Like Rosenberg and Rodker, Silkin perceives a trajectory of moral universalism between Old Testament and new American visions. This is the same trajectory which Silkin claims, in *The Life of Metrical and Free Verse* (1997), stretches from Hebrew poetry to Walt Whitman:

> For Whitman does indeed desire to be the epic poet, perhaps of democracy even more than of America, and for this the

energy must thread its delicacy in the most delicate way. This may be one reason why Whitman in the main relinquishes metricality *and* uses the parallelism found *unlineated* in the English Bible. (See Benjamin Hrushovski in *The Penguin Book of Hebrew Verse* (parallelism).) One must be epic but in the new mode of democracy – the new faith – and so find a different 'metric' – a rhythmic form appropriate to new requirements.[14]

As for Rosenberg and Rodker, so for Silkin, Whitman becomes a modern touchstone ('new') of what is also Old Testament ('*Hebrew*') universalism. Diversity is key to this universalism. In 'Isaiah's Thread' (1974), for instance, Silkin presents the many gathered together as one:

> The fly will be appointed, the sweated ox;
> And a furred leopard, over the kids it has pastured.
> Lie together, grin, creep, pant, assemble;
> Convene the kingdom.[15]

Like the 'Prologue' to *The Peaceable Kingdom*, 'Isaiah's Thread' depicts an heterogeneous assembly of species, from the 'fly' to the 'leopard', come 'together' to form one 'kingdom'. Similarly, 'A peaceable kingdom' (1980) has 'all converge'.[16] Again, in *The People* (1976)[17] humans behave like peaceable, various animals when they form a collective:

> Raising a peaceable commune recessed in
> The brain, where creatures join, and form a pact.

This 'pact' may be socially or sexually political:

> In that decent stillness we did nothing that day.
> As though over the moss, each plant, each flower, we lay
> between
> fitted the intent self to a peaceable kingdom, toxic leaves
> and petals, by lively consent, being sucked
> of poisons by elements they had with care selected.[18]

Post-coital calm ('that decent stillness') is also a type of 'peaceable kingdom'. Like a social 'pact', its political significance relates to the 'lively consent' of discrete 'egotisms'.[19]

Silkin's affiliation with political collectives finds corroboration in the Hebrew Bible. 'What Can We Mean?' (1976)[20] evokes God's 'covenant' as a moral touchstone:

> Were it in us to be
> as God, and break his covenant,
>
> we'd rive soul
> to the spongy equivalence
> of torn life.

Here God's 'covenant' is not dissimilar to the 'universal compact'[21] that Silkin considers in *The Life of Metrical and Free Verse*. When he writes of D. H. Lawrence's poems 'Snake' (1921) and 'Mountain Lion' (1923)[22] that the dramatised mistreatment of the animals demands 'expiation', Silkin deploys further traces of a biblical discourse. He goes on to describe a trajectory from Lawrence's poetry back to Isaiah's Peaceable Kingdom: 'No less than in "Snake", the burden of "Elephants in the Circus" represents the broken compact of the Peaceable Kingdom.'[23]

Here 'compact', like 'covenant' in 'What Can We Mean?', invokes the biblical 'covenant' between God, Noah and the planet's creatures of Genesis 9:8–13:[24]

> And God spake unto Noah, and to his sons with him, saying, And I, behold, I establish my covenant with you, and with your seed after you; And every living creature that *is* with you, of the fowl, of the cattle, and of every beast of the earth with you, to every beast of the earth. And I will establish my covenant with you; neither shall all flesh be cut off any more by the waters of a flood; neither shall there any more be a flood to destroy the earth. And God said, This *is* the token of the covenant which I make between me and you and every living creature that is with you, for perpetual generations: I do set my bow in the cloud, and it shall be for a token of a covenant between me and the earth.

Indeed, affiliation with a biblical 'covenant' reverberates throughout Silkin's poetry. The 'Prologue' of *The Peaceable Kingdom*, for example, begins with Noah's ark ('The animals in my poems go into the ark') and echoes Genesis at the time of the covenant ('all that go out of the ark'). Moreover, in the morally charged context of 'What Can We Mean?', other biblical covenants are suggested; for instance, that of Exodus 24:1–8 where Moses writes the words of God in 'the book of the covenant'. Famously, Exodus 20:1–17 relates the rules that the Jews are obliged to obey as their part in the covenant. These Ten Commandments remain central to Silkin's vision. Like Rosenberg, Silkin would seem to locate universal morality in the 'Ten immutable rules'[25] of the Hebrew Bible.

Understandably, Jon Glover remarks on Silkin's 'religious view of the purpose of poetry'.[26] Titles such as 'A prayer cup' (1976) and 'Psalmists' (1992) suggest as much.[27] However, Silkin's vision is not bounded by Judaism. Indeed, the fact that 'his covenant' (in 'What Can We Mean?') is lower-case implies a cautious distancing in relation to Judaism.[28] Judaism, I suggest, allows Silkin to remain unbounded by Englishness, and vice versa.

In Israel in 1967 for a symposium of Anglo-Jewish and Israeli writers, Silkin emphasised:

> My awareness of being a Jew has forced me – not into saying to myself: I will learn Hebrew and have bi-focal judgements, but I will read omnivorously and form my consciousness from as many cultures, humanistically speaking, as possible. Thus my Jewish self-awareness has forced me into humanism and into a cosmopolitanism, cautioned, as it were, by English and Jewish specifics.[29]

Silkin espouses a 'humanism' and 'cosmopolitanism' which are not bounded, but merely 'cautioned', by the relatively parochial 'specifics' of Englishness and Judaism. Further, Silkin intimates that both English and Judaic 'specifics' are constricting. He remarks of Rosenberg's 'God Made Blind' (1915):

> What Rosenberg is doing ... is not only subverting the religious authoritarian image of Judaism but is also (not simply symbolically) attempting to fight against authoritarian codes of the English society in which he was also immersed. So that by subverting the Judaic authoritarian system, or trying to, he is at the same time making equal gestures in the direction of English authoritarianism.[30]

Here, Silkin implies that Judaic and English systems are similarly parochial and 'immersed' in 'authoritarian codes'. By contrast, he praises Rosenberg for being a non-parochial Jew beyond such arbitrary 'codes', 'trying to realign the forces in society so that it will include not only a class but a community such as the Jews'. Silkin's conception of Jews as one 'community' among others allows for the possibility of a humanistic, cosmopolitan Jewishness.

By contrast, he rejects the constrictions of 'orthodox' Judaism:

> I don't doubt that most orthodox Jews are on a certain level sincere in their religious beliefs. I want to ask whether you have to be religious to be a Jew. Now, from their point of view, the answer is yes. From my own, I don't believe it.[31]

Silkin expounds on Judaic parochialism in 'A Word about Freedom and Identity in Tel Aviv' (1971).[32] Here a parrot speaks:

> into the claw it raised
> at its hooked face, the word
> 'torah, torah' in the hoarse, devotional
> grief religious men speak with
> rendering on God the law
> their love binds them with. Done,
> it cried its own cry, its claws tightening
> onto its beak, shaking slowly
> the whole face with the cry
> from side to side. This cry was placed
> by one Jew inside another. Not belonging though;
> an animal of no distinct race,
> its cry also human, slightly;
> wired in, waiting; fed on
> good seed a bit casually
> planted. Granulated, sifted,
> dry. The torah is:
> suffering begets suffering, that is.

Like the Jews, Silkin's parrot belongs to 'no distinct race'. However, its 'devotional' activities suggest a 'dry', repetitive Judaism ('The torah is: / suffering begets suffering'). Indeed, 'suffering begets suffering' parodies both Old Testament genealogies and a restrictive Judaic mind-set ('binds', 'tightening', 'wired in').

Through humour, the poem distances itself from 'sealed-off'[33] Judaic ritual which would delimit a universalistic Jewishness.

Amana Grass (1971) features several other poems set in Israel,[34] including 'Jaffa, and Other Places':

> Inertia heaps:
> mounds of boots, motionless and brown, remains of the
> mandate army, dispersed in England now.
> Done with in worse places: shoes, crutches, irons, many
> oddments, each similar, the inert teeth, ash, hair, dust
> winnowed between grains of soil or not winnowed between
> them;
> most of each category useful, separated. The flesh gets
> isolated from these,
> the goods and its body harrowed apart. Each item heaps on
> one of its kind, itself buried. Wardresses help sort each class.
> And not the negro his hunted skin finding each shadow not
> as dark as he
> offers an absence as blank.

The English who ruled in former British Mandate Palestine resemble diasporic Jewry in being 'dispersed' survivors ('remains of the / mandate army'). In a witty conceit, this comparison suggests a 'fusing'[35] between Jews and Englishmen. However, the conceit collapses in the context of victimhood. Whereas the English army left 'mounds of boots', Jewish victims of the Holocaust were themselves piled in mounds: 'shoes, crutches, irons, many / oddments, each similar, the inert teeth, ash, hair, dust'. Further, the taxonomy associated with Nazi concentration camps ('winnowed', 'each category useful, separated', 'isolated', 'harrowed apart') suggests English attempts to categorise people according to a more benign, but similarly wrong-headed, criterion of class ('sort each class'). Jews and other victims, the poem implies, are freely uncategorisable outside Nazi and imperial classifications.

To be sure, the poem also expresses empathy with 'the negro'. Unlike Sassoon and Rodker, Silkin affiliates with blacks unambivalently. 'Jaffa, and other places' depicts Jews and 'the negro' as fellow victims of prejudice who struggle against persecution and annihilation ('his hunted skin',[36] 'an absence as blank'). The poem implies a common stand against Nazism ('ash') in a post-colonial ('mandate') world.

By contrast, 'Divisions' (1971)[37] considers an ongoing source of strife in the Israeli–Palestinian conflict:

> Creatures with two legs come, and sit against a Cedar that
> no longer moves
> forward. They spread a map over their legs, engross a frontier;
> a document embossed by lines that divide one bit of land
> from the same bit,
> the first of these trees from the last of them. The line is
> arbitrary as a fish-hook. As if two iron hooks
> stuck like picks into the ground, and their shafts pulled,
> until in the earth a gap opened. A small, neat structure of stones,
> in fact, marks the hostile step which it is death to step.

Divisions of land according to ethnic affiliations are certainly deadly ('death to step'), yet also 'arbitrary'. Considered in a humanistic light ('Creatures with two legs'), they are ridiculous attempts to impose boundaries on the naturally unbounded ('divide one bit of land from the same bit'). Like 'Jaffa, and other places', 'Divisions' warns against racial boundaries ('frontier', 'hostile step') in the name of a humanistic pluralism.

Significantly, the narrator of 'Baited' (1958)[38] refuses to kill:

> I hurl that creature
> Back into the stream.
> Its life, small as a pool of soft blood in
> The hunter's hand it was
> Not worth the tremor of my hand to kill.

Unlike Rodker, whose representations of fish evoke a slippery freedom, Silkin depicts fish as victims deprived of freedom. Moreover, the narrator's refusal to act as a predator suggests some empathy with the fish as a creature which is 'baited'. That this empathy is compounded by a post-Holocaust *Weltanschauung* is made plainer in 'Flatfish' (1971).[39] Not merely 'baited', as a Jew might be by an antisemite, the netted flatfish suffer:

> A gradual pain
> Until the fish weaken. Could they cry
> We might gas them to concert
> Their distress.

Possibly, 'gas' refers to the death camps of the Holocaust, further linking fish and Jews in victimhood.

Inevitably perhaps, Silkin's vision of conflict in the Middle East is overshadowed by the European Jewish experience of concentration camps. For example, 'Jews without Arabs' (1989)[40] concludes:

> The milk in our mouths is burnt for ever.
> Friends, friends, what may we change to?

The first of these lines echoes Paul Celan's Holocaust poem 'Todesfuge' (1952):[41] 'Schwarze Milch der Frühe wir trinkin sie abends' ('Black milk of daybreak we drink it at sundown'). Thus, Silkin invokes Jews as a collectivity ('we') that has suffered the Shoah, and consequently 'may' choose not to mistreat Arabs. Of course, the 'change' may also imply a switch in affiliation from victim to master status. As the poem states: 'We're Jewish Pharoahs / Flicking water, whipping it.' In this instance, Silkin suggests that the Israeli–Palestinian conflict has inverted the Passover story, with Jews now in the position of 'Pharoahs' rather than Hebrew slaves.

Originally published in the *Tel Aviv Review*, 'Jews without Arabs' illustrates the socio-political concerns which Silkin felt he shared with Israel as a Jew ('We're Jewish'). Throughout his life, Silkin remained involved with Israeli literature. For instance, he jointly translated a collection of verse by the Israeli poet Natan Zach, *Against Parting* (1967).[42] He also contributed regularly to anglophone Israeli journals,[43] as well as anthologies of Israeli poetry in translation, such as *The Burning Bush: Poems from Modern Israel* (1977).[44] Only a few weeks before his death in November 1997, Silkin was finalising plans to publish translations of Amir Gilboa's Hebrew poetry.[45] Indeed, Silkin incorporates Gilboa's verse into his own poetry. In the middle of *The People*, for instance, he inserts:

> If my people were to forgive the enemies of my people there would be no forgiveness for my people. Mother, Mother![46]

Nonetheless, Silkin depicts Israel primarily as a parochial place of post-Shoah refuge ('Jaffa, and other places'), restrictive Judaic ritual ('A Word about Freedom and Identity in Tel Aviv') and inter-ethnic conflict ('Divisions', 'Jews without Arabs'). The poet's affiliation with Israel remains 'cautioned' by a 'humanism and ...

cosmopolitanism' which refuse delimitation by what he terms 'Jewish specifics'.[47] For freedom, Silkin looks to the diaspora:[48]

> Whose
> is this land that, like waiting flesh, turns
> with a kiss, domestic, but yet is
> a local habitation with no substance or name
> sustaining it? It is the ship's pasture,
> its interlinking husk of submarine,
> sea-spike, the sleeted fields of destruction:
> for payment, for emolument. I am
> a part of this – the bee, cutter of wood,
> whose timbered house is unimaginably
> hospitable. This is what it is. Northwards,
> a new Jerusalem with the lamb lies separate,
> its shade dense and lovely. The woman
> starts again, as though each portion of this
> were knit afresh.

In 'The ship's pasture' (1986), the speaker is affiliated to 'a new Jerusalem' in the North of England with 'the lamb' of Isaiah 11 ('the wolf also shall dwell with the lamb').[49] His Peaceable Kingdom is situated in 'a local habitation' and connubial domesticity ('domestic', 'timbered house', 'lovely. The woman'). However, he also raises an awkward question: 'Whose / is this land ... ?' A sense of otherness, rather than entitlement to 'the fields of England', is thus conveyed. The speaker reassures himself: 'I am / a part of this.' He rejoices in the 'unimaginably / hospitable', where he is not persecuted. However,

> some people here are brutal, the fist,
> because of standing in the wrong place,
> at the cheekbone. Fist, or snide
> arrowy word.

Possibly, 'snide / arrowy word' implies antisemitic abuse. In this manner, otherness within a sometimes 'brutal' society is juxtaposed with a diasporic paradigm of the Peaceable Kingdom. Northern English and Old Testament 'specifics'[50] interrelate ('as though each portion of this / were knit afresh') through the unifying narrator's affiliation with ('a part of this') and cautious distance from ('separate') both. I want to suggest that it is this tension between affiliation and otherness which offers the speaker a diasporic home.

In a similar vein, 'The Jews in England' (1997)[51] concerns the interrelation of minority Jewish poetry with English:

> Hear my speech, love, take notice, and stay within my acts.
> I am your tender gentile woman and you, Jew, have brought
> us this,
> a poem that is a single note, of praise, the psalms
> fresh as a changing glance, a fragrant look
> in an English we had not, but on our tongues
> makes our lives new. Yet now, she is she, this tongue,
> who will not come again, although I sit in grasses,
> their flowering, their mutual forgiving allowance
> of space, like feathery cats at a dish – the prairie,
> with its miles of sound, which adjusted to each newcomer.

Minority Jewish poetry ('the psalms') has changed the English language ('speech', 'changing', 'tongues') in a 'mutual forgiving allowance'. Further, 'prairie' evokes America and an immigrant culture. Rosenberg and Rodker also looked to America as an exemplary, pluralistic culture where Jewish immigrants could readily contribute to a 'new' poetry, free from the 'echoes' of England's past.[52] Efraim Sicher shrewdly remarks that 'Silkin's concern for language, like ... Rosenberg's, is that of a Jew coming to his native language as to a foreign tongue'.[53] As the grandson of immigrants,[54] Silkin identifies with the non-English 'newcomer' *and* the Jew habituated to English 'space'. Indeed, the 'Jew' of the poem imagines death as a literal *assimilation* into his adopted land:

> I have no notion of how I shall die. I saw it die.
> I see it, my brain, nails, digestion, all to decay into new earth.
> Revolving its cutting edge, a thresher,
> where wheat, stalk, haulm, and staff of floury seeds
> like torches, stand, each eye broaching the same vision.
> We face our God. And eat.

Here, Gentiles and Jews are indistinguishably (thanks to the 'thresher') transformed into a non-sectarian 'new earth' and 'same vision'. From this perspective, 'Jew' and 'gentile' even share the same 'God'. Indeed, the poem reaches for a Gentile-Jewish synthesis through universalistic 'love'. Each lover's reciprocally projected otherness ('gentile', 'Jew') is subsumed within Silkin's humanism.

Evidently, 'The Jews in England' glosses over Anglo-Jewish tension. This is the tension which Silkin identifies elsewhere with Anglo-Jewish poetry: '[Rosenberg] is the tension that exists between the two societies, and in this, he is truly Anglo-Jewish.'[55] Moreover, 'tension' is a recurrent concern of Silkin's other poems and literary criticism. As he states in *The Life of Metrical and Free Verse*:

> The meaning of [poetic] unity is not singleness and homogeneity, but heterogeneous elements momentarily unified in interaction. A state of continuous active tension. Reconciliation in singleness and homogeneity brings entropy.[56]

'Poem' (1971)[57] exemplifies Silkin's desideratum of 'continuous active tension':

> From the bare peak bluish light
> tilts, where life isn't, showing upwards
> each facet assured and monstrous
> of bent and pointed squareness.
> Wind opens the tense parts
> coolness contracts the mass, enlarging
> on it the water: one impulsion
> with two effects on the rock. The upright heaviness
> will shift, snow stone and sky break
> from each other. Here the bridge is rock,
> rock cut that cut stays rock:
> a curved stillness in air raised between two banks.

In its emphasis on the hugeness of the rock, 'Poem' deploys a vocabulary reminiscent of Rosenberg's *Moses* (1916). 'Monstrous', for example, echoes the verse-play's 'monstrous baulked perfection', while 'the mass, enlarging' suggests *Moses*'s 'I have a trouble in my mind for largeness'. Similarly, 'one impulsion / with two effects' may draw on the verse-play's 'I'll shape one impulse through the contraries'.[58] Tension and change are keynotes here, as 'the tense parts' of the rock 'shift'. Indeed, 'Poem' formally displays such a 'shift', its perspective changing ('Here the bridge is rock') to present an image of inbetweenness: 'A curved stillness in air raised between two banks.' Unlike Rosenberg and Rodker, however, Silkin presents suspension ('stillness in air') as powerfully dynamic ('mass, enlarging', 'one impulsion', 'upright heaviness') rather than a species of Anglo-Jewish 'emptiness'[59] or 'hanging in the void'.[60]

Silkin returns to the ethnically significant image of a bridge in 'Centering' (1974):[61]

> No centre can be formed
> here or by the next bridge. The trains
> pass on a tier above the road.
>
> Nor here; the road belts between
> the strength of the region fused into two spans,
> gone.
>
> Two precipitate banks, where water pushes
> within a moment of the quick of you, bituminous
> and rank.
> If you were made
> at the river-side
> you have to be a spanning, at least.

Here again, it is possible to see the bridges 'spanning' riverbanks in an Anglo-Jewish light. Since they live in diaspora, Anglo-Jews occupy a similarly liminal position 'between' their ancestral homeland and English 'habitation'.[62] Abandoning the search for a single place of reference ('No centre can be formed'), the narrator opts for a no-man's-land above the 'water'. Like the 'cosmopolitan' rat who crosses the 'sleeping green between' armies in Rosenberg's 'Break of Day in the Trenches' (1916),[63] the bridges catalyse understanding of opposing sides. They suggest a synthesis, or fusion ('fused into two spans'), which makes sense 'of the region'. Rather than exist as merely Other, like the 'bituminous / and rank' water which 'pushes' between 'two precipitate banks', the poet discovers a place in synthesising oppositions through 'the strength' of 'a spanning'.

Social hubs and, correspondingly, peripheral spaces are also significant in Silkin's poetry. 'The Centre' (1961)[64] merits extended quotation:

My ancestors made love
In the hot pastures of the near east
And got me my seed there.
I should be drawn to the Mediterranean.
I suppose I am. Greece
Was the shudder of the bird from the high hills.
But Italy; those with gold teeth
Are plucked of these by the Italian;
His main industry is fools.
His landscape gathers on the surface,
Not deepening into
The scents of heat, that delicate
Strength which breaks through
The white, Greek rock
In veins of darkness
That smell of the mineral
Origins of men.
So there is Greece. But my mind stays
In a place I saw little of.
The river drifts through
The town, falling massively
Under a low bridge.
Geneva. Was it fixed
I should choose your cool streets
Hinted of by the south?
Round this place move
The ornate schisms, intertwined
And made fast by the vicious and costly
Emblem of puissant Europe.
Is it strong only? It is also
Absurd. It is a continent
Caught in its intellect
At which centre it drops
Into a great lake;
Like some bath with its plug out.
And it is here I am
Constrained by having both
Prevailing intensities
As locked, and as formed
As the coolness is formed here
In precision from the clash

Of oppositions. Such firmness
Seems pre-determined
And intertwined in a gap
That is the weave and the space
Made by Europe in struggle,
Where choice flickers, but does not choose.
It is where the tensions meet.

Geneva, like the bridges of Silkin's other poems, 'is where the
tensions meet'. Mutually Other cultures 'clash' in 'Prevailing
intensities', creating a hybrid identity for the locale. In so far as
Geneva is compelled to be hybrid ('the clash / Of oppositions'), it
resembles the situation of Anglo-Jews. Further, like the Jews of
biblical discourse, the Swiss town is chosen: 'choice flickers, but
does not choose'.[65] Chosen without choosing, Geneva suffers a
quasi-Judaic centrality in Europe. This is a situation of 'intensities',
'oppositions', 'tensions' and 'struggle'.

Similarly, mankind's Greek 'Origins' are praised for the
dynamism of 'delicate / Strength which breaks through', rather
than a static pastoral ('pastures'). Indeed, 'The Centre' suggests that
the 'continuous active tension'[66] of political struggle ('breaks
through') has ancient 'Greek' roots. While acknowledging a
'Mediterranean' ancestry ('ancestors'), the poem's persona locates it
in a Hellenic rather than Hebraic landscape. Thus Silkin engages
with an English verse tradition which prioritises Hellenic over
Hebraic universalisms.

Silkin looks to centres rather than peripheries, and to depths
('deepening') rather than surfaces ('His main industry is fools. /
His landscape gathers on the surface'), for historical orientation; so
it may be no coincidence that 'Depths'[67] (1961) appears alongside
'The Centre' in *The Re-ordering of the Stones*:

Textures. Why always textures?
The fuss. It is enough
You take and hold the thing:
That being warm it gives you
A special sense of permanence.
Since but for the whole shape
There would be no texture. Despair
Has texture. It is constructed
From a total helplessness.

Despair is texture; without it
We should not know how to face
The thing with such certainty
Of loss. But touching it
We very gently feel
The whole paralysis
Of agony give way
Into the steadfastnesses
Of reality,
The differing planes of surface
We cannot avoid contact with
Which employs the sunk depths.

As in 'Poem' (1971), Silkin alludes to Rosenberg here. The final line's 'sunk depths' suggest the 'sunk silences' of 'Dead Man's Dump' (1917),[68] which is cited elsewhere in *The Re-ordering of the Stones*: 'The sunk silences / Rosenberg speaks of' ('Deficient').[69] In *The Penguin Book of First World War Poetry*, Silkin praises Rosenberg precisely for the 'deeper level of response'[70] he demands of readers. Such references to Rosenberg prompt an Anglo-Jewish reading of 'Depths'.

Here, historical 'depths' proffer a 'special sense of permanence' and 'the steadfastnesses / Of reality'. Conversely, 'textures' invoke 'paralysis' and 'Despair'. Possibly, the poem suggests that without connection to the past, diasporic surfaces bring 'total helplessness', such 'helplessness' as Rosenberg depicts, and Silkin discusses, in 'Chagrin' (1915–16).[71] Silkin, I want to argue, is depicting the interaction of England's 'differing planes of surface / We cannot avoid' with 'the sunk depths' of Jewish history which are 'the thing' itself.

'Jew' (1997)[72] develops this dichotomy between diasporic surfaces and Jewish depths. As in Rosenberg's 'The Slade and Modern Culture' (1911–1912),[73] diasporic suspension is associated with sexual desire:

Things feather
like oar-blades across water, light
flips over this sordid little bar.
Desire is so strange. Fool.
I want to feather the Christian woman who stares
At my concealed treasuries, finger-tips on the bar,
Her stillness at my restless core. Jew. Foolish Jew.

Sexual attraction to a 'Christian woman' makes Silkin's persona feel like a 'Fool' precisely because it suggests superficiality ('oar-blades across water', 'finger-tips on the bar') in diaspora. Since he affiliates with a Jewishness of centrality and depth ('at my restless core. Jew'), Silkin's persona apprehends otherness among 'Christian' surfaces. Thus, 'the Christian woman' is both 'Alien and close': 'close' sexually, and 'alien' because related to rootless diasporic surfaces. As in 'Depths', otherness brings despair:

> Creatures in wine jars mouth 'I want to die'
> Whose owner loves me. I must not say ... but his skull's heat –
> 'nothing more, thanks.' Stay
> in your bottles, you gentiles.

Such desperation ('I want to die') may be linked to antisemitism which the speaker associates with Gentiles ('Stay / in your bottles, you gentiles'). In the face of potential Jew-hatred, the poet remains silent: 'I must not say ... ' Thus, he experiences diasporic otherness as a Jewish silence which is both 'foolish' and desperate in a superficial environment. Further, the poet articulates Gentile silence and affiliation ('Whose owner loves me') with Jews as short-lived, 'his skull's heat' suggesting an imminent explosion of animosity against the Jewish Other.[74]

Silkin's meditations on Anglo-Jewish history in the North of England chronicle further examples of Gentile and Jewish silences. 'Astringencies' (1961),[75] for example, concerns the complicit silence of Christians regarding Jews who chose to take their own lives during the York pogrom of 1190 ('To escape christian death / By christian hand'); and the related fact that 'there has been / No synagogue since eleven ninety' in York:

> Absence of Jews
> Through hatred, or indifference,
> A gap they slip through, a conscience
> That corrodes more deeply since it is
> Forgotten – that deadens York.

Here the unacknowledged ('Forgotten') Jewish dead are a felt 'Absence', or 'gap', in York's monocultural narrative of itself. (As Silkin remarks in a note to another poem about the York pogrom, 'Malabestia' (1974), interested readers will only encounter 'the City guide-book's coy paraphrases'.[76]) A city's history is re-written, its expendable Jewish Other barely mentioned.

Similarly, 'Centre of Absence' (1976)[77] considers Newcastle's willed amnesia towards Jewish, and other, histories which formed the place:

> Pampedon is *Pantheon*. The Roman site
> opens a Greek name: *pantes theoi*
> all the gods. Oh, yes;
>
> the city will scrape this
> from itself.

The Romans are forgotten, and with them the Greek 'gods'. Forgotten too is the northern city's long Jewish history:

> First, Jew-gate: rain sluices silver
> braiding usury on the stones
>
> with workmanship. Newcastle buys
> the Jews' expulsion. The King
>
> is all gold; Judas bit small
> in the coin's realm. So, the King's light
>
> clatters upon the streets. 1656,
> 'Come in again,' Cromwell stutters.

The poem's final words are 'Ye divvent / knaa nowt heor', possibly evoking the denial of witnesses to Holocaust atrocities that they knew ('knaa') about the murders. Certainly, 'Astringencies'[78] links the North's treatment of medieval Jews to the Holocaust:

> All Europe is touched
> With some of frigid York,
> As York is now by Europe.

Interviewed in relation to the York pogrom, Silkin remarks: 'History continues in some ways to live.'[79] 'Resting Place' (1980)[80] echoes this conviction that historical depths resonate among present surfaces.

The poem concerns a car park built over a medieval Jewish cemetery:

> we are
> oil creeping to the Foss
> where a sword rests its two edges:
>
> it is not nothing to lie anywhere
>   that they will let you. The sword
> rusts like a child,
>
> the Jewish child, the gentile sword; earth
>   sells itself to us.
>
> Camphored in oil, I lose all memory.

The double negative – 'not nothing' – challenges twentieth-century English silence which would deny Anglo-Jewish landscapes and history. Further, 'Resting Place' addresses fellow Jews ('we are') and hints at an apologetic Anglo-Jewry[81] anxious to please Gentiles ('anywhere / that they will let you'). Silkin appeals to Jew and Gentile alike for recognition of a minority Anglo-Jewish history: 'What is it then, is it nothing?' Indeed, the absence of such recognition leaves only cultural amnesia ('Camphored in oil, I lose all memory').

Interestingly, 'Resting Place' represents Jews in the figure of 'the Jewish child'; a figure which is juxtaposed with 'the gentile sword'. Such symbolism suggests that Jews are innocent victims of Gentile aggression. As Silkin remarks in 'Astringencies':[82]

> Perhaps, they are haunted; for the cold
> Blood of victims is colder,
> More staining, more corrosive
> On the soul, than the blood of martyrs.

It seems that Silkin is similarly 'haunted' by the image of Jewish 'victims'. In his note to an extended chronicle of Jewish victimhood, 'Footsteps on the downcast path' (1984),[83] Silkin writes: 'This poem is not concerned with heroes or martyrs, but victims.' Rodker also associated Jewish history with victimhood. The Holocaust, however, is the historical backdrop for Silkin's bleak assessment:

                              Girls
    in a row, on fire. Hot sheen, blood
    in ashes beside that. And wiring
    that trails, then snaps – the blue cobbles slashed.
    Armour's chain rickets on the flesh.
    Sinewy cries, anfractuous crying; sweat, petals, shit,
    and everything that one must do, to resist
    in a Polish sewer. The House
    up-ends its beard of flame, Warsaw, feathery
    with soot; a fossil
    gets smelted to a wall.[84]

Further, the poet is keen to distinguish such victimhood from the
voluntary deaths of Christian martyrs.[85] Indeed, 'Footsteps on the
downcast path' disassociates Jewish victims from traditional
Anglo-Christian symbols of martyrdom: 'the English pennant
shook its cross, / I mean blood.'
    Nonetheless, martyrdom is evoked in Silkin's 'Death of a Son'
(1954).[86] This poem, I suggest, taps into a Christian discourse
concerning the martyrdom of Jesus:

          this was
    Something religious in his silence,

        Something shining in his quiet,
    This was different this was altogether something else.

Silkin's mentally defective son ('who died in a mental hospital aged
one') has an aura ('Something shining') of divinity ('Something
religious'). Possibly, this is one reason Philip Larkin chooses to
anthologise 'Death of a Son' alone among Silkin's poems in *The
Oxford Book of Twentieth-Century English Verse* (1973).[87] The poem
echoes (Larkin's) Christian awe at the crucifixion:

    He turned over on his side with his one year
    Red as a wound
    He turned over as if he could be sorry for this
    And out of his eyes two great tears rolled, like stones, and he
                                                                    died.

Here 'wound' suggests Christ's death on the Cross, which is in turn

associated with His forgiveness ('as if he could be sorry for this').
Further, 'stones' evokes the rock which was removed from Christ's
burial place at the resurrection. Jesus, according to Christian
theology, accepts martyrdom for the sake of all mankind. In that
sense, Silkin is not comparing his dead son to Christianity's Son of
Man. However, 'Death of a Son' does champion the universal pity
and compassion preached by Christian theology.

Similarly in 'Endomorphic' (1997),[88] Silkin speaks of Jesus as
universal:

> Mother it is time to be lyrical.
> There was a saviour,
> and such was his unaggressing nature
> the constitution of the kingdom was set up to accept all.
> Don't even think it. No king ever was,
> only the idea, his grief over each parted soul.

Steering clear of Christian belief ('Don't even think it. No king ever
was'), Silkin nevertheless affiliates with 'the idea' of Christian
universalism ('to accept all'). Rosenberg also associates Christianity
with universalism when he writes: 'Christ perceives a larger
reachless love.'[89] Like Rosenberg, Silkin finds nothing Other in the
Christian 'idea' of universalism free from the theological taint of
anti-Judaism.

Further, I contend that Silkin espouses the notional
universalisms of Jewish victimhood *and* Christian martyrdom. Over
time, Silkin suggests elsewhere, such universalisms merge as
victims come to be recalled as martyrs, 'So that even if martyrology
is not to the exact taste of most Jews it is an ingredient produced by
history, and can only be ignored. It cannot be dismissed.'[90] In a post-
Shoah context, 'Polish fragments of dust' (1992)[91] compares a
martyred Christian saint to the Jews:

> You are Sebastians
> and Christian infantry
> with arrows in your flesh, as they are
> in our quarrelsome bodies, which are homeless, too,
> as sins disremembered.

Here Saint Sebastian represents both the martyrdom of Catholic
Poles ('You are Sebastians') and the Jews they persecuted in Poland.

Indeed, the figure serves to unite Catholics and Jews in pain and suffering ('with arrows in your flesh, as they are / in our quarrelsome bodies'). Silkin deploys 'Sebastians' to emphasise what Polish Jews and Catholics have shared, rather than what separates them. Nonetheless, post-Holocaust Jews 'are homeless' in Poland:

> Poland
> touch our ghosts with care, they will scream all day,
> and you'll be in tears for ever, whole angels
> in the religious skies, where they use
> the time for petitions of injured souls.

In the interests of Judaeo-Christian unity, 'Polish fragments of dust' blurs 'religious' boundaries. Significantly, Catholic (purgatorial) 'petitions' are evoked in a Judaic 'religious' context to urge peace and reconciliation: 'Now cross the ice in bliss and peace.'

By contrast, the Holocaust intervenes to prevent such Judaeo-Christian universalism in 'A prayer cup' (1976):[92]

> As if steel, but a silvery
> tar creeps upon Isaac
> in Abraham's hand. Our Bible
>
> is clasped in darkness. And for wine
> three inches of the blood
> of six million. The cup
>
> wells Hebrew, and my grandparents
> have tracked their kind into
> the lake over-flowing
>
> our curious feet. I who write
> a factious poem want the means
> to bless a Christian. Breath
>
> from the two locomotives *Work*
> and *Freedom* steams over
> the numbered faces.

Here the 'wine' has become Jewish 'blood / of six million' in a figure of Christian transubstantiation. Further, the invocation of the stalled sacrifice of Isaac by his father Abraham – the *akedah*[93] – suggests a symbolically completed sacrifice in the Holocaust[94] ('a silvery / tar creeps upon Isaac/ in Abraham's hand'). If Isaac is now dead, Judaism resembles Christianity in having its own martyred son. However, the Shoah prevents a Judaeo-Christian synthesis. Silkin writes with passionate irony: 'I who write / a factious poem want the means/ to bless a christian.' Denied their humanity by Christians ('our curious feet' refers to a long history of literature on Jews' satanic hooves and later Nazi fictions),[95] Jews have also been denied the Church's supposed universality. In a double-bind, the Church portrays Jews as 'factious', and Other, whatever their universalist aspirations.

Following Rosenberg, Silkin mines 'Hebrew' ritual and 'Our Bible' for *minority Modernist* purposes in 'A prayer cup'. From a post-Holocaust perspective, the upper-case 'H' and 'B' suggest morally viable Judaic referents in modern England. Conversely, Silkin's lower-case 'christian' implies both a post-Christian, universalistic view of Jewish–Gentile relations, and the moral bankruptcy of twentieth-century Christianity. Like Rosenberg, again, Silkin insists on complexity. In *The Life of Metrical and Free Verse*, he cites the First World War poet approvingly: 'Simple *poetry* – that is where an interesting complexity of thought is kept in tone and right value to the dominating idea so that it is understandable and still ungraspable.'[96]

Silkin's emphasis on 'complexity' as a prerequisite of good poetry may be significantly affected by the Nazis' categorisation of Jews as mere numbers. Similarly, 'A prayer cup' portrays 'numbered faces' that have been denied their 'ungraspable' human otherness by simple, fascist solutions.

However, I want to argue that Silkin is also guilty of categorising Jews. In defining them as victims-cum-martyrs, he posits Jewish universal significance while denying local diasporic choices: 'Victims, / Neither chosen nor choosers, but they die' ('The Victims' (1958)).[97] The critic and publisher Michael Schmidt is surely right to remark that Silkin fights back as a 'hero or martyr' who is fully prepared to meet the most 'severe conditions'.[98] Silkin's anthology of First World War verse further suggests an affiliation with such martyrological combat.

Silkin universalises Jewish victimhood. As the poet stresses in interview: 'In a sense one felt almost obliged to see outside the Jews and their condition. The Jews are only one instance of victims.'[99]

Additionally, Silkin's oeuvre displays an unflagging affiliation with the struggle for universal justice. Like Rosenberg, Silkin finds a 'useable'[100] tradition of moral universalism in the Hebrew Bible:

> Wisdom, in the Old Testament, was often associated with the prophets – 'I am no prophet' – and the prophets in their turn were often maverick perhaps, but dissident in their opposition to kings and their nations. Wisdom becomes the possession of the tribe but is often compounded out of singleness of position, opposition to and dissent from, the worldly conduct of power. It is not the romantic position of deriving strength from opposition, though that is not the easy thing so many contemporary intellectuals claim it to be; were it so far fewer university professors would have supported Hitler, out of fear, presumably. The strength of the prophets lay in their moral singularity.[101]

Thus, Silkin looks to the 'Old Testament' for a politics of 'moral' 'dissent' against 'the worldly conduct of power'. Concomitantly, he associates power with the absence of good poetry: 'I do not subscribe to the naïve notion that destitution and/or suffering are predicates for good writing, but I do believe that power is probably alien to it.'[102]

Consistently, Silkin depicts the majority of humanity united in victimhood, like Jews, but always free to take a martyrological stand against their oppressors' 'power'. Poetry remains his preferred medium because it deals with 'universal relationships' and 'the universal compact'.[103] In the wake of the Holocaust, Silkin categorises those who do not affiliate with this 'compact' as allies of 'Hitler'.

NOTES

1.   See, for example, Raymond Williams, 'Commitment', *Stand* 20:3 (1979), pp. 8–11, where Williams notes that 'the argument for commitment was usually taken as an argument for being a Left writer'. See further 'The Small Magazine since 1960: a recorded conversation with Jon Silkin', in Michael Schmidt and Grevel Lindop (eds), *British Poetry Since 1960: A Critical Survey* (South Hinksey: Carcanet, 1972), pp. 193–201, where Silkin is interviewed about the 'Northern experience'. See also Terry Eagleton, 'Nature and Politics in Jon Silkin', *Poetry Review* 69:4 (1980), p. 7, where Silkin is described as an 'ecologist *avant la lettre*'.
2.   See, for example, Romana Huk, 'Poetry of the Committed Individual: Jon Silkin, Tony Harrison, Geoffrey Hill, and the Poets of Postwar Leeds', in James Acheson

and Romana Huk (eds), *Contemporary British Poetry: Essays in Theory and Criticism* (New York: State University of New York Press, 1996), pp. 175–219. See also William A. Johnsen, 'The Treacherous Years of Postmodern Poetry in English', in Ann Massa and Alistair Stead (eds), *Forked Tongues?: Comparing Twentieth-Century British and American Literature* (London: Longman, 1994), pp. 75–91, where Johnsen considers 'Silkin, Hill, and Political Poetry' in a discrete section of his essay. See further Neil Corcoran, *English Poetry Since 1940* (Harlow: Longman, 1993), pp. 84, 136.

3.   Peter Forbes (ed.), *Scanning the Century: The Penguin Book of the Twentieth Century in Poetry* (London: Viking, 1999), pp. 210–11.

4.   Forbes (ed.), pp. 204–12.

5.   Jon Silkin, 'Anglo-Jewish Poetry', *Jewish Quarterly* (spring 1967), pp. 22–4.

6.   See Jon Silkin, 'Editorial', *Stand* 4:1 (1958), p. 3 and pp. 3–4: '*Stand* was begun, in 1952, because I felt then, as now, that I lived in a society marked by its casual indifference to the individual and his suffering […] For some the victim is seen in focus most sharply in the context of the concentration camp.'

7.   An earlier volume, *The Portrait and Other Poems* (1950), was 'printed by a pay-for-it-yourself publisher called Arthur H. Stockwell, of Ilfracombe': see Jon Silkin, 'The First Twenty-Four Years', in *Contemporary Authors Autobiography Series*, vol. 5 (Detroit: Gale, 1987), pp. 243–65.

8.   Jon Silkin, *The Peaceable Kingdom* (London: Chatto & Windus, 1954), p. 3.

9.   See Isaiah, in *The Holy Bible* (Oxford: Oxford University Press, 1862).

10.   Peter Lawson, 'Interview: Jon Silkin', *Sphagnum* 11 (1981), pp. 24–33.

11.   Silkin, *The Peaceable Kingdom*, p. 7.

12.   See Deuteronomy 6:4–9, 11:13–21, in *The Holy Bible*. See also Louis Jacobs, *Concise Companion to the Jewish Religion* (Oxford: Oxford University Press, 1999), pp. 153–4.

13.   Lawson, 'Interview: Jon Silkin', *Sphagnum* 11, p. 33. Edward Hicks (1780–1849) was a Quaker preacher and artist, resident in Pennsylvania. At least sixty of his *Peaceable Kingdoms* survive. See Eleanor Price Mather, *Edward Hicks: His Peaceable Kingdoms and Other Paintings* (London: Cornwall Books, 1983), p. 21.

14.   Jon Silkin, *The Life of Metrical and Free Verse in Twentieth-Century Poetry* (Basingstoke: Macmillian, 1997), p. 187. See also Benjamin Hrushovski, 'Notes on the Systems of Hebrew Versification', in T. Carmi (ed.), *The Penguin Book of Hebrew Verse* (London: Penguin, 1981), p. 58: 'The system of this type of rhythm may be described as semantic-syntactic-accentual free parallelism. It is based on a cluster of shifting principles, the most prominent one being the semantic-rhetorical, the most obviously restricted one being the rhythmical'; 'No systematic rhyme is to be found in the Bible, but there is a very pervasive usage of alliteration, sporadic end-rhyme, puns, acrostics and formulas, either embellishing or reinforcing the major principles of parallelism'.

15.   Jon Silkin, *The Principle of Water* (Cheadle: Carcanet, 1974), p. 95.

16.   Jon Silkin, *The Psalms with their Spoils* (London: Routledge, 1980), p. 63.

17.   Silkin, *The Principle of Water*, p. 48.

18.   Jon Silkin, 'Amana Grass', in *Amana Grass* (London: Chatto & Windus, 1971), p. 23.

19.   Silkin, 'Amana Grass', in *Amana Grass*, p. 20: 'To enlarge, amid these natures, whose heraldic egotisms silently conflict.'

20.   Jon Silkin, *The Little Time-Keeper* (Old Woking: Carcanet, 1976), p. 66.

21.   Silkin, *The Life of Metrical and Free Verse*, p. 211.

22.   Vivian de Sola Pinto and Warren Roberts (eds), *The Complete Poems of D.H. Lawrence*, 2 vols. (London: Heinemann, 1964), pp. 349, 401.

23.   Silkin, *The Life of Metrical and Free Verse*, p. 213.

24.   See Genesis 9:8–13, in *The Holy Bible*.

25.   See Isaac Rosenberg, 'The Jew' (1916), in Ian Parsons (ed.), *The Collected Works of Isaac Rosenberg* (1979; London: Chatto & Windus, 1984), p. 101: 'Moses, from whose loins I sprung, / Lit by a lamp in his blood / Ten immutable rules, a moon / For mutable lampless men.'

26.   Jon Glover, 'The Critic as Poet', *Poetry Review* 69:4 (1980), pp. 16–20.

27.   Jon Silkin, *Testament Without Breath* (Manaccan: Cargo Press, 1998), pp. 15, 27.

28.   Lawson, 'Interview: Jon Silkin', p. 27: 'Lawson: "You're prepared to *give* but

always hold something back?" Silkin: "Yes. I think I would describe that as caution, really."'

29. Silkin, 'Anglo-Jewish Poetry', *Jewish Quarterly*, pp. 22–4.
30. Silkin, 'Anglo-Jewish Poetry', *Jewish Quarterly*, p. 24.
31. Silkin, 'Anglo-Jewish Poetry', *Jewish Quarterly*, p. 24. Lawson, 'Interview: Jon Silkin', p. 31.
32. Silkin, *Amana Grass*, pp. 26–7.
33. Silkin, *Amana Grass*, p. 26.
34. See Silkin, *Amana Grass*, pp. 26–36. The other poems are 'Reclaimed Area', 'What are the Lights ... ', 'Conditions', 'Ayalon', 'Bull-god', 'A Word about Freedom and Identity in Tel Aviv' and 'Divisions'.
35. Silkin, 'Jaffa, and Other Places', in *Amana Grass*, p. 36: 'the hardened grains / fusing'.
36. Several of Silkin's nature poems concern hunted animals, which are explicitly or implicitly compared to Jews. 'First it was Singing', for example, is one of four poems in *The Peaceable Kingdom* which features hunted foxes: 'It was their speech, and my speech, / The Jewish stone and the / Animal rock // Rolling together that made me sing / Of our common lash, the white raised weal across / Our black back, I and / The hunted fox.' The others are 'The Cunning of an Age', 'No Land Like It' and 'This Dreaming Experience'. In *Beyond Marginality: Anglo-Jewish Literature After the Holocaust* (Albany: State University of New York Press, 1985), p. 144, Efraim Sicher links Silkin's image of a 'hunted fox' to a 'modern victim with whom the poet, as a Jew, identifies'.
37. Silkin, *Amana Grass*, pp. 45–6.
38. Jon Silkin, *The Two Freedoms* (London: Chatto & Windus, 1958), pp. 10–11.
39. Silkin, *Amana Grass*, pp. 40–1.
40. Jon Silkin, *The Lens-Breakers* (London: Sinclair-Stevenson, 1992), pp. 71–2.
41. Paul Celan, *Poems*, trans. and ed. Michael Hamburger (London: Anvil, 1988), pp. 60–1. Celan (1920–1970) was a Romanian-Jewish poet who wrote in German. Silkin remarks of poets who have tackled the Holocaust that 'the great instance is the German poet who committed suicide, Paul Celan': Lawson, 'Interview: Jon Silkin', p. 28.
42. Natan Zach, *Against Parting*, trans. Nathan Zach and Jon Silkin (Newcastle: Northern House, 1967).
43. See, for example, *The Tel Aviv Review* 2 (fall 1989/winter 1990), pp. 166–76 and *The Jerusalem Review* 4 (2000), pp. 174–7. The poems in the second of these journals were published posthumously.
44. Moshe Dor and Natan Zach (eds), *The Burning Bush: Poems from Modern Israel* (London: W. H. Allen, 1977). Silkin translated poems by Amir Gilboa, Yechiel Mar and Natan Zach for this volume. His co-translator for Amir Gilboa's 'Isaac' was Zach. Bat-Sheva Sheriff collaborated in Silkin's translation of Yechiel Mar's 'Hope' and 'An appended poem'. Silkin translated Zach's 'Sergeant Weiss' with Avraham Birman: pp. 36, 41–2, 73–5.
45. Anthony Rudolf, 'Jon Silkin Obituary', *Jewish Chronicle*, 12 December 1997, p. 22.
46. See Lawson, 'Interview: Jon Silkin', pp. 25–6: 'Silkin: "I'm glad you chose that little poem, which is tiny, and not mine. It's the work of an Israeli poet (in translation, of course) called Amir Gilboa."'
47. Silkin, 'Anglo-Jewish Poetry', *Jewish Quarterly*, pp. 22–4.
48. Jon Silkin, 'The ship's pasture', in *The Ship's Pasture* (London: Routledge & Kegan Paul, 1986), p. 84.
49. Silkin, *The Peaceable Kingdom*, p. 3.
50. Silkin, 'Anglo-Jewish Poetry', *Jewish Quarterly*, pp. 22–4.
51. Jon Silkin, *Making a Republic* (Manchester: Carcanet/Northern House, 2002), p. 34.
52. See Rosenberg, 'Emerson' (1913), in Parsons (ed.), p. 288.
53. Sicher, p. 151.
54. 'Five major pogroms took place in Russia during the last twenty years of the nineteenth century and the first years of the twentieth, impelling my grandparents, on both sides of the family, from Baltic Russia (Lithuania) to Britain': Silkin, 'The First Twenty-Four Years', p. 243.

55. Jon Silkin, 'The Poetry of Isaac Rosenberg', in *Isaac Rosenberg 1890–1918: A catalogue of an exhibition held at Leeds University May–June 1959, together with the text of unpublished material* (Leeds: Partridge Press, 1959), p. 3.
56. Silkin, *The Life of Metrical and Free Verse*, p. 61.
57. Silkin, *Amana Grass*, p. 42.
58. Rosenberg, *Moses* (1916), in Parsons (ed.), pp. 144, 150.
59. Rosenberg, 'Chagrin' (1915–16), in Parsons (ed.), p. 95.
60. John Rodker, 'Note', in *Collected Poems 1912–1925* (Paris: The Hours Press, 1930), p. vii.
61. Silkin, *The Principle of Water*, p. 11.
62. Silkin, 'The ship's pasture', in *The Ship's Pasture*, p. 84. For a wide-ranging discussion of Jewish diasporic narratives, see Sidra DeKoven Ezrahi, *Booking Passage: Exile and Homecoming in the Modern Jewish Imagination* (London: University of California Press, 2000).
63. Parsons (ed.), pp. 103–4.
64. Jon Silkin, *The Re-ordering of the Stones* (London: Chatto & Windus, 1961), pp. 29–30.
65. See Dan Jacobson, *The Story of the Stories* (London: Secker and Warburg, 1982), pp. 59–60, for a discussion of Jewish belief in a chosen status, and the ensuing anxieties of not choosing for oneself.
66. Silkin, *The Life of Metrical and Free Verse*, p. 61.
67. Silkin, *The Re-ordering of the Stones*, p. 37.
68. Parsons (ed.), pp. 109–11.
69. Silkin, *The Re-ordering of the Stones*, pp. 27–8.
70. Jon Silkin (ed.), *The Penguin Book of First World War Poetry* (Harmondsworth: Penguin, 1979), p. 36.
71. Parsons (ed.), p. 95. See also Jon Silkin, *Out of Battle: The Poetry of the Great War* (1972; Oxford: Oxford University Press, 1978), pp. 264–5. See further Chapter 2.
72. Silkin, *Testament Without Breath*, pp. 31–2.
73. Parsons (ed.), p. 302.
74. See Lawson, 'Interview: Jon Silkin', pp. 25–6, where Silkin remarks: 'I suspect that lurking in the Christian psyche is some question mark which they hang over the body of the Jews – and it's not usually a friendly question mark.'
75. Silkin, *The Re-ordering of the Stones*, pp. 12–15.
76. Silkin, *The Principle of Water*, pp. 83–7.
77. Silkin, *The Little Time-Keeper*, pp. 57–8.
78. Silkin, *The Re-ordering of the Stones*, pp. 12–15.
79. Lawson, 'Interview: Jon Silkin', p. 24.
80. Silkin, *The Psalms with their Spoils*, pp. 5–6.
81. See Bryan Cheyette, *Contemporary Jewish Writing in Britain and Ireland: An Anthology* (London: Peter Halban, 1988), p. lviii.
82. Silkin, *The Re-ordering of the Stones*, pp. 12–15.
83. Silkin, *The Ship's Pasture*, pp. 51–62.
84. Silkin, *The Ship's Pasture*, p. 60.
85. For a discussion of the difference between martyrdom and victimhood in Silkin's work, see Massa and Stead (eds), p. 84.
86. Silkin, *The Peaceable Kingdom*, pp. 23–4.
87. Philip Larkin (ed.), *The Oxford Book of Twentieth-Century English Verse* (1973; Oxford: Oxford University Press, 1998), pp. 594–5.
88. Silkin, *Making a Republic*, pp. 64–5.
89. Rosenberg, 'Creation' (1913), in Parsons (ed.), pp. 50–1.
90. Silkin, Foreword to 'Footsteps on the downcast path', in *The Ship's Pasture*, p. 51.
91. Silkin, *The Lens-Breakers*, pp. 66–7.
92. Silkin, *The Little Time-Keeper*, p. 40.
93. See Genesis 22:1–19, in *The Holy Bible*. See further 'Isaac', a revised version of the *akedah*, which Silkin translated with Natan Zach from Amir Gilboa's Hebrew original, in Moshe Dor and Natan Zach (eds), p. 36. In Gilboa's post-Shoah poem, it is Isaac's father who has already been killed by the Nazis: 'It is me that's butchered, son / And my blood already on the leaves.' Here the *akedah* has not

stopped short of murder. In a post-Shoah twist, it has also been inverted, since it is the father rather than the son who has been sacrificed.

94. See further my discussion of Karen Gershon's 'Kaddish' (1966), 'Easter' (1966), 'The Flight into Egypt' (1990) and 'The Bethlehem Babies' (1990) in Chapter 6.

95. See Joshua Trachtenberg, *The Devil and the Jews* (1943; Jerusalem: The Jewish Publication Society, 1983), p. 208: 'It is instructive to compare the graphic representations of the sorcerer and the witch in medieval art, which consistently emphasize their demonic characteristics – horns, tails, claws, cloven hoof, and the attendant demons or devils – with the pictures of the Jew ... The latter are at once seen to be nothing but slavish reproductions of the former.' See further Sander Gilman, 'The Jewish Foot: A Foot-Note to the Jewish Body', in *The Jew's Body* (London: Routledge, 1991), pp. 43–4 and pp. 38–59: 'In the Viennese fin-de-siècle humor magazine, *Kikeriki*, the flat and malformed feet of the Jew served as an indicator of the Jewish body almost as surely as the shape of the Jewish nose ... By the 1930s the image of the Jew's feet had become ingrained in the representation of the Jewish body. The Nazi caricaturist Walter Hofmann, who drew under the name of 'Waldl', illustrated how the Jew's body had been malformed because of the Jew's own refusal to obey his own God's directives.'

96. Silkin, *The Life of Metrical and Free Verse*, p. 312. See also Rosenberg, Letter to Gordon Bottomley, dated 23 July 1916, in Parsons (ed.), p. 238.

97. Silkin, *The Two Freedoms*, pp. 47–8.

98. Michael Schmidt, 'Stand: Symposium on "Commitment"', *Stand* 20:3 (1979), pp. 12–15.

99. Lawson, 'Interview: Jon Silkin', p. 28.

100. Rosenberg, *Moses* (1916), in Parsons (ed.), p. 151.

101. Silkin, *The Life of Metrical and Free Verse*, p. 100. See also Rudolf, 'Jon Silkin Obituary', *Jewish Chronicle*, p. 22. Rudolf maintains that Silkin writes in 'the Jewish prophetic tradition'.

102. Silkin, *The Life of Metrical and Free Verse*, p. 295.

103. Silkin, *The Life of Metrical and Free Verse*, p. 211.

6

Karen Gershon: Exile and Diaspora

Unlike the other poets in this study, Karen Gershon was not born in England. She began life as a German Jew, Kaethe Loewenthal, and came to the United Kingdom as a refugee from Nazism. In December 1938, a month after the German pogrom known as *Kristallnacht*,[1] the fifteen-year-old Kaethe arrived at Harwich on a *Kindertransport* (children's transport).[2] Among the other European children who were similarly sent by their parents to England were the future Anglo-Jewish poets Lotte Kramer and Gerda Mayer.[3] Gershon, I suggest, is the most significant of these writers.

Though in exile, the young Kaethe Loewenthal had no plans to return to Germany. Rather, Kaethe considered her home to be in British Mandate Palestine.[4] Even after changing her name to Karen Gershon and establishing a family in England, she had no intention of adopting a multi-hyphenated Anglo-German-Jewish life in the diaspora. Pertinently, Gershon is Hebrew for 'stranger in a strange land'.[5] After more than fifty years in England, the poet was only prepared to say: 'Here I am reconciled.'[6]

I want to argue, however, that Gershon's sense of being 'reconciled' to England accords with a diasporic literary tradition. Her verse expresses a tension – common to Anglo-Jewish poetry and poetics – between 'social'[7] exile and an 'imaginary homeland'.[8] This chapter also considers Gershon's novels and autobiographies as diasporic literature.

THE POETRY OF KAREN GERSHON

An imaginary Israel inspired Karen Gershon. As the German-Jewish Kaethe Loewenthal, she constructed her own textual homeland: 'I began to write stories, and essays, and poems, and a whole sequence of 'Letters from Jerusalem'; in my imagination I lived there.'[9] Vitally, the topic about which she wrote was the Israel of her 'imagination': a fictional Israel where she felt at home. 'Writing, writing,' Gershon stresses, 'I almost stopped being homesick.'[10] The poet's provisional ('almost') home was in the text. Indeed, Zionism inspired Gershon's first attempt at a poem:

> The poem began, 'Wake up, Jews!' and went on to say that they ought not to leave it to others to decide what their Jewishness meant, that they should learn to see it as an asset instead of as a burden, that they should decide to emigrate to the Land of Israel not because they were no longer wanted in Germany but because that was where they should want to be.[11]

From the beginning, Gershon's 'Israel' was more imagined than known in reality.

Some thirty years after settling in England, Gershon's first collection of verse, *Selected Poems* (1966), was published.[12] Here, Gershon mined the Hebrew Bible to impose a stabilising narrative on disorientating Jewish experience under Nazism. Again, such a narrative suggests an imaginary home, in so far as it implies Jewish continuity in texts. Indeed, it resembles what Isaac Rosenberg describes in 'Zion' (1906)[13] as Israel's 'story'. For example, Gershon deploys the Haggadahic[14] tale of Moses leading the Israelites out of Egypt in 'The Children's Exodus' (1966):[15]

> When we went out of Germany
> carrying six million lives
> that was Jewish history
> but each child was one refugee
> we unlike the Egyptian slaves
> were exiled individually
> and each in desolation has
> created his own wilderness

By setting the displacement of refugees ('exiled individually') in a traditional Judaic context ('Jewish history', 'Egyptian slaves'), Gershon frames and delimits it. Typologically, she suggests that after wandering in the 'wilderness' from Nazi Germany, the 'children' of Israel are destined to rediscover their homeland. Like

Rosenberg, Gershon draws upon the Hebrew Bible to shape her Zionist dreams.

Moreover, Gershon lived in Israel from 1968 to 1974.[16] I want to suggest that her Israel-based poems, *Legacies and Encounters* (1972), continue to champion Jewish narrative continuity by reaffirming the diasporic tension between European exile and a Zionist homeland. Claiming affinity with Israel, Gershon simultaneously expresses exile from the 'unredeemable *and indestructible ruin*'[17] of her forever lost German-Jewish home. For example, 'Israel Notebook 1966'[18] juxtaposes Jerusalem with the Holocaust ash left behind in Germany:

> Ancient Jerusalem is ruin-grey –
> the ash of history raked to a crown;
> oriental Jewish children play
> within the range of rifles pointed down.
> From desert stone, in legendary places,
> an ancestry of pride is being built
> by survivors with contaminated faces –
> all people whom the Germans would have killed.

Here, affiliation with Israel is clearly set in opposition to the death offered the immigrants ('killed') in their former 'contaminated' homes. The 'survivors' have chosen life in the *altneu* (old-new)[19] Jewish homeland ('an ancestry of pride is being built'). For the present, however, they occupy a provisional space between exile and a potential home: they are being orientalised so as to become Israeli ('oriental Jewish'). Even the narrator exists somewhere between 'Jerusalem' and 'the Germans'. 'Israel Notebook 1966' remains, in Sidra DeKoven Ezrahi's phrase, 'open-ended':[20]

> God's dereliction where he pottered man,
> green orchestration of Messianic dreams,
> are the south and north of both exile and home,
> where every year of the expectation of life
> is represented by another nation –
> all people whom the Germans would have killed.

In 'exile', this stanza implies, one experiences 'Messianic dreams' of 'home'. Such 'dreams' bring 'man' to Israel. The poem mines Judaic texts ('God's', 'Messianic') in the service of the Zionist project to return 'home'. However, history ('every year') determines that Jewish survivors from 'the Germans' reach Israel in 'exile' from their former domiciles. Everything is provisional, as the title's reference to a 'notebook' suggests. Gershon explains: 'My poems tell of my life like diary entries taken at random.'[21]

'Time Which Has Made Ruins' (1966)[22] was written in England, but also evokes ongoing exile from European destruction:

> Time which had made ruins of
> many places I have loved
> has no power to destroy
> what exists in memory
> our temple which was burned
> stands for ever in my mind
> built of substances which can
> defy the practices of man
>
> The eternal light which laid
> its mercy on my childhood days
> and commanded me to be
> servant of its mystery
> lodged a splinter of its grace
> in my consciousness and throws
> on the reality I face
> a radiance it cannot lose

The 'temple' of Gershon's German home town[23] remains 'for ever in my mind' and in 'ruins'. To this extent, it replaces Solomon's Temple in the traditional diasporic narrative.[24] Moreover, the poem offers consolation in language bearing traces of religious discourse. It transcends the tensions of diasporic reality by invoking such 'ungraspable'[25] signifieds as 'eternal light', 'grace' and 'radiance'. Interestingly, 'I Set Out for Jerusalem' (1972)[26] links such transfiguration to both Zionism and childhood:

> When my infant senses met
> reality instead of home,
> I set out for Jerusalem.
>
> I belong with those who kept
> a Jerusalem of thought

as a refuge from the world,
guardians of splinters which
constitute our heritage.
Two thousand years of wilderness
from which the caretaker has swept
the excrements of history
are kindled to a radiance

These lines evoke an ineffable 'Jerusalem of thought' as 'a refuge from the world', which is associated with childhood ('infant senses'). From a Zionist perspective, 'Jerusalem' constitutes the transcendent opposite – 'radiance' rather than 'excrements' – of Jewish 'reality' in diaspora. Indeed, 'Jerusalem' encourages the speaker to jettison adult experience ('history') for childlike innocence:

Need to belong has made me come
to help rebuild Jerusalem,
where everyone is family –
all descendent from Abraham
and sharing one inheritance.
Where every step is taken by
one entering my father's house,
and every stone is laden with
the honey of remembrances

Childhood ('my father's house'), transcendence and Israel are merged here to suggest a childlike 'home' presided over by the Judaic father figure 'Abraham'. Similarly, 'Naomi in Jerusalem' (1972) and 'My Children Walk in Jerusalem' (1972)[27] imply that Israel is childlike. 'Naomi in Jerusalem' begins:

One generation past the holocaust
my golden daughter matches Jerusalem:
all she expends herself on contributes to make her.

Unlike the speaker, the 'golden daughter' is in harmony with ('matches') the golden stones of Jerusalem. Significantly, Naomi is 'One generation past the holocaust'. She is unambivalently at home because she is too young to know diasporic history. Again, 'My Children Walk in Jerusalem' contrasts Israeli innocence with the speaker's diasporic experience:

A German girl came to my door,
saying she was the daughter of
someone I played with as a child.
I thought of how I was allowed
to use Margaret's garden swing:
that such a thing was event enough
forty years later to be recalled
implies the weight of the chains I wore.
I have lived with my memories for so long,
by now the poison has drained out.

My children walk in Jerusalem
engaged in life and unconcerned
that history makes use of them
to balance old iniquities.
They have no ghetto memories:
English country children who
belong to the Messianic age

The speaker's 'ghetto memories' of Nazism ('chains I wore') are distinguished here from her children's 'engaged' and 'unconcerned' life in Jerusalem. They transcend diasporic 'history' in a 'Messianic age' of return to Israel. By contrast, the speaker recalls a 'garden swing' which she was 'allowed', rather than entitled, 'to use'. This swing belonged to her Gentile ('German') friend 'Margaret'. Paradoxically enough, its 'chains' came closest to offering escape from German-Jewish reality in the speaker's own childhood.

Gershon's novel *Manna to the Hungry* (1990–91) depicts the protagonist, Eva, as similarly split between childlike affiliation with Israel and adult experience of diaspora. On arrival in Tel Aviv, Eva feels as though she has entered a fairy tale. After the initial disorientation – 'an Alice-in-Wonderland-like feeling of being the wrong person even to herself' – she meets her deceased brother's best friend Achim: 'Eva first saw him from ground level while he was standing at the top of the stairs leading up the side of the house to the Gilboas' flat. She felt like Jack at the foot of the beanstalk.'[28]

Israel is imagined as a world of children's stories. Eva thinks: 'This is the place I set out for as a child.' However, since Eva has a subsequent diasporic history, she remains outside Israeli reality: 'Her passions were here in Jerusalem ... She saw herself as standing *outside life's shop-window* – as she had stood as a child coveting sweets, as an adolescent clothes.' [*my italics*] Consequently, Eva behaves like 'a child' or 'adolescent'; and, as young people do, she strives to belong to a group: 'They passed the intersection where all the lights for pedestrians change at once, so that at intervals the road is altogether claimed by people crossing; like a child she had twice gone out of her way to join in.'[29] Childlike affiliation ('to join in') is a desideratum in Israel. Eva 'knew no better than to believe that the State would provide for her as if it were her parents'. In the care of parental Israel, Eva feels transformed – like Alice in Wonderland – to pre-adult, post-diasporic safety. Significantly, it is while she is visiting parental figures that Eva decides to make *aliyah* (adopt Israeli citizenship):

> Being in the home of people of her parents' generation ... turned time back for her, made her feel like a child again so that, washing her hands, the face she caught sight of in the mirror above the basin astonished her. It felt to her as if she were only pretending to be an adult, a married woman, a mother ... It was in this mood of being a stranger to herself that, over a frugal salad lunch, served European style, she told them that she was going to settle in Israel.[30]

'As if she were only pretending to be an adult', Eva finds the moment propitious to affiliate with Israel. Only when imagining herself a child ('like a child again') does Eva manage to jettison her sense of otherness in the country. Adult experience ('the face ... in the mirror above the basin astonished her') is replaced by twinned affiliations with childhood and the young State of Israel. Consequently Eva, still a diasporic woman, is left 'in this mood of being a stranger to herself'.

To be sure, Eva's affiliation with Israel relates to her own survival as a *Kindertransport* girl:

> She had fallen in love ... with the country. Or perhaps what she had fallen in love with was the idea of Jewish survival. What she had so whole-heartedly reached out for and wanted to hold on to at no matter what cost was the Jew in herself.

As 'an only survivor' of her family since the Shoah, Eva identifies Israel inextricably with both 'the idea of Jewish survival' and 'the Jew in herself'. Indeed, Israel resembles the *Kind* Eva was, as well as the childlike person she becomes again through affiliation with the new country:

> As she had always reacted to any child's crying as if it were aimed at her, so ever since coming to Israel she had been responding to the signs of its ongoing rebirth all about her with the urge to join in, to become a part of it all and be absorbed into it, mixed with a sense of guilt because of all that had already been achieved without her.[31]

Rather than reacting as an adult on hearing a 'child's crying', Eva identifies with it by wanting 'to join in, to become a part of it all and be absorbed into it'. She desires nothing less than to be 'a stranger to herself', as an adult, by merging with the youthful Israeli crowd she imagines. Eva's reaction to *'any* child's crying' [*my italics*] recalls her own orphan condition, while reinforcing her childlike affiliation with the State.

However, Eva also feels that she has arrived too late. She has 'a sense of guilt because of all that had already been achieved without her'. Feeling childlike, she re-experiences a *Kind* survivor's guilt in being ineffectual when most needed ('achieved without her'). After all, there have been three wars in Israel (1948, 1956 and 1967) for which she was absent. Eva survives, but many Israelis have died in battle. Her childhood guilt at surviving her murdered German-Jewish parents endures in transmuted form.

To be sure, there is more than a sprinkling of autobiography in *Manna to the Hungry*. While Gershon was safe in Britain, both her parents were enslaved and murdered by the Nazis. After deportation to the Riga ghetto, her father died in 1942 or 1943, and her mother probably in 1944.[32] Consequently, the poet fell prey to survivor's guilt. 'In the Park' (1966)[33] sets this out:

> As I walked alone in my home town's loveliest garden
> the past I remembered moved further out of my reach
> that so much remained made what was lost to me certain
> a sole survivor cannot commemorate much
>
> This was no suitable setting for one in mourning
> I thought of my dead and felt guilty to be alive
> a multiple shadow lay at my feet as a warning
> to the past I pledged all I am all I do all I have

How loved I must have been as a child in this Eden
where the perfect are unselfconscious before their fall
by the dead in whose debt I am I felt myself bidden
to celebrate being alive on behalf of them all

Gershon writes a 'Kaddish'[34] (prayer in memory of the dead) to the
dead, but feels 'bidden / to celebrate being alive on behalf of them
all'. Interestingly, since 'home' is associated with 'my dead', the
very fact of being a 'survivor' necessarily becomes some sort of
post-Holocaust exile. The flip-side of a kaddish is a plea for home.
As Emma reflects in *The Last Freedom* (1986):

> The Holocaust ... had more or less by-passed her. It was an
> exemption she had not sought and if she had understood it at
> the time would not have wanted; she had always found it too
> difficult to live with ... She wished that it were not for ever
> too late for her to share in her Jewish birthright of suffering
> for the world – though according to the Gentiles the only Jew
> who had ever done so was Jesus. She did not think that it
> would have been too high a price to pay for belonging. Now
> at last she understood what was meant by 'the guilt of
> survival'.[35]

Exempted from the Holocaust, Emma wishes to suffer 'for the
world'. She seeks martyrdom ('Jesus') which, in the wake of the
Shoah, she considers 'her Jewish birthright'. Her 'guilt of survival'
drives her to affiliate ('belonging') with the dead.

Gershon goes further than Jon Silkin in explicitly depicting Jesus
as a martyred Jew. Whereas Silkin deploys traces of Christian
discourse in 'Death of a Son' (1954) and 'Polish fragments of dust'
(1992),[36] Gershon states baldly in 'Kaddish' (1966): 'Christ
persecuted was a Jew'; and in 'Easter' (1966):

> The Christian world commemorates
> the crucifixion of a Jew.[37]

To be sure, there is a twentieth-century Jewish literary tradition of
appropriating Christian symbolism.[38] Siegfried Sassoon empathised
with Christianity's noblest Jew: 'I shut my eyes, seeing on the
darkness a shape always the same – in spite of myself – the
suffering mortal figure on a cross, but the face is my own.'[39]

If Christianity has traditionally insisted on typologically reinterpreting the Old Testament as presaging the New, Gershon re-reads the New Testament as presaging the Holocaust. For example, 'The Flight into Egypt' (1990) and 'The Bethlehem Babies' (1990) are New Testament tales of 'refugees' and 'the mess of bodies in the common grave', respectively.[40] Like Rosenberg, Sassoon and Silkin, Gershon finds much to admire in Christianity. Indeed, she internalised the values of the ostensibly Christian majority in Germany 'before Hitler came to power'.[41] As Gershon explains in an autobiographical text, *A Tempered Wind* (1992): 'Having grown up in a Christian environment, I was aware that Christianity offers to mourners more comfort and hope (one of the reasons why it instead of Judaism was adopted by the pagan Romans).'

She also internalised other, not so universal, attitudes. From 1930, 'Bielefeld was putting out its first anti-Semitic newspaper'. Amid a burgeoning atmosphere of social and political antisemitism, Gershon became 'ashamed of being a Jew'. The very word 'Jew' was an 'execration' to her ears. She and her sister Lisa 'did not believe what they read [in *Der Stürmer*]. But they did not totally disbelieve it either'. As a girl influenced by the dominant culture in Germany, Gershon 'was incapable of believing that it was everybody else who was wrong [about Jews]'.[42] Thus, she absorbed antisemitism:

> Suddenly she was seeing the Jews as the Nazis saw them; the years of indoctrination had finally taken effect. Her indifference – beginning on that day [*Kristallnacht*] – was confined to the men, and it included her father. The only thing about him which still mattered was that he was a Jew and Jewish men did not matter.[43]

Elsewhere, Gershon admits: 'I hated myself and did not feel anyone's equal and there was nothing I could do about it.'[44] Again, Inge in *The Bread of Exile* (1985) 'frequently called herself a Jewish shit' and 'Jewish rubbish', while the Anglo-German-Jew Barbara in *The Fifth Generation* (1987) 'cursed herself' as a 'shitty misfit'.[45] Such sentiments and representations suggest Jewish self-hatred. The cultural historian Sander Gilman states: 'Self-hatred results from outsiders' acceptance of the mirage of themselves generated by their reference group – that group in society which they see as defining them – as a reality.'[46]

Gilman is speaking specifically about German Jews. Projecting self-hatred onto her father, Gershon attempts to escape pariah status as a Jew among antisemites. Gilman explains: 'Jews see the dominant society seeing them and ... they project their anxiety about this manner of being seen onto other Jews as a means of externalising their own status anxiety.'[47]

Possibly, Gershon dismisses 'Jewish men' with a view to distancing herself as a *woman* from the immediate targets of Nazi antisemitism.[48] As we shall see in Chapter 7, Elaine Feinstein similarly Judaises some of her male protagonists in order to depict the women within her texts as comparatively more empowered. However, 'My Mother' (1966) suggests that Gershon also wishes to distance herself from 'appalling tortured'[49] Jewish women. Here Gershon confesses:

> I have disowned her for life's sake
> her hands once hesitant and white
> have touched me with the Jewish plague
> she is my enemy because
> I am burdened with her fate

Antisemitism and the Holocaust have led Gershon to associate her mother with what Nazis described (and she repeats) as 'the Jewish plague'. Consequently, Gershon must reject her in order to carry on living: 'I have disowned her for life's sake.' Yet the projection of 'Jewish plague' onto her mother is not the end of Gershon's psychological move. The mother, in turn, has touched her daughter with this 'plague'. If self-hatred before the Shoah led to attempts at assimilation in Germany,[50] after the Holocaust a German Jew cannot decently deny her Jewishness. Thus, Gershon concludes 'My Mother': 'I am burdened with her fate.' The poet affiliates with a diasporic Jewishness which she nonetheless considers irksome ('burdened'). Similarly, the speaker in 'Kaddish'[51] states:

> Simple must be the words I use
> to commemorate all these
> Jews and those who died like Jews;

while also admitting:

> I mourn my parents without pride
> I see them as their killers did

> who by degrading me as well
> are beyond death victorious

Simultaneously, Gershon declares a duty to bear witness ('commemorate') for the German-Jewish dead ('all these / Jews') and her humiliation ('degrading') in doing so. This is one source of the tension in her verse.

To be sure, Gershon is writing Anglophone poetry. Unlike Jon Silkin, however, her verse is not orientated around English 'specifics'.[52] Moreover, her choice of language is relatively arbitrary. Before leaving Germany, Gershon was not interested in English: 'the only language she was interested in mastering was Hebrew'.[53] On arrival in England, she knew 'more Hebrew than English'.[54] David Hartnett remarks: 'Unlike [Paul] Celan, who spent a lifetime exploiting the linguistic riches of the oppressor, or [Dan] Pagis, who wrote in Hebrew, Gershon chose, or was chosen by, the language of her country of exile.'

Hartnett continues: 'The speaker's aggrieved alienation from the experience she is driven to imagine is at one with her sense of linguistic exile.'[55] Discussing Kafka, George Steiner writes similarly 'of estrangement, of the artist unhoused in his language'.[56] Indeed, Gershon's sense of exile remains strong because she is not writing in her natal tongue. Her estrangement from the German language began during the Nazi years: 'Her mother had begun to say to her, "How can you make poems in the language in which we are being cursed!"'[57]

English reminds Gershon why she is not writing in German. It also suggests provisionality: being 'between languages'. This may explain the awkwardness which some readers discern in Gershon's poetic phraseology. Gershon, I suggest, conveys precisely in her language a refugee's 'inbetweenness'. She chooses, or is chosen by, a 'minor literature' in English.[58]

'Home' (1966)[59] evokes the fear felt by a refugee:

> The people have got used to her
> they have watched her children grow
> and behave as if she were
> one of them – how can they know
> that every time she leaves her home
> she is terrified of them
> that as a German Jew she sees

them as potential enemies
Because she knows what has been done
to children who were like her own
she cannot think her future safe
her parents must have felt at home
where none cared what became of them
and as a child she must have played
with people who in later life
would have killed her had she stayed

The speaker envisages her neighbours as neither friends nor enemies. They are ambiguously situated indeterminates, strangers who are thus also 'potential enemies'. Similarly, the 'German Jew' in England sees herself being seen by 'them' as a stranger. Indeed, the vulnerable 'her' is an example of 'the stranger ... the person who comes today and stays tomorrow'.[60] The German-Jewish sociologist Georg Simmel notes that such a person becomes estranged because she 'is considered a stranger in the eyes of the other', adding, 'the classical example is the history of European Jews'.[61]

Zygmunt Bauman goes further: 'To the stranger himself ... freedom appears first of all as acute uncertainty. Unmitigated by at least a part-time availability of safe harbour, it tends to be experienced as a curse rather than a blessing.'[62] Following enforced separation from parental protection, Gershon describes herself as 'constantly ... insecure'. There ensues a stranger's 'acute uncertainty' in England. 'My wish to be of use was hampered by my fear of being found inadequate,' Gershon writes, 'I feared being confronted with strangers, feared needing to speak to them, did not know what to say, or not how to say it in English; my shyness magnified by embarrassment must have made me appear rather stupid.'[63]

Clearly, this is '"literal" exile'[64] experienced as a curse ('insecure', 'fear', 'inadequate'). However, Gershon's description of 'shyness', 'embarrassment' and a sense of social stupidity are not dissimilar to the awkwardness evoked by Isaac Rosenberg in his short story *Rudolph* (1911), and in his letter of the same year to Miss Seaton. In the latter, Rosenberg writes: 'I find it difficult to make myself intelligible at times; I can't remember the exact word I want, and I think I leave the impression of being a rambling idiot.'[65]

Feeling 'socially isolated',[66] the First World War poet portrays a gaucherie similar to that depicted a generation later by the German-

Jewish 'voice of the *Kindertransport* generation'.[67] Such a correspondence between Jewish poets in England suggests that Gershon's 'shyness' and 'embarrassment' are affected by a sense of social exile, as a Jew among Gentiles, as well as linguistic infelicities ('how to say it in English').

Gershon's empathy with First World War poetry is significant. As she writes in the foreword to her *Collected Poems* (1990): 'My English mentors were the poets of the First World War, especially Wilfred Owen.'[68] In *A Tempered Wind*, she explains, 'I can't remember how I discovered him [Owen] and Siegfried Sassoon – whose *Selected Poems* are on sale; I've bought a copy – I feel as if I had always known them. I relate to them and therefore I feel related.'[69]

Gershon's situation as a poet whose life is radically changed by the Second World War goes some way to explaining this literary affiliation with an earlier generation of war poets. Indeed, she might be described as a war poet herself. C. B. Cox comments, 'It's sometimes said that 1939–45 produced no major war poets, but this is what Karen Gershon becomes by her unpretentious, honest account of her deprivation.'[70]

Significant too is Gershon's sense of social embattlement as a Jew in Nazi Germany, and then as a German-Jewish refugee in England. Antisemites continue to abuse Jews in periods of civil calm. Jews are compelled to fight fascists even in peacetime. As the character Peter Heine reflects in *The Fifth Generation*:

> It was not true that anti-Semitism had disappeared [in Germany], it had merely been disestablished and gone underground ... If that part of the war wasn't over yet, if Jews and Nazis were still fighting each other, then his place was certainly at the battle front.[71]

Like Jon Silkin, Gershon takes a stand against fascism. Sensing embattlement, she also emphasises united fronts. For example, a Gentile character, Paul, states in *Burn Helen* (1980): 'We're all on the same side.'[72] By contrast, in *The Last Freedom* (1986), an elderly *Kind*, Emma, remarks of a German, Bruno: 'Some of his looks had gone into her like bullets.' Here, Gershon suggests that any German-Jewish intercourse is metaphorically bellicose. However, Emma also opines that 'enmity is a relationship'.[73] Gershon says something similar in her poem 'Explosion' (1972): 'enmity is the closest relationship of all'.[74] From this perspective, all relationships resemble war ('enmity'), as opposed to the peace and loneliness of solitude. Of course, the social complications of being an Anglo-German-Jewish woman contribute to this embattled *Weltanschauung*. Significantly, Emma chooses to leave Bruno in Germany and return to England, where she can resume her life alone rather than engage conflictually with (German or English) Gentile males in a battle of the sexes underpinned by antisemitism.

Fleeing conflict, the protagonists of Gershon's novels face alienation. For example, Inge in *The Bread of Exile* is 'beset by the unfamiliar'. 'Being a refugee', she reflects, 'was like being in Looking-Glass country.'[75] References to 'Alice-in-Wonderland',[76] mirrors-images and 'fairyland' abound in Gershon's novels. They convey a sense of unreality and self-estrangement catalysed by imagining one's reception in a new language and society. When Emma becomes involved with Bruno in *The Last Freedom*, she slips into a 'Looking-Glass' sense of unreality: 'Surely they were partaking in a fairyland ritual: had it addled their brains? – an almost unknown old man with a doubtful past and questionable intentions was saying things that made her feel a stranger to herself.'[77]

Whether in England, Israel or Germany, Gershon's protagonists eventually come to see themselves as exiles in search of social, cultural or biographical continuity. Such characters experience 'insecurity'[78] in the face of others' distorting representations ('Looking-Glass Country'), and 'a fairyland' abandonment of personal control ('a stranger to herself') over their painstakingly constructed lives. In contrast to reality, imagination furnishes Gershon's protagonists with bounded and comforting self-representations. Emma, for example, wonders whether 'perhaps she had chosen a seventy-year-old man to fall in love with so as to get the benefit of all the emotions and none of the reality'.[79] Rather than feeling solipsistic, Emma finds a reassuring imaginary home in front of a mirror:

> Since what little she knew of the reality of him had been moulded by her daydreams in accordance with her needs, she made her purchases with an ideal self in mind. And when she got home, and tried the things on in front of her full-length mirror – tried the complete trousseau – it reassured her about Bruno to see her reflection so acceptable to herself.[80]

Alone with 'her full-length mirror', Emma's imagination transfigures 'reality'. She is at 'home' with her private reflection of an 'ideal self', since it conforms to 'daydreams' of being 'acceptable'. Home lies in solipsistic self-reflection. Exilic estrangement lurks on the other side of the mirror in a 'Looking-Glass country', and the eyes of strangers.

Love and sexuality also provide a refuge for Gershon's protagonists. Gershon's first novel, *The World Was Old* (1956), portrays a sexual rebel, Stella: 'She lit his cigarette before lighting her own and, giving the matches back, let her fingers touch his. Why should it always be left to the man to make the advances? She thought.'[81]

In prison, Stella is visited by a Christian chaplain:

> When the chaplain came into the cell Stella moved back against the wall, trembling: so long was it since she had been alone with a man. 'Now my child,' he said, 'I have not come to scold you. I am coming to you with the mercy of Jesus Christ.'
>
> Stella was not listening to him. She was studying his clothes, wondering what he was wearing underneath.[82]

Here, sexuality transcends a claustrophobic ('cell') Christian ('Jesus Christ') environment. Though Stella is not Jewish, she is certainly not affiliating with a Christian *Weltanschauung* ('Stella was not listening to him').

Significantly, one of the two books[83] translated by Gershon is a treatise concerning sexuality in literature. In *Obszön: Geschichte einer Entrüstung* (1962) [*Obscene: The History of an Indignation* (1965)],[84] the German-Jewish social philosopher Ludwig Marcuse traces the associations between antisemitism and censorship, as well as between strangers and sexuality. 'Sexual release,' Marcuse claims, 'means the dissolution of all social bonds.' During coitus, he continues, 'the human being ceases to be his own master'.[85] In other words, sex makes strangers of us all. Marcuse adds that Nazi propaganda castigated Jews as sexually unacceptable. '*Der Stürmer* later portrayed the Jewish lecher in greater detail,' he observes; 'National-Socialistic anti-Semitism was imbued with sexuality.' Thus, the Jewish Other in Nazi Germany became identified with 'this accursed little devil sex'. Sexuality and Jews were imagined as 'dirty, filthy, beastly'. Both were associated with 'the dark powers beneath the illuminated world'.[86] Together, they were perceived as a menace by totalitarian minds that refused to countenance individual freedom.

By contrast to what Marcuse identifies as a damaging metaphysics of 'Christian-German-Idealistic dogma' regarding sexuality, *Obscene* praises the Old Testament for its eschewal of hypocrisy: 'Is it an accident that it [the obscene] is mentioned neither in the Old Testament nor in other evidence of early cultures? They probably did not contain anything sexual which was forbidden.'[87] Thus, Marcuse makes his case for unrepressed sexuality in the Hebrew Bible (along with other, implicitly pre-Christian, 'early cultures').

Correspondingly, Gershon's biblical novels, *The Boy with the Sling: A Life of King David* (c.1984) and *The Historical and Legendary Esther* (c.1980), are frank in their depiction of sexual desire.[88] Indeed, Gershon's pronouncements on sex echo Marcuse's in their yoking of the Hebrew Bible to non-repressed sexuality. As Eva muses in *Manna to the Hungry*:

> She had never understood why the human body which was said to be made in God's image should even in part be something to be ashamed of or why so many aspects of the sexual activity without which mankind would not have survived should be regarded as sinful.[89]

Rejecting what Marcuse identifies as 'the Christian dualism of body and soul',[90] Gershon extols sex in 'Love Song' (1975):[91]

> Love me familiarly,
> without humility,
> as Adam did Eve who had
> once been a part of him;
> shine on me directly
> so that no chink of doubt
> can take your warmth from me;
> don't let me fail to be
> the instrument you think:
> be masterful, make me
> respond in harmony.

Since sex relates to the original Old Testament couple Adam and Eve, it partakes of Jewish tradition and appears 'familiarly'

Hebraic. Sex also resembles lyrical poetry in so far as it transcends life's tensions ('respond in harmony'). Significantly, Gershon associates love and lyricism: 'The first poem in the English language which made an impression on me was "The force that through the green fuse drives the flower" ... Dylan Thomas made me fall in love with the English language.'[92]

Further, she echoes Thomas's poem[93] in 'Married Love' (1975):[94]

> you lie green in the membranes of my senses
> and rise like sap in my experiences.

Gershon's linkage of connubial sex with lyricism suggests that both defuse diasporic tensions. Further, to frame lyrical intoxication, the poet sets it within 'familiarly' domestic Old Testament narratives. For example, the speaker in 'Uphold Me' (1975)[95] urges her husband to:

> be David to make me Bathsheba,
> elaborate me with legends

In the midst of transcendent lyrics, such Hebraic references offer a countervailing affiliation with an ongoing Jewish story ('legends') of domestic love.

Gershon's personae commonly retain an awareness of potential estrangement in England:

> That was the moment I stopped being orphaned:
> not when you married me but when you took
> a share in our responsibilities.

For a former *Kindertransport* child, marriage exists in the tension between sharing an English home ('a share') and being adopted ('orphaned') into it. Such a home is always provisional:

> I sought a home it would not hurt to lose
> Which would outweigh for me the one I lost.[96]

Gershon's novels *Burn Helen* and *The Fifth Generation* also depict domesticity as provisional. In the former, Helen is a Gentile orphan 'who had always believed that she thought, compulsively, I wish I were dead, because she felt guilty about having survived her family'.

Helen is suffering an Anglicised species of Holocaust survivor's guilt. Like Gershon, she is an orphan of the Second World War: '*They were killed in the blitz. Her whole family was.*' Helen's affiliation with a dead family ('I wish I were dead') is challenged when she is diagnosed as terminally ill. The imminence of her own death situates Helen more intensely between affiliations with her dead and her living adoptive family. Committed as a wife and mother, Helen nonetheless feels estranged as an orphan:

> When she had been 'a gamble' in her uncle's house she had believed that once she grew up and made her own family she would stop being an orphan; but there was nothing inevitable about being related to [her husband] Paul.[97]

The dual clauses of the above sentence serve to emphasise the contrast between Helen's arbitrary marriage ('nothing inevitable') and her 'orphan' state. Implicitly, the death of Helen's original 'family' during the blitz *was* 'inevitable'. Thus, she shares an Anglicised variant of Gershon's 'Jewish fate'.[98] Like Gershon again, Helen cannot shed her estrangement ('being an orphan') simply through marriage.

Helen's fatal disease moves her closer to her dead, and further from her living, family. However, she chooses to affiliate with the living: 'We are a close family, Helen had thought – it needed a stranger at their table to make this apparent.' A reminder of estrangement is required ('it needed a stranger') for Helen to appreciate her adoptive home.

The stranger in *Burn Helen* is Anglo-Jewish. Helen's son, Terence, wants his mother to meet Kim: 'She did not want her [Kim] to come. "I don't like strangers in the house," she argued. "It made me feel not at home when Zelda was staying."' Kim is explicitly Anglo-Jewish, whereas the novel's earlier stranger only had a Jewish-sounding name ('Zelda'). Gershon narrates a Gentile's discomfort around Jews:

> Helen had never knowingly met a Jew; she felt afraid of them because of their history. She thought, that is why she is willing to settle for Terence.
> They heard a cuckoo and Kim smiled at her.[99]

Helen fears Jews according to the poet's definition of them. As Gershon writes in *Notes of a Heart-Patient* (1993): 'a Jew is a Jew by his history'.[100] To Helen, Jews are also synonymous with the unknown, the strange: she 'had never *knowingly* met a Jew' [*my italics*]. It is precisely this difficulty of recognising – of *knowing* – a Jew which causes anxiety. Kim is a Jew in being a stranger: 'a cuckoo' in an English home. Zygmunt Bauman remarks:

> The stranger is assigned no status inside the cultural realm he wants to make his own. His entry will therefore signify a violation of the culture he enters. By the act of his entry, real or merely intended, the life-world of the natives that used to be a secure shelter is turned into a contested ground, insecure and problematic.[101]

Certainly, Helen feels that her home is threatened by the entry of Kim. However, as Kim strives to jettison her '*neither/nor*'[102] condition of indeterminacy, Helen begins to appreciate strangers. She reflects: 'All their babies had been born in hospital; it had always moved her to think what strangers had done for them.'[103] Helen's definition of 'strangers' as those outside the family home universalises the term. Strangers cease to be threatening, Jewish Others when viewed as merely extra-familial. Significantly, Helen recalls 'strangers' in the context of a life-affirming ('babies') and benevolent institution ('hospital'), associated here with families. Thus, she relates the impersonality of the hospital to the security of home, and in the process attempts to reconcile the tensions of her own orphaned but married life. Further, Helen's attempts at self-reconciliation enable her to understand the Anglo-Jewish Kim:

> She [Kim] was saying: ' ... if while they're [my parents are] abroad I could think of this as my – as my – ' Was it 'home' she was unable to say? the effort was making her blush. Looking down, plucking at the grass, she finished: 'as somewhere for me to come to.'[104]

Empathetically, Helen hazards that the 'cuckoo' Kim is trying to say 'home'. Moreover, in her stammering ('as my – as my – '), Kim resembles Gershon's self-portrait as a tongue-tied refugee in *A Tempered Wind*.[105] Thus, I want to suggest, Gershon's depiction of Kim implies the author's identification with Anglo-Jewish discomforts and tensions.

The familiar figure of an orphan re-appears in *The Fifth Generation*: '[Barbara] had come to England ... in the winter before the war with a children's transport and been raised in a Jewish orphanage.' Barbara has married a Gentile in the aftermath of the war, believing 'that, living in Somerset with a Gentile husband, she would be able to escape her Jewishness'.[106] She considers her Jewishness as devoid of meaning, except as defined by antisemites:

> At the time [of her marriage] she said that her Jewishness did not matter: she was not a Jew by religion since she did not believe in God; that she was a Jew by race mattered only to people like Hitler; she and PS [Peter, her adopted son] were Jewish by their history but in time and with Luke's help, she believed, they would grow out of it.[107]

Barbara's attempted assimilation into Englishness through her husband Luke is seriously undermined when she learns that her adopted child is, in fact, Hitler's secret son.[108] Suddenly, Peter resorts to antisemitic stereotypes in his interpretation of Barbara's behaviour; and the distance between mother and son grows. Peter thinks 'stupid Jewish bitch' about Barbara; and when she offers him food: 'Yiddishe Moma'. Meanwhile, Luke begins to recruit Peter into a Gentile alliance against the Jewess in their midst:

> If Barbara could not bear to have Hitler's son in her home ... then he would take him away: he sealed the unspoken promise with a kiss on Peter's cheek ... They would have to wean their Peter, emotionally, from his Barbara.[109]

Barbara now feels isolated. 'The security of England' has metamorphosed to estrangement. Concomitantly, she comes to feel that 'an English Gentile' lacks 'the background necessary for a proper understanding' of her different German-Jewish experiences.[110] Barbara's knowledge of 'the Holocaust as her home ground'[111] suddenly changes to anxiety about its possible repetition. Such a 'Looking-Glass'[112] reversal of Barbara's domestic security is reflected in what Peter calls a 'fairy tale' inversion of his situation from adopted Jew to son of Hitler. In a final twist of the plot, Peter Heine discovers that he is not Hitler's son, Peter Sanger:

> He had invented himself; he was a figment of other people's imagination ... He could not remember what the other Peter had looked like and, thinking of him as his alter ego, visualized him as looking rather like himself: an idealized mirror-image.[113]

Peter has 'invented himself' as a Nazi by imagining an 'idealized mirror-image'. He is behaving as one who feels more at home in imagination than reality ('He could not remember what the other Peter had looked like'). In this, he resembles Emma in *The Last Freedom* whose 'ideal self' is also found in a 'mirror'. Mirrors reassuringly bound identities. In the case of Nazis, however, such a framing denies life to Jews and others outside its 'idealized' parameters.

All's well that ends well, even in melodramatic Nazi narratives. Mossad secret-service agents reassure Peter that he is a Jew, and will prove useful as a bogus Nazi bait in their planned capture of Adolf Eichmann. Peter's affiliation with Israel is effected through camaraderie with the agents: 'Gone was the antagonism he [Peter] had at first felt towards Morry [of the Mossad]; since he knew him to be a fellow Jew, and an Israeli at that, all he could feel for him was comradeship.'[114] Finding an apparently fated ('all he could feel') 'comradeship' with a 'fellow Jew', Peter also imagines an idealised 'Israeli' state free of 'antagonism'.

By contrast, in her foreword to the second edition of *We Came as Children: a collective autobiography* (1966; 1989), Gershon confronts the tensions of her Anglo-Jewish situation:

> When I came to this country I was on my way to what was then called Palestine. While working on this book I realised that, for me, England would always remain a foster-home. I then continued my journey, together with the family I had made. Perhaps I had left it too late.
>
> I feel more at home in Israel than I do in England, but I don't feel at home there either, and that is worse, because there I still expect to be able to feel at home. Here I am reconciled.[115]

Two years after the first edition of *We Came as Children*, the poet made *aliyah*. Her foreword to the 1989 edition suggests why she returned to the Anglo-Jewish diaspora in 1974. Evidently, Gershon did not 'feel at home' in Israel. To be sure, she realises that England will 'always remain a foster-home'. Possibly for all Jews, the diaspora stays 'a *foster* homeland, perhaps a *step*-homeland, benevolent or stern, yet once removed at all times'.[116] From this perspective, Gershon's poem 'Foster-England' (1975)[117] appears to carry immense symbolic weight. In claiming to be 'reconciled' to

England, the poet implies a coming to terms with inherently diasporic tensions. These, I contend, resemble the tensions voiced from Isaac Rosenberg to Elaine Feinstein by Anglo-Jewish poets writing between 'social' exile and an 'imaginary homeland'.[118]

NOTES

1. On the night of 9–10 November 1938, Germans burned and looted synagogues and other Jewish establishments. The quantity of smashed glass lent this first nation-wide pogrom the name *Kristallnacht*. See Saul Friedländer, *Nazi Germany and the Jews: The Years of Persecution 1933–39* (1997; London: Phoenix, 1998), pp. 269–76.
2. For an account of *Kindertransport* experiences in England, see Karen Gershon (ed.), *We Came as Children: a collective autobiography* (1966; London: Papermac, 1989).
3. See Lotte Kramer, 'Reflections', in Stephen W. Massil (ed.), *Jewish Year Book 2000* (London: Vallentine Mitchell, 2000), pp. 69–75; and Gerda Mayer, 'Flight to England', *Poetry Review* 88:4 (winter 1998/1999), pp. 25–7.
4. Karen Gershon, *The Bread of Exile* (London: Gollancz, 1985), p. 14.
5. See the television documentary on Karen Gershon, directed and produced by John Pett, *Stranger in a Strange Land* (Channel 4, 1990).
6. 'Foreword', in Gershon (ed.), *We Came as Children*, p. 9.
7. See Terry Eagleton, *Exiles and Emigrés: Studies in Modern Literature* (London: Chatto & Windus, 1970), p. 18: 'I am concerned ... with the "social" exiles.'
8. Bryan Cheyette, '"Ineffable and usable": towards a diasporic British-Jewish writing', *Textual Practice* 10:2 (1996), p. 303 and pp. 295–313.
9. Karen Gershon, *A Tempered Wind: autobiography* (unpublished, 1992), p. 49.
10. Ibid., p. 50.
11. Karen Gershon, *A Lesser Child* (London: Peter Owen, 1994), p. 130.
12. Karen Gershon, *Selected Poems* (London: Gollancz, 1966).
13. Ian Parsons (ed.), *The Collected Works of Isaac Rosenberg* (1979; London: Chatto & Windus, 1984), p. 4.
14. The Haggadah relates the narrative from the book of Exodus, in which Moses leads the Children of Israel out of slavery in Egypt towards the Promised Land. See *Passover Haggadah*, trans. Rabbi Nathan Goldberg (1949; New York: Ktav Publishing House, 1966).
15. Karen Gershon, *Collected Poems* (London: Papermac, 1990), p. 22 and pp. 22–4.
16. 'Foreword', in Gershon, *Collected Poems*, p. 2 and pp. 1–3.
17. Sidra DeKoven Ezrahi, *Booking Passage: Exile and Homecoming in the Modern Jewish Imagination* (London: University of California Press, 2000), p. 139.
18. Gershon, *Collected Poems*, pp. 66–8.
19. Theodor Herzl's utopian novel, *Altneuland, Roman* (Leipzig: Hermann Seemann Nachfolger, 1902), was the first to imagine a revival of ancient Israel in the modern world.
20. Ezrahi, p. 35.
21. 'Foreword', in Gershon, *Collected Poems*, p. 2 and pp. 1–3.
22. Gershon, *Collected Poems*, p. 8.
23. See Gershon, *A Tempered Wind*, p. 48, where the poet discusses her 'Jewish community in Bielefeld'.
24. Louis Jacobs, *Concise Companion to the Jewish Religion* (Oxford: Oxford University Press, 1999), p. 267: 'The First Temple, built by King Solomon, as told in the book of Kings, was destroyed by Nebuchadnezzar in 586 BCE.'
25. Rosenberg, Letter to Gordon Bottomley, dated 23 July 1916, in Parsons (ed.), p. 238.
26. Gershon, *Collected Poems*, pp. 69–70.
27. Gershon, *Collected Poems*, pp. 71–2.
28. Gershon, *Manna to the Hungry* (unpublished, 1990–1), pp. 24, 27–8.

29. Gershon, *Manna to the Hungry*, pp. 38, 45, 186.
30. Gershon, *Manna to the Hungry*, pp. 145, 144.
31. Gershon, *Manna to the Hungry*, pp. 138, 22, 137.
32. Gershon, *A Tempered Wind*, p. 195.
33. Gershon, *Collected Poems*, p. 32.
34. Gershon, *Collected Poems*, pp. 14–17.
35. Gershon, *The Last Freedom* (unpublished, 1986), pp. 146–7.
36. See, respectively, Jon Silkin, *The Peaceable Kingdom* (London: Chatto & Windus, 1954), pp. 23–4; and Jon Silkin, *The Lens-Breakers* (London: Sinclair-Stevenson, 1992), pp. 66–7.
37. Gershon, *Collected Poems*, pp. 15, 18. See further Gershon, *Manna to the Hungry*, p. 50: 'Standing in the sunshine in that courtyard on Mount Zion she [Eva] could believe that he [Jesus] had existed and in that case – why had this never occurred to her, why had she never heard anyone say this or seen it written? – he must have been a Jew.'
38. See David G. Roskies, *Against the Apocalypse: Responses to Catastrophe in Modern Jewish Culture* (London: Harvard University Press, 1984), pp. 258–310.
39. Diary entry for 23 January 1917, in Rupert Hart-Davis (ed.), *Siegfried Sassoon Diaries 1915–1918* (London: Faber, 1983), p. 124.
40. Gershon, *Collected Poems*, pp. 156, 157.
41. Gershon, *A Tempered Wind*, p. 178.
42. Gershon, *A Lesser Child*, pp. 24, 69, 42, 115.
43. Gershon, *A Lesser Child*, p. 179.
44. Gershon, *A Tempered Wind*, p. 60.
45. Gershon, *The Bread of Exile*, pp. 139, 144; and Karen Gershon, *The Fifth Generation* (London: Gollancz, 1987), p. 43.
46. Sander Gilman, *Jewish Self-Hatred: Anti-Semitism and the Hidden Language of the Jews* (Baltimore, MD: Johns Hopkins University Press, 1986), p. 2.
47. Gilman, *Jewish Self-Hatred*, p. 11.
48. For a discussion of the relationship between women and 'that *other* outsider, the Jew', see Jacqueline Rose, 'Dorothy Richardson and the Jew', in Bryan Cheyette (ed.), *Between 'Race' and Culture: Representations of 'the Jew' in English and American Literature* (Stanford, CA: Stanford University Press, 1996), p. 116 and pp. 114–28.
49. 'My Mother' (1966), in Gershon, *Collected Poems*, p. 30.
50. See David Sorkin, *The Transformation of German Jewry 1780–1840* (1987; Detroit: Wayne State University Press, 1999), p. 4: 'Self-denial is thought to have engendered self-hatred, and self-hatred, in turn, hatred by others.'
51. Gershon, *Collected Poems*, pp. 14–17.
52. Jon Silkin, 'Anglo-Jewish Poetry', *Jewish Quarterly* (spring 1967), pp. 22–4.
53. Gershon, *A Lesser Child*, p. 157.
54. 'Foreword', in Gershon, *Collected Poems*, p. 1 and pp. 1–3.
55. David Hartnett, 'Traces of darker times', *Times Literary Supplement*, 21–27 September 1990, p. 1007.
56. George Steiner, *Language and Silence: Essays 1958–1966* (1967; London: Faber, 1985), p. 148.
57. Gershon, *A Lesser Child*, p. 157.
58. 'Foreword', in Gershon, *Collected Poems*, p. 1 and pp. 1–3; George Szirtes, *The Budapest File* (Newcastle: Bloodaxe, 2000), p. 15; Gilles Deleuze and Félix Guattari, *Kafka: Toward a Minor Literature* (1975; Minneapolis: University of Minnesota Press, 1986), p. 19.
59. Gershon, *Collected Poems*, p. 44.
60. Georg Simmel, 'The Stranger' (1908), in Kurt H. Wolff (ed.), *The Sociology of Georg Simmel* (New York: Collier-Macmillan, 1964), pp. 402–8.
61. Kurt H. Wolff (ed.), p. 403.
62. Zygmunt Bauman, *Modernity and Ambivalence* (Cambridge: Polity Press, 1991), p. 79. See also Zygmunt Bauman, 'Allosemitism: Premodern, Modern, Postmodern', in Bryan Cheyette and Laura Marcus (eds), *Modernity, Culture and 'the Jew'* (Cambridge: Polity Press, 1998), pp. 143–56.
63. Gershon, *A Tempered Wind*, pp. 9, 17, 115.
64. Eagleton, p. 18.

65. Rosenberg, Letter to Miss Seaton, dated 1911, in Parsons (ed.), p. 182.
66. Rosenberg, 'Rudolph', in Parsons (ed.), p. 281 and pp. 276–83.
67. 'Obituary: Karen Gershon', *AJR Information* (May 1993), p. 15.
68. 'Foreword', in Gershon, *Collected Poems*, p. 2.
69. Gershon, *A Tempered Wind*, pp. 163–4.
70. C. B. Cox, 'Patriots and Exiles', *The Spectator*, 5 August 1966, p. 180.
71. Gershon, *The Fifth Generation*, p. 142.
72. Karen Gershon, *Burn Helen* (Brighton: The Harvester Press, 1980), p. 99.
73. Gershon, *The Last Freedom*, pp. 49, 179.
74. Gershon, *Collected Poems*, p. 68.
75. Gershon, *The Bread of Exile*, pp. 28, 20, 79.
76. Gershon, *Manna to the Hungry*, p. 24; Gershon, *The Fifth Generation*, p. 90.
77. Gershon, *The Last Freedom*, p. 97.
78. Gershon, *The Last Freedom*, p. 114.
79. Gershon, *The Last Freedom*, p. 101.
80. Gershon, *The Last Freedom*, p. 113.
81. Karen Loewenthal, *The World Was Old* (London: The Bodley Head, 1956), p. 157.
82. Loewenthal, p. 113.
83. Gershon also translated Arthur Ruppin's *Memoirs, Diaries, Letters* (London: Weidenfeld & Nicolson, 1971). Ruppin was the first professor of sociology at the Hebrew University, Jerusalem.
84. See Ludwig Marcuse, *Obszön: Geschichte einer Entrüstung* (Munich: Paul List Verlag, 1962); and Ludwig Marcuse, *Obscene: The History of an Indignation*, trans. Karen Gershon (London: MacGibbon & Kee, 1965).
85. Marcuse, *Obscene*, pp. 29, 33.
86. Marcuse, *Obscene*, pp. 182, 181, 170.
87. Marcuse, *Obscene*, pp. 15, 34.
88. See, for example, Karen Gershon, *The Boy with the Sling: A Life of King David* (unpublished, *c*.1984), p. 141: 'He [David] was thoroughly gratified ... that she should be so blatant about wanting him, which promised a livelier sexual exchange than he had been getting'; and Karen Gershon, *The Historical and Legendary Esther* (unpublished, *c*.1980), p. 52: 'Esther got into Xerxes' bed: she raised the coverlet from his feet and kissed it, and kissed his feet, and then his knees, then his thighs –'.
89. Gershon, *Manna to the Hungry*, p. 127.
90. Marcuse, *Obscene*, p. 14.
91. Gershon, *Collected Poems*, p. 109.
92. Gershon, *A Tempered Wind*, p. 107.
93. 'The force that through the green fuse drives the flower', in Walford Davies (ed.), *Dylan Thomas: Selected Poems* (Harmondsworth: Penguin, 2000), pp. 18–19.
94. Gershon, *Collected Poems*, pp. 100–1.
95. Ibid., pp. 108–9.
96. 'Married Love', in Gershon, *Collected Poems*, pp. 100–1.
97. Gershon, *Burn Helen*, pp. 77, 2, 86.
98. See, for example, 'The Children's Exodus', in Gershon, *Collected Poems*, p. 24: 'at Dovercourt we were taught that / our share of the Jewish fate / had not been left behind'.
99. Gershon, *Burn Helen*, pp. 16, 37, 39.
100. 'On Being a Jew', in Karen Gershon, *Notes of a Heart-Patient and Other Poems* (unpublished, 1993), p. 20. See also Gershon, *The Fifth Generation*, p. 41: 'He was as good a Jew as she, was a Jew by his history.'
101. Bauman, *Modernity and Ambivalence*, p. 78.
102. Bauman, *Modernity and Ambivalence*, p. 56: 'Undecidables are all *neither/nor*; which is to say that they militate against the *either/or*. Their underdetermination is their potency: because they are nothing, they may be all.'
103. Gershon, *Burn Helen*, p. 47.
104. Ibid., p. 41.
105. Gershon, *A Tempered Wind*, pp. 9, 17, 115.
106. Gershon, *The Fifth Generation*, pp. 16, 30. Compare Gershon, *Manna to the Hungry*,

pp. 5, 14, where Anglo-German-Jewish *Kind* Eva has married an English Gentile because, 'as she was bound to see it, being a Jew got you killed'. Further, 'the whole point of her coming to England, she had believed, was that there she would be like everybody else'.

107. Gershon, *The Fifth Generation*, p. 23.
108. See also Ira Levin, *The Boys from Brazil* (New York: Random House, 1976), of which Gershon's story is a variant.
109. Gershon, *The Fifth Generation*, pp. 43, 85, 92–3.
110. Gershon, *The Fifth Generation*, pp. 129, 140.
111. Gershon, *The Last Freedom*, p. 36.
112. Gershon, *The Bread of Exile*, p. 79.
113. Gershon, *The Fifth Generation*, pp. 133, 156.
114. Gershon, *The Last Freedom*, pp. 113, 152, 155.
115. Gershon, *We Came as Children*, p. 9.
116. Bauman, *Modernity and Ambivalence*, pp. 171–2.
117. Gershon, *Collected Poems*, pp. 98–9.
118. Eagleton, p. 18; Cheyette, '"Ineffable and usable": towards a diasporic British-Jewish writing', p. 303 and pp. 295–313.

7

Elaine Feinstein: Transcendence and Continuity

Like Karen Gershon, Elaine Feinstein writes with a pronounced awareness of the Shoah. Indeed, I want to discuss her lyrical poems of transcendence against the background of the Holocaust. However, I also want to emphasise that Feinstein does not depict the Shoah as the determining event of Jewish history. Rather, she mines the Hebrew Bible precisely to stress Jewish continuity before and beyond the Holocaust.

Further, Feinstein's poetry, novels and biographies are significant in relation to a transcendence of 'Little Englandism'[1] and the Anglo-Jewish diaspora. I approach her work relating to English insularity and delimited Jewish families with such socio-political concerns in mind. Feinstein resembles Jon Silkin, I suggest, in choosing to distance her poetic personae from the English and Jewish specifics of her oeuvre. Instead, she asserts a solitary and universal 'I' in the tradition of English Romantic and American Black Mountain poetry.[2]

To be sure, Feinstein also wishes to address a community of readers. Running through her potentially solipsistic verse is a countervailing tendency towards affiliation with communities of women, Jews and other groups she perceives as peripheral.

Feinstein's self-centring as the 'I' which sings her lyrics serves to compensate for her peripherality – as a Jew, a woman and a northerner – in English literature and society.[3] Further, this 'I' posits a different centrality to that traditionally allotted to women in Jewish families. Other Anglo-Jewish women poets, such as Ruth Fainlight and Joanne Limburg, have also found ways to challenge familial roles. In Feinstein's case, personal freedom and escape from taxonomical fixity are articulated in the 'ungraspable'[4] position of the '*luftmensch*',[5] or Jewish diasporic dreamer. Additionally, Feinstein re-deploys a biblical discourse of patriarchal power for feminist purposes.

This final chapter argues that Feinstein's affiliation with historical continuity in diaspora co-exists in 'continuous active tension' (Silkin's phrase[6]) with a desire for imaginative transcendence of her historical circumstances through art.

THE POETRY OF ELAINE FEINSTEIN

Elaine Feinstein is undaunted by Theodor Adorno's anti-transcendent, post-Holocaust admonition that 'to write lyric poetry after Auschwitz is barbaric'.[7] Indeed, her poems are replete with phrases such as 'elation' ('New Year '66'), 'exultation the / street sings' ('Votary' (1971))[8] and 'the sunlight is euphoric' ('Picnic' (1997)).[9]

The Holocaust may not be far from such expressions of euphoria. As Feinstein notes in 'Lisson Grove' (1997):[10]

> At your bedside, I feel like someone
> who has escaped too lightly
> from the great hell of the camps,
>
> except that I don't altogether escape.

Again, in Feinstein's novel *Children of the Rose* (1975) escape from emotional fall-out following the Holocaust is the desired goal. Alex wants a child: 'To teach *someone, somehow* to be free of it all. Everything that destroyed Lalka and me. To escape.' Further, Lalka's sister Clara remarks: ' – None of us really escaped.'[11] 'Song of Power' (1966) goes further, since it juxtaposes the 'fire' of the camp crematoria with an assertion of strength to protect the next generation against Jew- and other 'baiting'.[12]

In an autobiographical essay, Feinstein remarks:

> [Adolescent] security was exploded once and for all, at the war's end, when I read what exactly had been done to so many children as young as I was, in the hell of Hitler's camps. You could say that in that year [1945] I became Jewish.[13]

Her semi-autobiographical novel *The Survivors* (1982) affirms the impression made by the Holocaust, once again, during the Eichmann trial:

Then, in 1961, came the trial of Adolf Eichmann, and the horror of that daily newsprint bit like acid into Diana's unbelieving mind all year. Of course, she had read the newspapers after the war. She knew the facts. She had seen the photographs. But now, every day, the newsprint in *The Times* brought the truth into her consciousness in a new way.

Now she read as if for the first time what had been done to the Jews of Europe.[14]

Thus, the references to 'escape', 'rescue' and 'release' in Feinstein's poetry appear to be more than simply expressions of lyrical transcendence.[15] That is, they seem to express something besides 'a moment of insight or heightened perception'.[16] When Feinstein extols 'golden hours' in a 'supernatural city',[17] she is doing so, I suggest, in counterpoint to 'the great hell of the camps'. When she writes of 'flying' or 'rising' to some sort of lyrical paradise, she may also be counterbalancing 'Jewish' memories of 'the hell of Hitler's camps'.[18]

For example, 'To Cross' (1971)[19] juxtaposes an idyllic English awakening with the flight of wartime fugitives:

> Nobler, they wrote on the
> run   in holes   lonely
> unloved
>   what respite
> to have an August morning green at five
> young men lying in their clothes between
> blankets ash about them
> their unfrightened faces.
> Now in this bare room
> I speak with love only
> of those who keep their way in
> a mad calm bearing uncertainly
> the trap in which they are taken

Although the speaker is not herself 'on the / run', she identifies with those who were to the degree that she compares her own peace now with theirs as 'respite'. The 'young men' around her are part of the pastoral ('green') assembly. However, the relaxation suggested by cigarette 'ash about them' and 'unfrightened faces' carries a counter-image of crematorium 'ash' and, hence possibly Jewish, frightened 'faces'.

What the speaker recalls in the midst of this transcendent space – 'this bare room' like a *tabula rasa*, speaking 'with love only' – is 'the trap' of a hellish world. Further, she relates empathetically to this 'trap', as her switch to the present tense in describing fugitives implies ('they are taken'). Indeed, the poem suggests that the speaker may also be one 'of those who keep their way in / a mad calm'. Although she feels 'respite' for the moment, she is aware of the discrepancy between recent Jewish persecution ('mad') and England's apparently safe haven ('calm'). Feinstein's 'mad calm' resembles Silkin's 'continuous active tension'[20] in positing the dynamic unease of Anglo-Jewish poets since the Holocaust.

'Patience' (1977),[21] too, indicates an empathy with those fleeing persecution. Here, 'the fugitive / enters the river, she is washed free'. The poem concludes:

> The trees hiss overhead. She feels their shadows.
> She imagines herself clean as a fish,
> evasive, solitary, dumb. Her prayer:
> to make peace with her own monstrous nature.

Like 'To Cross', 'Patience' evokes freedom from the world's evil, as the swimmer attempts to conjure an Edenic *tabula rasa*: a 'clean' place of 'peace' and 'prayer'. However, serpent-like evil has already entered Eden ('The trees hiss overhead'). Moreover, the speaker recognises evil within 'her own monstrous nature'. Thus, transcendence remains an ongoing aspiration in the face of tense social and psychological circumstances.

Although Feinstein is clearly not fleeing political persecution in England, she is all too aware of 'the mist of invisible / English power' ('Exile' (1971)). 'Out' (1971),[22] for instance, expresses the wish to get beyond the subtle, pervasive force of the dominant culture:

> The diesel stops. It is morning. Grey sky
> is falling into the mud. At the waterside
> two builders' cranes are sitting like birds
>
> and the yellow gorse pushes up
> like camel-thorn between oil-drums and old cars.
> Who shall I take for my holy poet

to lead me out of this plain? I want an
innocent spirit of invention   a Buster Keaton
to sail unnaturally overhead by simple leverage and

fire the machinery. Then we should all spring out of our
heads, dazzled with hope, even the white-faced ticket
collector dozing over his fag, at such an intervention

suddenly in this stopped engine, we should
see the white gulls rising out of the rain over
the fen   and know our own freedom.

Clearly, the speaker wants to rise 'up' and 'out' of this English ('fen') landscape; to escape it and 'sail unnaturally overhead'. All around her is English deliquescence ('Grey sky / is falling into the mud'), and the only human represented ('the white-faced ticket collector') is inert ('dozing'). Whereas for poets writing before the Shoah, such as T. S. Eliot in 'Burbank with a Baedeker: Bleistein with a Cigar' (1920),[23] Jews epitomised the amorphous threat of degeneration, for Feinstein, conversely, it is English inertia ('dozing', 'mud') which suggests the threat of 'falling into the mud'. Possibly, 'mud' also implies a powerlessness which Feinstein associates with Jews unable to escape the Shoah. As she writes in her novel *Mother's Girl* (1988): 'He [Janos] tackled the central agony of the twentieth century, not as a remote fact for intellectuals to whom the Jews of Europe had become ghosts. For him, the horrors were personal. His own family had disappeared into mud.'[24]

'Out' contrasts England with imagined dynamism and energy ('fire the machinery'). Indeed, Feinstein may be invoking a Jewish transcendence of English inertia. She pleads for a 'holy poet / to lead me out of this plain'. Possibly, this prayer ('holy') echoes those of the Israelites following Moses through the Sinai desert[25] ('yellow', 'camel-thorn', 'oil-') to the Promised Land.[26] Feinstein appears to find biblical inspiration for a poetry which can transfigure England into the Edenic ('innocent').

Moreover, Feinstein's persona aspires to escape England's dominant social and literary definitions of a gradually evolving national identity; to 'spring out' of English 'mud' by an immigrant 'intervention', as it were, 'unnaturally'. As we have seen, Rodker refused cultural applications of Darwinism ('the psychology of Apes') for similar immigrant reasons. Again in 'Fishing' (1971), the narrator's son 'is watching for / a single gudgeon to fly up / out of the silver mud'; while in 'Aviation' (1990) the speaker imagines literally flying ('on skinny leather wings') clear of her English life, but: 'These marshlands / clog the feet.'[27]

Like Rosenberg, Rodker and Silkin, Feinstein also looks to America ('Buster Keaton') as an immigrant culture beyond England's literary traditions. Further, it seems significant that 'Buster Keaton' made movies at the beginning of the twentieth century, around the time that Feinstein's grandparents immigrated to Britain. Feasibly, he signifies the juncture at which Feinstein's immigrant tradition became Anglophone. Indeed, 'Keaton' suggests the new ('innocent spirit of invention'), artificial ('leverage', 'fire the machinery') and transcendent ('to sail unnaturally overhead') 'intervention' of immigrant imagination in England. 'Keaton' is an exemplary *'luftmensch'*: 'someone who walked and lived on air, with only his wits to help him survive'.[28] In this sense, 'Keaton' – an American gentile – also signifies the diasporic Jewish imagination, sailing with Chagall-like otherness over England.

Thus signified, Keaton stands, or rather floats, in contrast to the 'white-faced ticket / collector'. He rises up, the 'ticket / collector' sinks down ('dozing'). Further, Keaton's levitation 'overhead' resembles the movement 'up' of the 'yellow gorse'. Possibly, Feinstein is associating 'Keaton' with the colour yellow in contradistinction to the 'white-faced' Englishman. Yellow has a long history of association with Jews. In *A History of the Jews in England*, Cecil Roth explains how after 1275:

> A piece of yellow taffeta, six inches long and three broad, cut in the same shape as before, was henceforth to be worn over his heart by every Jew above the age of seven years … Two years later an inquiry was instituted into the manner in which this and other regulations were being obeyed. The result was seen in 1279 when orders were issued once more emphasizing the necessity for Jewish women as well as men to wear the Badge of Shame.[29]

Roth continues:

> The entire body of medieval legislation which reduced the Jew to the position of a yellow-badged pariah, without rights and without security other than by the goodwill of the

sovereign, remained on the statute book ... As late as 1818 it
was possible to maintain in the courts Lord Coke's doctrine
that the Jews were in law perpetual enemies.[30]

More recently, Jews in Germany and across Nazi-occupied Europe
were obliged to wear a yellow badge between 1941 and 1945.[31]
Considered in this historical context, it may be significant that the
colour yellow proliferates throughout Feinstein's poetry; for
example in 'Mother Love' (1966), where 'shit slides out / yellow';
and 'Urban Lyric' (1990), which frames a 'face yellow in its frizz of
hair'.[32] Again, the extended poem 'Gold' (2000), ostensibly narrated
by Mozart's Jewish librettist Lorenzo da Ponte, describes in its
opening stanza 'a yellow flare in the mirror'.[33]

  Yellow is often transformed to gold in Feinstein's writing, as
though lyrical transfiguration were a type of aesthetic alchemy:

> In February the weather changed ... Yellow light
> everywhere. Even the grey walls of Lalka's town garden
> turned yellow. The twigs of the bare trees had an aureole of
> sunlight like golden smoke in their branches ... Katie had
> found a new man. She was walking in the garden of Eden.
> Everything was changed for her; she was every dead thing in
> which love wrought new alchemy.[34]

'Yellow' is the colour of 'sunlight' which transforms ('turned') the
'grey'. It also resembles the colour of gold ('golden'), which
'alchemy' derives from base everyday metals. Possibly,
Feinstein's strategy here is to transmute ('Everything was
changed') the shame and victimhood of both the medieval Jewish
badge and the Nazi *Jude* patch into a text of value and beauty
('love'). In *Children of the Rose*, Lalka visits the Jewish cemetery in
Krakow:

> The Shammus [synagogue caretaker] was determined to
> finish his task. He showed them the wall, in which the names
> of the thousands who had been murdered by the Nazis had
> been etched. It was all that remained of them now, that
> golden etching.[35]

From Holocaust fire, something alchemically precious remains: a
'golden etching'. Feinstein's own writing may be an attempt to

similarly transcend and transform the hell of the Shoah and its yellow *Jude* badges into the 'golden etching' of her words.

Moreover, 'golden' relates to imaginative transformation of England. For example, 'Renaissance Feb. 7' (1971)[36] begins:

> In the true weather of their art
> these silver streets bustle, skin lit towers:
> we have broken some magic barrier into
> the daylight of the Duc de Berry's golden hours
> and now in a supernatural city what is
> possible changes

The poem's reference to the 'golden hours', or illuminated manuscripts,[37] of a French Renaissance aristocrat ('the Duc de Berry') suggests imaginative transformation of restrictive circumstances. Indeed, 'we' have risen above English constrictions on several levels by breaking through 'some magic barrier': barriers of time ('hours'), place ('streets') and social status ('Duc'). Consequently, 'possible changes' are intimated as much for the speaker on the 'streets' as for the 'streets', through the 'art' of the poem. In being a manuscript which transfigures the quotidian, the poem itself resembles the Duc's 'golden hours'.

By contrast, the 'yellow and bitter' Jew in 'The Old Tailor' (1986)[38] has failed to transform his situation. Yet his wife, who may also be Jewish, remains courageous in the face of his 'miserable' existence. She is described with traces of a discourse surrounding cheery, English war veterans. In the face of her husband's bellicose 'sneers', this 'plucky wife smiled through'. The old tailor's wife transcends her husband's failure by coming 'through' it.[39]

In summary, I want to suggest that Feinstein categorises Jews as 'yellow' rather than white. Further, overlapping discourses of semitic and sexual otherness enable her to distinguish a *female* Jew's imaginative transcendence from a male Jew's 'certainty of failure'.[40]

Feinstein's biographies tend to Judaise embittered men in order to construct female subjects as free from failure. For example, her biography of the black American blues singer Bessie Smith presents the performer as empowered, while Smith's male partner Jack, like the subject of 'The Old Tailor', is portrayed as simply vengeful:

> Whatever Jack did for the rest of his life he could never get free of his Empress, or fail to understand that his relationship

with her was the thing which most interested people about him ... By far the cruellest of his acts was his trying to get back at Bessie through her adopted son, Jack Gee, Jun. The fact that the child carried his name did not mean that Jack had any affection for him, and it's hard to see how Jack's intention could have been anything other than simple vengeance.[41]

Concurrently, traces of an empowering Judaic discourse are applied to Smith. For example: 'Bessie's idea of luxury ... was to be uprooted and Empress of her own domain'; 'in some of her own lyrics she wrote as if she was one of the poor herself in the tradition of wandering singers like Leadbelly or Blind Lemon'; 'there was no easy way out of the ghetto'. 'Uprooted' and 'wandering' Bessie may be, but she is also upwardly mobile beyond 'the ghetto': she displays the 'aspiration' of 'ambitious blacks'. Further, 'What had once seemed a barrier to acceptance has nowadays come to signify the very self-confidence that was lacking, the confidence that Bessie was asserting.'[42] Bessie's lyrical 'asserting' breaks through the 'barrier to acceptance'. Her 'aspiration' is realised, while 'self-confidence' propels her beyond socially restrictive racial and gender barriers.

To an extent, Feinstein appears to empathise with her biographical subject here. Indeed, Feinstein's biographies may be read in terms of her own preoccupations. As she remarks of Ted Hughes, 'Pushkin's letters do not quite bear out Ted's conviction that Pushkin was a changed man after his marriage and it may be that Hughes' insight was autobiographical.'[43]

Empathetically, Feinstein writes of Bessie Smith as a woman and a lyrical artist whose 'phrasing is unhurried and subtle. She knows exactly where to place an extra syllable, where to stress a word ... On long-haul drives across country it is Bessie's voice I hear in my ears as I make up my own songs to her music.'[44]

Here, Smith's singing is elided with Feinstein's writing ('where to place an extra syllable, where to stress a word'), and Feinstein's writing with Smith's singing ('I make up my own songs to her music'). Possibly, Smith's 'music' and Feinstein's poetry meet somewhere near Black Mountain College, North Carolina, and the American poet Charles Olson's emphasis on 'phrasing' in poems according to the duration of a breath.[45]

To be sure, trans-racial affiliation with blacks is evident in *Bessie*

Smith. Bessie is a black version of a Jewish woman who makes it out of the ghetto to the Promised Land of transcendence through her art. Most blacks are not so fortunate, and remain signified as Hebraic slaves fleeing Pharaonic Egypt:

> In those days the South spilled over into Northern cities, as hopeful blacks fled from poverty and racism. The North was Canaan; and they came out of slavery looking for the land that had been promised to them. What they usually found was a black ghetto.[46]

Traces of Judaic discourse overlap with descriptions of American blacks to such an extent in *Bessie Smith* that it sometimes seems as though Feinstein considers blacks and Jews to be identical. When, for example, Smith's 'voice and Louis [Armstrong's] trumpet exchange brazen and derisive comment',[47] the 'contemptuous Yiddish phrases' of Feinstein's father[48] are transposed to a black context. Similarly, Bessie takes 'refuge' from a 'white' world by 'being offensive',[49] while the subject of 'Dad' (1977)[50] is rudely 'unconcerned with pleasing anyone'.

Further, Feinstein's novels and poems are replete with descriptions of Jews as black. In *Loving Brecht* (1992), for instance, Frieda Bloom's hair is categorised by her 'English nanny' as 'too thick. Like an animal or an African'. Thus, Feinstein depicts her Jewish protagonist as racially resembling 'an African' in the eyes of the Other: a white English woman. Moreover, Frieda is a Jewish singer who loves 'black jazz'. Feinstein writes, 'She [Lotte Lenya] had an opera voice in those days that was finer than mine; I [Frieda] already had smoky, growling notes in my voice that I had learnt not from Lenya herself but American black voices.'[51] Frieda situates herself between a (white, European) 'opera voice' and 'American black voices'. This is no coincidence. Frieda is Other to 'black' Americans and Gentile Europeans. Victimised in Europe during the 1930s, Frieda also resembles blacks in America. Like Sassoon and Rodker, Feinstein suggests that Jews are coloured indeterminately.

Feinstein resembles Silkin in being readily empathetic towards blacks.[52] The poet describes her adolescence, when 'skinny and black I went / dancing at the Palais' ('Poor Relations' (1966)). Similarly, 'Moon' (1971) expresses hopes for 'strange black / people of the sun' to liven up 'East Anglian' whites with 'an alien drum'.

'Song of Power'[53] boldly states that 'black is the / mirror you gave me'. Nevertheless, 'Song of Power' celebrates a gendered, more than a racial, power:

> For the baiting
> children in my
> son's school class who
> say I am a witch:
> black is the
> mirror you gave me.
>
> Drawn inward at siege
> sightless, mumbling:
> criminal, to bear three
> children like fruit
> cannot be guarded
> against enemies.
>
> Should I have lived sterile?
> The word returns me.
> If any supernatural power
> my strangeness earns me
> I now invoke, for
> all Gods are
>
> anarchic even the Jews'
> outside his own laws, with
> his old name
> confirms me, and I
> call out for the
> strange ones with wild hair
>
> all the earth over to
> make their own coherence,
> a fire their children
> may learn to bear at last
> and not burn in.

The poem's persona embraces 'black' otherness as 'a witch', protecting her vulnerable Jewish son. Indeed, the sole intimation of racial power occurs through the figure of Yahweh ('the Jews'' God).

Possibly, the narrator is doubly empowered: as a woman ('witch') and Yahweh-like defender ('even the Jews' / ... / ... / confirms me') of a son who must 'be guarded / against enemies'. Like 'The Old Tailor' and *Bessie Smith*, 'Song of Power' depicts the male ('my son's') as weak, and the female as strong.

Feinstein, I suggest, looks to the Hebrew Bible for a discourse of Yahweh-like Jewish power which is useable by women. How she relates this patriarchal discourse to an ethnic discourse of Jewish male vulnerability is exemplified in 'A Legendary Hero' (1983), an essay about her father. Here, the poet describes how as a girl she regarded her father with 'uncritical idolatry'.[54] This phrase insists that the writer sees her younger self as substituting her father for Yahweh ('idolatry'). Similarly, in Feinstein's novel *All You Need* (1989), the narrator recalls some childhood confusion about the relationship between God and her father: ' "God," he said, ruffling those curls [of hers] with a big soft hand. Did he really feel so intimate with God? She hadn't been sure.'[55]

By contrast, 'A Legendary Hero' relates a recurring childhood dream concerning paternal vulnerability:

> I began to dream, obsessionally, that my father was being attacked by a man with a bread knife. As I watched helplessly the strength went out of my father's huge arm; I always woke, screaming, before his assailant brought down the knife on his head. I suppose it was a dream that acknowledged my fear that he was more vulnerable in the world than I wished. There are other readings. It probably sealed my own dependence on every weak man I have loved since.[56]

One of the 'readings' of Feinstein's dream is that all Jewish men are somehow weak 'in the world', and 'every weak man' to some extent displays Jewish vulnerability.

Significantly, it is a domestic 'bread knife' which fells the father in Feinstein's dream. Since the domestic is traditionally a female realm, such an image suggests Feinstein's dream association of her Jewish mother with 'strength' over her 'weak' Jewish father. Clearly, the image also evokes a metaphorical castration which deprives the father of his power ('the strength went out of my father's huge arm'). However, since it is 'a man with a bread knife' who attacks Feinstein's 'father', that 'man' may be read as embodying dominant Gentile power which serves to emasculate Jewish men.

To be sure, Feinstein is aware of the complexity of her relationship with her parents. Indeed, 'A Legendary Hero' tends towards a demystifying self-'psychotherapy'. Perceiving both the idolatry of her father and his vulnerability, Feinstein is also able to acknowledge that her mother's 'strengths' were real enough but 'invisible to me'.

Despite such apparent demystification, however, Feinstein concludes 'A Legendary Hero' with a prayer addressed to her deceased father. Such a prayer suggests that for Feinstein her father after death has resumed his psychological role as a substitute for Yahweh:

> Father, forgive me, lying under the earth, unforgotten still. Forgive me my cowardice. The way my life has bent since you died. Forgive me living without your fierce courage. I have been cowed, I have been downed, I have let small shocks better me; as you never did.
>
> And if I still feel under your protection it is not from some imagined heaven (you lie next to my mother in the cemetery in Groby Road, Leicester) but as a voice in my own heart pointing up my anxieties in contemptuous Yiddish phrases. The *why worry?* of my childhood which would serve me so well now.
>
> And my prayer?
> It is to make me bolder.[57]

Here the adult supplicant and aspiring child unite to plead for pardon ('forgive me' is repeated thrice) for falling short of an idealised male role model ('I have let small shocks better me; as you never did'). Feinstein prays that she may resemble the God-like figure her childhood self imagined her father to be; and move closer to invulnerability: 'I modelled myself on my father. And ... nothing downed his spirits for long.' Indeed, the prayer suggests that once dead Feinstein's father reassumes those Yahweh-like qualities which the poet still wishes to emulate.

In the same essay, Feinstein recalls distancing herself from a mother she perceived as submissive: 'what I came to fear most, I suppose, was turning *into* her [my mother]; to be servant and silent support'.[58] As a feminist, Feinstein wishes to assert self-empowerment ('And my prayer? It is to make me bolder'). However, she turns to her father rather than mother for a powerful role model. Pertinently, Feinstein's first published poem was 'Father' (1961).[59] It concludes with an emphatic reference to paternal strength: 'shabby and powerful as an old bus'. Again, 'Dad' (1977)[60] asserts a father's 'courage' and 'uncowed' resolution.

Many Anglo-Jewish women before the Second World War resembled Feinstein's mother in being restricted to the disempowering domestic sphere. According to Rickie Burman:

> By the 1920s ... this generalization about Jewish women [not taking jobs] was becoming increasingly accurate. Increased prosperity and a striking decline in family size meant that the once crucial economic contribution of women was often no longer required. By refraining from paid work, women increased the level of domestic comforts of their husband and children, and also furthered the status of the family, by demonstrating that the husband earned sufficient to keep his wife at home.[61]

Consequently, Feinstein is obliged to look to earlier generations of Jewish women for role models of extra-domestic power. Moreover, such earlier role models furnish Feinstein with a tradition of loving and protecting – indeed, *mothering* – 'weak'[62] Jewish men.

Burman illustrates the proximity of such a tradition. She shows that Feinstein's Russian-Jewish immigrant grandmothers would have drawn upon

> a different tradition: whilst they also perceived the woman's domestic role as of primary importance, this did not necessarily entail exclusion from the economic sphere. Rather, it was opposed to the male sphere of religious study and scholarship, and assigned to her the more general responsibility to provide for her family and contribute to the household economy in whatever way she could.[63]

According to Paula Hyman, immigrants such as Feinstein's grandmothers would have been likely to follow a tradition of 'Ashkenazic women in Central and Eastern Europe'. Hyman continues:

> They were traditionally responsible for much of what we would now describe as masculine roles. It was not

uncommon, for example, for the Jewish wife to be the primary breadwinner of the family, particularly if her husband was talented enough to be able to devote himself to study.[64]

Daniel Boyarin makes a similar point regarding the traditional differentiation of gender roles in East European Jewish families.[65] Indeed, the Jewish tradition of women taking jobs to provide for their families allows Feinstein to formulate a feminist matriarchal affiliation. For example, she writes in 'The Celebrants VI' (1973)[66] of 'my desert grandmother' as a key ancestor whose diasporic 'daughters have seen Babylon / Persepolis, Delphi'. Again, in the novel *Dreamers* (1994) Feinstein places a Jewish protagonist in the tradition delineated above: 'She [Hannah] came from generations of women who had run mills and workshops, while their menfolk dreamed and studied.'[67]

In *The Survivors* (1982), a semi-autobiographical[68] novel, the worldly, powerful Rasil is introduced (like the Judaised Bessie Smith) as a sort 'of father and mother in one':[69]

> Rasil never thought much about God. Abram said that was all right for a woman.
>
> Rasil thought about practically everything else. She kept chickens in the back yard, and fought off marauding cats with her bare hands. She couldn't read or write, but she could count; and no tradesman cheated her, because she could add up faster in her head than they could scribble. It would be a tough local man who would take her on, anyway, with her huge upper arms, muscled from swabbing floors and chopping wood. She was a handsome woman, and even with all her children pulling her about, and chastely dressed as she was, she couldn't disguise the heavy sexual health of her body under the folds.[70]

Rasil is a Jewish grandmother and feminist role model: powerful ('It would be a tough local man who would take her on'), 'sexual' and intelligent ('she could add up faster in her head than they could scribble'). Feinstein illustrates what critics and historians argue: how Ashkenazic Jewish tradition empowered women in daily life. Despite Old Testament *patriarchy*,[71] it is possible that Jewish communities in diaspora have traditionally been *matriarchal* since they have revolved around the family home. As Aviva Cantor remarks, 'For Jewish women ... [exile] was not different in kind, only in degree – more stress, more problems, but not a discontinuity: the real ruler was still at home.'[72]

According to Batya Bauman, there are continuous elements of the matrilineal, matrilocal and matrifocal in Jewish social practice.[73] *Halakhah* [Jewish religious law] states that someone is a Jew only if his or her mother is Jewish; thus, Judaism is a matrilineal religion.[74] Largely focused on the home in diaspora, where the 'real ruler'[75] is the mother, Jewish life can fairly be classified as matrilocal. That the Jewish mother is traditionally at the centre of such a culture also ensures her matrifocal pre-eminence.

Since Jewish women are accorded a central role within Ashkenazic life as mothers, it may not be surprising that Feinstein identifies maternal love as her strongest emotion. 'My strongest impulse is maternal,' she claims.[76] Titles such as 'Mother Love', 'At Seven a Son' (1966) and 'Prayer for my Son' (2000) further attest to the importance of motherhood and family within Feinstein's oeuvre.[77] In an interview, Feinstein declares: 'Family is very important. The family has kept me going, really.' Thus, while identifying her position within English literature and society as peripheral – as a woman, a Jew and a northerner[78] – Feinstein finds an empowering Ashkenazic centrality within her family as a mother.

Such centrality subjects the poet to emotional pressure of great intensity. Since family in this socio-cultural context may well be the primary locus for emotional expression, it can also become a place identified with claustrophobia. Indeed, it may be no coincidence that incest features as a significant theme of Feinstein's novels. In *Loving Brecht* (1992), for example, Frieda's father enters her room unannounced:

> One night, however, he [father] appeared in my room, as if by mistake, and there was something in his face which I did not understand.
> 'Are you all right?' I asked.
> 'My dear girl,' he said hopelessly and put out his arms for an embrace. He looked very handsome and oddly happy. Almost without thinking I assumed the mothering position, with his big handsome face held against my breasts. He lay there for a time, sighing as I stroked his hair.
> 'What a good girl you are,' he said.[79]

Here the incest is mainly psychological, as Mr Bloom attempts to treat Frieda like a wife; and his Jewish daughter, 'without thinking', assumes 'the mothering position'. There is an implication here that the father wants his daughter to imitate his wife by behaving as a mother towards him. Since Mr Bloom is vulnerable as a Jewish man in 1930s Berlin, he seeks a version of maternal comfort and protection.

Feinstein dreamt of her own father's vulnerability.[80] Following his wife's death, Feinstein's father turned to his daughter, seeking 'someone gentle and tireless as my mother. I knew that, and it prevented me responding warmly to his gestures of love. After our bitterest quarrels, he would open his arms. "Doesn't matter. You still love me, don't you?" '[81]

An almost identical picture of potentially incestuous emotional intensity is drawn in *The Shadow Master* (1978), where Belinda berates her dead father:

> And what you wanted, what you *expected*, was to move into my house and become my *child*. It was like a curse, to be denied children and be given an old man to tend. That's why I drew back. Do you understand *now* ? You never knew how hard it was for me, to *resist* becoming what you wanted; gentle and tireless like my mother had been. Cooking special foods, attending to every need.[82]

Here again a father 'wanted', nay '*expected*', to be treated like a '*child*' by his daughter, as his wife had treated him in her time.

Feinstein's most recent novel, *Dark Inheritance* (2000), places the imagination of incest between a stepmother and son at the heart of its plot.[83] Moreover, when the protagonist Rachel O'Malley hears that her own son is in danger, she re-affirms the centrality of her maternal identity: 'No one else matters, she thought. He's all there is. And, since she had not realised how central a place he [her son] occupied in her emotional landscape, how could Tom have known it?'[84] Similarly, *The Shadow Master* places the reconciliation between a Jewish mother, Lilian, and her son, Paul, close to the climactic conclusion of the novel's apocalyptic plot.[85]

In *The Survivors*, Benjy Katz finds such an emotionally intense Anglo-Jewish family atmosphere somewhat claustrophobic. Driving around with a friend, he feels 'delighted to be out of the small, tight world of the house and synagogue which clenched round his own family so protectively. Out.'[86]

The repetition of 'out' calls to mind Feinstein's poem of that name. It suggests the wish to escape a claustrophobic[87] Jewish family home ('the small, tight world of the house'), as 'Out' invokes transcendence of England's restrictions beyond that home. Like the persona of that poem, Benjy desires ('delighted') diasporic otherness and 'freedom'[88] ('out'). He yearns for a life beyond Jewishness, as the persona of 'Out' aspires to escape Englishness. Both Benjy and the speaker of 'Out' seek a centred 'I', which is not centred, however, within Jewish or English traditions perceived as similarly claustrophobic.

Feinstein depicts such an 'I' as exilic, and her poetry as correspondingly produced on the peripheries of both Jewish and English traditions. Indeed, she has written three poems with the title and theme of 'Exile'[89] and declared to an interviewer: 'I always felt myself to be an exile.'[90] In a similar vein, the poet's biographies narrate peripheral or exilic lives: Bessie Smith, 'uprooted and Empress of her own domain'; the Russian poet and 'natural outsider' Marina Tsvetayeva, 'more of a guest than a host' beyond her native Russia; D. H. Lawrence living 'outside the Christian traditions' in New Mexico; Pushkin, the 'African' 'outsider', banished from St Petersburg to the provinces; and Ted Hughes, a working-class northerner who, like Feinstein, went to Cambridge University in the 1950s and felt excluded from 'the English literary centre'.[91] In Feinstein's choice of biographical subjects, affiliations with those on the peripheries of dominant cultures are clearly evident.

Of course, it is nothing new for Anglo-Jewish poets to identify themselves as exilic. We have seen that Rosenberg, Rodker and Gershon all did so. Rosenberg and Gershon looked to Israel as the land from which Jews were exiles. By contrast, Rodker wrote of France as a place where he could comfortably be Other as a foreigner. Such *extraterritorial* spaces, in Israel and France, provided 'imaginary homelands'[92] for these diasporic poets: *textual* realms that might 'eclipse the parochial representations and received images' of Jews in Britain.[93]

Similarly, Feinstein explores Anglo-Jewishness in extraterritorial texts. Like Rodker, Sassoon and Gershon, she also promulgates an orientalism which she links with Jewishness. For example, in *The Shadow Master*:

Women were dressed in Turkish trousers of silken transparency. Some of them who spoke no English occupied themselves with bringing Belinda dishes of chicken shashlik, flavored with walnut sauces. Other skewers of kebab appeared before her. While she ate gluttonously, they poured red wine. One after another came and sat next to her and told their stories.[94]

There's more than a hint of *The Arabian Nights* in this harem-like environment of 'stories'. Significantly, 'English' Belinda is being acculturated to the 'Turkish' Orient in the home of a Jewish man. Feinstein looks at Jewishness through 'English' eyes: 'Even the alien, almost oriental tremble in the voice of the man singing from the [Torah] text (which he pointed along with a silver marker) seemed strangely moving to her [Belinda].'[95]

Here, the 'oriental' 'text' is the Hebrew Bible. Feinstein appears intent on producing a similarly Jewish and 'oriental' text, addressed to English auditors who resemble Belinda, in *The Shadow Master*.

As might be expected, Feinstein also writes of Jews in England. 'Amy Levy' (1997),[96] for instance, recounts a dream of the Victorian Anglo-Jewish poet. Indeed, as Silkin looks to Rosenberg for a point of Anglo-Jewish orientation, so Feinstein turns to Amy Levy (1861–89)[97] in this poem. The parallels between Levy and Feinstein extend beyond race, gender and poetic vocation. Levy, after all, was the first Jewish woman to be admitted to Newnham College, Cambridge, which Feinstein attended some seventy years later:

Precocious, gifted girl, my nineteenth-century
voice of Xanthippe, I dreamed of you last night,
walking by the willows behind the Wren,
and singing to me of Cambridge and unhappiness.

'Listen, I am the first of my kind and
not without friends or recognition,
but my name belongs with my family
in Bayswater, where the ghosts

of wealthy Sephardim line the walls,
and there I am alien because I sing.
Here, it is my name that makes me strange.
A hundred years on, is it still the same?'

Rhetorically, Feinstein suggests that 'a hundred years on' the situation of Anglo-Jewish women poets is 'still the same'. Like Levy, Feinstein must transcend Jewish 'family' claustrophobia ('line the walls') in order to express her lyrically individualistic 'I'. Further, such an 'I' remains 'alien' in the context of traditional Jewish roles allotted to women. Beyond the Jewish family, within an insular English literature and society, the twentieth-century poet is similarly situated as Other ('my name ... makes me strange').

'Amy Levy' invokes an Anglo-Jewish textual tradition of the 'alien' which has much in common with the exilic and exotic scenarios of Feinstein's novels, biographies and other poems. To this extent, Levy's displacement provides Feinstein with a useable tradition of 'social'[98] exile in England. The tension between living 'Here' and being 'strange', as between 'family' and the 'alien', is not dissimilar to the 'tension' which Silkin identifies in Rosenberg's poetry as 'truly Anglo-Jewish'.[99]

Speaking in an interview, Feinstein focuses on Levy's peripheral positioning in English literature and society: 'The danger of being at the periphery is that you never quite penetrate sufficiently not to disappear into darkness, rather as Amy Levy did.'[100] In 'Night Thoughts' (1973),[101] she dramatises this fear of disappearing into socially exilic 'darkness':

> Uncurtained, my long room floats on
>   darkness, moored in rain,
> my shelves of orange skillets
>   lie out in the black grass.
> Tonight I can already taste
>   the wet soil of their ghosts.
> And my spirit looks through the glass:
>   I cannot hold on for ever.
>
> No tenure, in garden trees, I
>   hang like a leaf, and stare
> at cartilaginous shapes
>   my shadow their visitor.
> And words cannot brazen it out.
>   Nothing can hold on for ever.

'Night Thoughts' may be read as a reflection on diaspora. The poet's 'spirit looks through the glass' and sees a phantom ('ghosts. / And

my spirit') mirrored back at her. She is a 'shadow' floating ('floats')
above ('I / hang like a leaf') the land in which she, as a 'visitor',
holds 'no tenure'. Indeed, the poem resembles Rosenberg's
'Chagrin' (1915–16)[102] in its presentation of seemingly endless
suspension ('I / hang', 'I cannot hold on for ever'). Alone and,
therefore, lyrically unbounded by constrictions ('my spirit'
'uncurtained'), the poet faces her diasporic isolation. Rather than
'sail unnaturally overhead' like the *'luftmensch'*[103] of 'Out', the not-
quite-white speaker of 'Night Thoughts' is (punningly) 'moored' in
'black' diasporic 'darkness'.[104]

Such a potentially desperate reflection on Anglo-Jewish
solipsism is avoided in 'Mirror' (1997), where family continuity is
celebrated[105]:

> Mirror, mirror, what's going on?
> A matron aunt or stubborn father
> these days looks out of the mirror.
> When I smile at them they are gone.
>
> A pace behind the silvered glass
> they wait like ghosts, though not so much
> scary as shy, eager to touch
> my present flesh with their own past.
>
> Within my body is a thread
> of which resemblance is the sign:
> my story is not only mine
> but an extension of the dead.

Here the poet considers 'the dead' and the 'past' in relation to her
'present flesh'. Rather than suggest the suicidal yearnings that
plague the solitary mirrored speaker of 'Night Thoughts', 'Mirror'
narrates a reassuring continuity ('thread', extension', 'story').

Since Feinstein's family 'story' was Russian-Jewish before her
grandparents immigrated to England, it may not be surprising that
she has translated several Russian poets, most notably Marina
Tsvetayeva.[106] As Feinstein records in her biography of Tsvetayeva,
the Russian poet famously wrote: 'In this most Christian of worlds
/ all poets are Jews.'[107] Reciprocally, Feinstein finds much that she
remembers from her Jewish childhood is also Russian:

> The first time I went there [to Russia] I visited the house of the poet Margarita Aliger, whom I also translated in that same book [*Three Russian Poets*]. I was really struck by the way her table looked like my mother's, even the tablecloth. Then there was the herring, the cream cheese – everything was so similar. And, of course, that's Russia. The food is similar. Even the flavour of the sour cucumbers was right: deliciously different from Polish cucumbers! I felt very at home.[108]

Indeed, Jewish continuity through 'unEnglish' food is suggested throughout Feinstein's oeuvre.[109] Moreover, the 'thread' of continuity to which 'Mirror' refers appears elsewhere, for example in *The Ecstasy of Dr Miriam Garner* (1976) and *Mother's Girl*:

> I know, what she [Miriam] *needs* desperately, to feel safe at all. It's *continuity*: Some sort of inner thread has gone.[110]

> You [David] are my future, thought Halina, I mustn't hurt you. I mustn't give you my pain to carry, or tell you too much of my story, or Leo's. It will damage you as Lucy and I have been damaged; or perhaps that damage is part of the human inheritance, and the only terrible burden is to have no inheritance at all.[111]

For Feinstein, continuity and 'inheritance' make life 'human', despite the 'damage' and 'pain' consequent on carrying the 'burden' of history ('my story'). *Dreamers* voices a similar sentiment: 'Was it possible, she [Clara] wondered, to become a complete human being in the strange situation in which she found herself – without family, without home, without any baggage from her past? She was unsure.'[112]

Feinstein's oeuvre answers this question in the negative. Evidently, affiliation with Jewish history ('baggage from her past') furnishes the poet with a 'family' context. However, she depicts this same history ambivalently. 'Allegiance' (1997),[113] for example, evokes 'my inheritance / – Kovno, Odessa, packing and running away'. On the one hand, such an 'inheritance' provides a stabilising sense of historical grounding. On the other, it repeatedly features escape from the quotidian ('packing and running away'). Feinstein's poetry of transcendence, I want to suggest, recreates the tension of such a history, offering a dialectic between lyrical escape and diasporic continuity.

NOTES

1. See Peter Conradi, 'Elaine Feinstein', in *Dictionary of Literary Biography, volume 14: British Novelists Since 1960, Part 1: A–G* (Detroit: Gale, 1983), pp. 293–4: '[Feinstein's] roots, if she had them and was not nomadic, were certainly not to be discovered in a nationalist version of "Little Englandism".'
2. See Pamela L. Shelton (ed.), *Contemporary Women Poets* (Detroit: St James Press, 1998), pp. 113–35, where Feinstein claims: 'What I'm looking for is a music which has the natural force of spoken feeling, the Wordsworthian "language really used by men".' She speaks here also of her 'one-time Black Mountain mentors'. See further Elaine Feinstein, *Mother's Girl* (1988; London: Arena, 1989), pp. 82–3: 'It came to me that I had been altogether on the wrong track; that with Keats I believed in the holiness of the hearts' affections and the truth of the Imagination.'
3. See Peter Lawson, 'Way Out In the Centre: In Conversation with Elaine Feinstein', *Jewish Quarterly* (spring 2001), pp. 65–9.
4. Isaac Rosenberg, Letter to Gordon Bottomley, dated 23 July 1916, in Ian Parsons (ed.), *The Collected Works of Isaac Rosenberg* (1979; London: Chatto & Windus, 1984), p. 238.
5. Elaine Feinstein, *Dark Inheritance* (2000; London: The Women's Press, 2001), p. 15.
6. Jon Silkin, *The Life of Metrical and Free Verse in Twentieth-Century Poetry* (Basingstoke: Macmillian, 1997), p. 61.
7. See Theodor Adorno, 'Commitment', in Rodney Livingstone, Perry Anderson and Francis Mulhern (eds), *Aesthetics and Politics* (London: New Left Books, 1977), pp. 177–95.
8. Elaine Feinstein, *Selected Poems* (Manchester: Carcanet, 1994), pp. 6, 51.
9. Elaine Feinstein, *Daylight* (Manchester: Carcanet, 1997), p. 26.
10. Ibid., p. 21.
11. Elaine Feinstein, *Children of the Rose*, (1975; Harmondsworth: Penguin, 1976), p. 170.
12. Feinstein, *Selected Poems*, p. 21. During an interview with Bryan Cheyette on 11 November 2001 at the New End Theatre, London, Feinstein acknowledged that 'fire' referred to the camp crematoria, since the poem was written in the wake of the Eichmann trial.
13. 'Elaine Feinstein', in *Contemporary Authors Autobiography Series*, vol. 1 (Detroit: Gale, 1984), p. 219 and pp. 215–24.
14. Elaine Feinstein, *The Survivors* (1982; New York: Penguin, 1991), p. 297. A similar point is made in Feinstein's biography *Ted Hughes: The Life of a Poet* (London: Weidenfeld & Nicolson, 2001), p. 18: 'When the war ended in 1945 the cinemas at Mexborough, like those of the rest of the country, showed the liberation of Belsen. The impressionable fifteen-year-old boy watched the bones of men, women and children being pushed by bulldozers into trenches for mass burial ... The imagination of a whole generation was marked by those newsreels.'
15. See 'Separations' (1997), 'Respite' (2000) and 'New Year '66' (1966), respectively, in Feinstein, *Daylight*, p. 22, Elaine Feinstein, *Gold* (Manchester: Carcanet, 2000), p. 35 and Feinstein, *Selected Poems*, p. 4.
16. David Lindley, *Lyric* (London: Methuen, 1985), p. 88.
17. See 'Renaissance Feb. 7' (1971), in Feinstein, *Selected Poems*, p. 66.
18. See 'Aubade for a Scientist' (1966) and 'At Seven a Son' (1966), in Feinstein, *Selected Poems*, pp. 8, 10. See also 'Elaine Feinstein', in *Contemporary Authors Autobiography Series*, p. 219.
19. Feinstein, *Selected Poems*, p. 47.
20. Silkin, *The Life of Metrical and Free Verse*, p. 61.
21. Feinstein, *Selected Poems*, p. 95.

22. Feinstein, *Selected Poems*, pp. 38, 27.
23. T. S. Eliot, *The Complete Poems and Plays of T. S. Eliot* (1969; London: Faber, 1978), pp. 34–5. See also Chapter 2.
24. Feinstein, *Mother's Girl*, p. 62.
25. Feinstein evokes the desert in several other poems. See, for example, 'The Celebrants VI' (1973) where she describes 'my desert / grandmother' who came from 'nomads, wilderness people'; 'June' (1977), which features an 'old cactus / yellowing' by which 'we remember the desert', and 'New Songs for Dido and Aeneas 9' (1986) with its 'cactus and desert grass'. See also 'Aviation' (1990): 'I have a monster in my head, yellow / and surly as a camel': Feinstein, *Selected Poems*, pp. 70, 98, 123 and 145.
26. Similarly, 'Regret' (1986) depicts a biblical leader guiding his 'children' up to a 'mountain ledge', while admonishing them to 'forget' what 'still lies below'. In this poem, the speaker to whom Feinstein refers is Lot leaving Sodom and Gomorrah. 'And here among these salty pillars / the unforgiving stand', s/he says: 'Forget the smoking city': Feinstein, *Selected Poems*, p. 109. John Rodker also warns against looking 'backward' through the biblical analogy of Sodom and Gomorrah in 'Hymn to Cold' (1916): Andrew Crozier (ed.), *John Rodker: Poems & Adolphe 1920* (Manchester: Carcanet, 1996), pp. 73–5.
27. John Rodker, *The Future of Futurism* (London: Kegan Paul, Trench, Trubner, 1927), p. 60; Feinstein, *Selected Poems*, pp. 40, 145.
28. Feinstein, *Dark Inheritance*, p. 15.
29. Cecil Roth, *A History of the Jews in England* (London: Oxford University Press, 1941), pp. 95–6.
30. Roth, p. 247.
31. See Raul Hilberg, *The Destruction of the European Jews* (London: Holmes & Meier, 1985), pp. 75 and 57–8: 'For the sake of uniformity [in November 1939], Reichsstatthalter Greiser of the Wartheland ordered that all Jews in his Reichsgau wear a four-inch yellow star sewed on the front and back of their clothes.' Wearing of the yellow star was extended 'to the entire Reich-Protektorat area' by a decree of 1 September 1941. The decree 'provided that Jews six years or over were to appear in public only when wearing the Jewish star'.
32. Feinstein, *Selected Poems*, pp. 14, 133.
33. Feinstein, *Gold*, pp. 9–26.
34. Feinstein, *Children of the Rose*, p. 77.
35. Ibid., p. 125.
36. Feinstein, *Selected Poems*, p. 66.
37. The Duc de Berry (1340–1416) 'invested fortunes on the treasures that remain as his monument – paintings, tapestries, jewelry, and illuminated manuscripts (including the world-famous *Très riches heures du duc de Berry*)': *The New Encyclopaedia Britannica*, vol. 2 (Chicago: Encyclopaedia Britannica, 2002), p. 158. Feinstein also mentions the Duc de Berry in her novel *The Circle* (1970; Harmondsworth: Penguin, 1973), p. 115: 'And the bowl interested her. It was a deep blue, as deep a blue as one of the skies from the Duc de Berry.'
38. Feinstein, *Selected Poems*, p. 112.
39. See also 'Photographs' (1990), in Feinstein, *Selected Poems*, p. 139: 'What you / think of as disadvantages will bring you through.'
40. 'The Old Tailor', in Feinstein, *Selected Poems*, p. 112. See also Jacqueline Rose, 'Dorothy Richardson and the Jew', in Bryan Cheyette (ed.), *Between 'Race' and Culture: Representations of 'the Jew' in English and American Literature* (Stanford, CA: Stanford University Press, 1996), p. 125 and pp. 114–28: 'Like being a Jew, being a woman can also be described as a state of non- or partial participation in the available or dominant cultures.'
41. Elaine Feinstein, *Bessie Smith* (Harmondsworth: Viking, 1985), p. 73.
42. Ibid., pp. 13, 43, 20, 34, 35.
43. Feinstein, *Ted Hughes*, p. 153.
44. Feinstein, *Bessie Smith*, p. 11.
45. See Paul Hoover (ed.), *Postmodern American Poetry* (New York: Norton, 1994), p. 3: 'For Olson, each line of poetry was both idiosyncratic and "necessary" as a result

of each speaker's particular breath.' See also Michele Roberts, 'Elaine Feinstein in Conversation', *PN Review* 23:3 (January–February 1995), pp. 45–7: 'After 1959, when I started a poetry magazine called *Prospect*, I was in touch by letter with Charles Olson.' See further Ruth Padel, 'Imports in England's Lane', *The Times Literary Supplement*, 16 November 1990, p. 1248: 'In 1959 a young British poet wrote to Charles Olson and he wrote back. Olson's letter – to Elaine Feinstein – is famous now, a Black Mountain credo which led to his first publication in England.' Padel continues: 'From Olson she learned to take risks with space and voice.' For Olson's letter to Feinstein, see Ralph Maud (ed.), *Selected Letters of Charles Olson* (London: University of California Press, 2000), pp. 264–6.

46. Feinstein, *Bessie Smith*, p. 40.
47. Ibid., p. 12.
48. Elaine Feinstein, 'A Legendary Hero', in Ursula Owen (ed.), *Fathers: Reflections By Daughters* (London: Virago, 1983), p. 167 and pp. 159–67.
49. Feinstein, *Bessie Smith*, pp. 31–2.
50. Feinstein, *Selected Poems*, p. 97.
51. Elaine Feinstein, *Loving Brecht* (London: Hutchinson, 1992), pp. 3, 38, 72. For an account of Jewish identification with blacks in America, see Michael Alexander, *Jazz Age Jews* (New Jersey: Princeton University Press, 2001).
52. See, for example, 'Jaffa, and other places', in Jon Silkin, *Amana Grass* (London: Chatto & Windus, 1971), p. 36: 'And not the negro his hunted skin finding each shadow not as dark as he / offers an absence as blank.' See further Chapter 5.
53. Feinstein, *Selected Poems*, pp. 15, 35, 21.
54. Feinstein, 'A Legendary Hero', p. 160.
55. Elaine Feinstein, *All You Need* (1989; New York: Viking, 1991), p. 193.
56. Feinstein, 'A Legendary Hero', p. 162.
57. Ibid., pp. 167, 160.
58. Ibid., pp. 160, 165.
59. See *Prospect* 5 (winter 1961), p. 24.
60. Feinstein, *Selected Poems*, p. 97.
61. Rickie Burman, 'Jewish Women and the Household Economy in Manchester, c.1890–1920', in David Cesarani (ed.), *The Making of Modern Anglo-Jewry* (Oxford: Basil Blackwell, 1990), p. 72 and pp. 55–75.
62. Feinstein, 'A Legendary Hero', p. 162.
63. Cesarani (ed.), p. 62.
64. Paula Hyman, 'The Jewish Family: Looking for a Usable Past', in Susannah Heschel (ed.), *On Being a Jewish Feminist: A Reader* (New York: Schocken, 1983), pp. 22–3 and pp. 19–26.
65. See Daniel Boyarin, *Unheroic Conduct: The Rise of Heterosexuality and the Invention of the Jewish Man* (California: University of California Press, 1997), p. xxii.
66. Feinstein, *Selected Poems*, p. 70.
67. Elaine Feinstein, *Dreamers* (1994; Basingstoke: Pan, 1996), p. 8.
68. Much of Feinstein, 'A Legendary Hero', pp. 159–67 and 'Elaine Feinstein', in *Contemporary Authors Autobiography Series*, pp. 215–24 is repeated verbatim in Feinstein, *The Survivors*, pp. 9–18.
69. Feinstein, *Bessie Smith*, p. 43.
70. Feinstein, *The Survivors*, p. 23.
71. See David Biale, *Eros and the Jews: from Biblical Israel to Contemporary America* (California: University of California Press, 1997), p. 11: 'The Bible is the origin of patriarchy: the male God of the Old Testament.'
72. Aviva Cantor, 'The Lilith Question', in Susannah Heschel (ed.), *On Being a Jewish Feminist: A Reader*, pp. 40–50.
73. Batya Bauman, 'Women-identified Women in Male-identified Judaism', in Susannah Heschel (ed.), *On Being a Jewish Feminist: A Reader*, pp. 88–95.
74. 'According to the traditional Halakhah, Jewish status depends either on the status of the mother or on conversion to Judaism. Thus, the child of a Jewish mother and a non-Jewish father is Jewish, but not the child of a non-Jewish mother and a Jewish father': see Louis Jacobs, *Concise Companion to the Jewish Religion* (Oxford: Oxford University Press, 1999), p. 111.

75. Heschel (ed.), p. 46. See further Claire R. Satlof, 'History, Fiction, and the Tradition: Creating a Jewish Feminist Poetic', in Heschel (ed.), pp. 186–206: 'The religious activities open to women are performed in private, at home.'
76. See A.S. Byatt, 'Writers in Conversation: Elaine Feinstein' (London: ICA Video, 1987).
77. Feinstein, *Selected Poems*, pp. 10, 14; and Feinstein, *Gold*, p. 36.
78. Lawson, 'Way Out In the Centre: In Conversation with Elaine Feinstein', *Jewish Quarterly*, pp. 66, 67.
79. Feinstein, *Loving Brecht*, p. 11.
80. Feinstein, 'A Legendary Hero', p. 162.
81. 'Elaine Feinstein', in *Contemporary Authors Autobiography Series*, p. 222.
82. Elaine Feinstein, *The Shadow Master* (New York: Simon and Schuster, 1978), pp. 65–6.
83. See, for example, Feinstein, *Dark Inheritance*, p. 84.
84. Ibid., p. 166.
85. Feinstein, *The Shadow Master*, pp. 243–6.
86. Feinstein, *The Survivors*, p. 64.
87. See also *Ted Hughes*, p. 11, where Feinstein empathetically evokes the Yorkshire poet's sense of claustrophobia in the family and its tight-knit community: 'Hughes speaks of climbing back down into the comfortable valley as a return to the pit, and of passionately wanting to escape the constricted life there.'
88. See 'Out' (1971), in Feinstein, *Selected Poems*, p. 27: 'and know our own freedom'.
89. See 'Exile' (1971), in Feinstein, *Selected Poems*, p. 38; 'Exile' (1997), in Feinstein, *Daylight*, p. 34, and 'Exile' (2000), in Feinstein, *Gold*, p. 39.
90. Byatt, 'Writers in Conversation: Elaine Feinstein'.
91. See Feinstein, *Bessie Smith*, p. 13; Elaine Feinstein, *A Captive Lion – The Life of Marina Tsvetayeva* (London: Hutchinson, 1987), pp. 35, 180; Elaine Feinstein, *Lawrence's Women: The Intimate Life of D. H. Lawrence* (London: HarperCollins, 1993), p. 148; Elaine Feinstein, *Pushkin* (1998; London: Phoenix, 1999), pp. 12, 164, and Feinstein, *Ted Hughes*, p. 24.
92. See 'Imaginary Homelands' (1982), in Salman Rushdie, *Imaginary Homelands: Essays and Criticism 1981–1991* (London: Granta Books, 1991), pp. 9–21.
93. Bryan Cheyette, '"Ineffable and usable": towards a diasporic British-Jewish writing', *Textual Practice* 10:2 (1996), p. 307 and pp. 295–313.
94. Elaine Feinstein, *The Shadow Master*, p. 82.
95. Feinstein, *The Shadow Master*, p. 172.
96. Feinstein, *Daylight*, p. 40.
97. See Melvyn New (ed.), *The Complete Novels and Selected Writings of Amy Levy* (Gainesville: University of Florida Press, 1993).
98. See Terry Eagleton, *Exiles and Emigrés: Studies in Modern Literature* (London: Chatto & Windus, 1970), p. 18: 'I am concerned not so much with the work of the "literal" expatriates but with the "social" exiles.'
99. Jon Silkin, 'The Poetry of Isaac Rosenberg', *Isaac Rosenberg 1890–1918: A catalogue of an exhibition held at Leeds University May–June 1959, together with the text of unpublished material* (Leeds: Partridge Press, 1959), p. 3. See further Chapter 5.
100. Lawson, 'Way Out In the Centre: In Conversation with Elaine Feinstein', *Jewish Quarterly*, p. 67.
101. Feinstein, *Selected Poems*, p. 73.
102. Parsons (ed.), p. 95.
103. Feinstein, *Dark Inheritance*, p. 15.
104. Feinstein, *Selected Poems*, p. 27.
105. Feinstein, *Daylight*, p. 57.
106. See Elaine Feinstein (ed.), *The Selected Poems of Marina Tsvetayeva* (Oxford: Oxford University Press, 1971). Two of Feinstein's free translations of Tsvetayeva's poems, 'Insomnia (3)' and 'An Attempt at Jealousy', were selected by Christopher Ricks for inclusion in *The Oxford Book of English Verse* (Oxford: Oxford University Press, 1999), pp. 652–3. See also *Three Russian Poets: Margarita Aliger, Yunna Moritz, and Bella Akhmadulina*, trans. Elaine Feinstein (Manchester: Carcanet, 1979).
107. Feinstein, *A Captive Lion*, p. 157.

108. Lawson, 'Way Out In the Centre: In Conversation with Elaine Feinstein', *Jewish Quarterly*, p. 69.

109. See, for example, Feinstein, *All You Need*, pp. 42–3: 'From the table rose a spicy odour that took Nell back to that same [Anglo-Jewish] childhood; the scent of pickles, smoked fish, cream cheese and rye bread … This was the smell of Eastern Europe. The smell of those houses of her childhood, carried on into contemporary London. And the tablecloth itself was familiar; stitched and patterned like those of her childhood aunts. And in another elusive resemblance, like the tablecloth in the flat of a Russian woman she had visited in Moscow in her final year. In Moscow she felt the same stirring of something warm and welcoming, something unEnglish, something altogether alien to Plumrose Crescent, something she liked and admired and had missed.' See also Feinstein, *The Circle*, p. 150: 'Afterwards they went out in the car to find the delicatessen. Found a strange collection of food to take with them; smoked cods' roe and pickled eggs and cold salami. Sour cucumbers. Rye bread and cracker biscuits.' The protagonists of *The Circle* are not referred to as Ashkenazic Jews, but are gastronomically signified as such.

110. Elaine Feinstein, *The Ecstasy of Dr Miriam Garner* (London: Hutchinson, 1976), p. 154.

111. Feinstein, *Mother's Girl*, p. 158.

112. Feinstein, *Dreamers*, p. 176.

113. Feinstein, *Daylight*, p. 52.

8

Conclusion

This is the first study of a literary history that has been ignored in England. Throughout the twentieth century, Jews have contributed immensely to English poetry. To be sure, these poets have found publishers and readers. However, they have been published for a readership which supposedly affiliates with the dominant culture. Within this received culture, Isaac Rosenberg and Siegfried Sassoon are canonised as First World War poets, John Rodker is remembered as a Modernist and Jon Silkin is appraised as a northern radical. Essays appear which classify Karen Gershon as a refugee writer, and Elaine Feinstein is pigeon-holed as a woman poet.[1] By contrast, this work reads these poets against the grain of the dominant culture. In championing minority Anglo-Jewish voices, it aims to challenge the notion of a monocultural English literature.

However, I do not mean to construct an hermetic canon of Jewish poetry. Although this is certainly a study of minority verse, it is not a prescriptive manifesto for the reading of such verse. All of the poets considered here can be read in a number of different, even competing ways. For example, Isaac Rosenberg and Siegfried Sassoon may be understood simply as poets of war. The Second World War poet Keith Douglas turns to Rosenberg in this manner when he writes:

> Rosenberg I only repeat what you were saying –
> the shell and the hawk every hour
> are slaying men and jerboas, slaying[2]

It is easier still to overlook the Jewishness of Siegfried Sassoon's poetry. Unlike Rosenberg, Sassoon does not write poems urging the Jewish people to collective action or evoking national re-birth through Zionism. Though he strove for clear bounds to his 'chameleon'[3] identity, Sassoon is not delimited by my placing him in an Anglo-Jewish poetic context. Both Rosenberg and Sassoon are canonical First World War poets, as well as minority diasporic voices.

Nor do I want to suggest that John Rodker has been reclaimed for an exclusive Jewish poetry. Andrew Crozier is entitled to wonder 'how content Rodker would have been to be subsumed within this category' of Anglo-Jewish poets, and to approach him simply as an 'indigenous Modernist'.[4] While Crozier wishes to underscore Rodker's position as an English Modernist, I want to stress his importance as a minority Anglo-Jewish Modernist. Without my emphasis, many resonances from Rodker's poetry would be lost. Further, Rodker is significant to this study as a representative of Anglo-Jewish poetry between the two world wars. More research has yet to be conducted into this period, for example into the poetry of Joseph Leftwich, Gilbert Frankau and A. Abrahams.[5]

It would be a mistake to underestimate the importance of class and gender affiliations for Anglo-Jewish poets. Both Rosenberg and Silkin, for example, espouse a working-class radicalism which is integral to their visions of social ameliorisation. By contrast, Sassoon orientates himself by the compass of a conservative aristocracy. Elaine Feinstein imagines being remembered 'as a precursor of the present richness of women poets', rather than as an ethnic writer.[6] Rodker affiliates with an artistic and intellectual elite, while championing revolution.[7] Thus a plurality of class and gender perspectives is valid and necessary in the reception of Anglo-Jewish verse.

In contrast to received critical opinion, there is an Anglo-Jewish poetic lineage. Indeed, I have edited an anthology, *Passionate Renewal: Jewish poetry in Britain since 1945* (2001),[8] in order to trace recurrent themes and concerns within this lineage. What emerges in my collection and this study are the diverse ways of writing about Jewishness. The focus of this book is on the diasporic tensions, and sense of suspension, between metaphorical exile and an imagined homeland in Anglo-Jewish poetry. What becomes clear is the sense of 'inbetweenness' shared by Anglo-Jewish poets. These poets do not express a common notion of origins or goals, but they do negotiate an ongoing 'story' which is always *in medias res*: in the middle of a diasporic narrative.[9]

Much Jewish poetry is also concerned with conclusions, and the narrative closure which they seem to guarantee. Karen Gershon's verse, for example, invokes Israel as a Zionist consummation of Jewish history and culture. On a more sombre note, Gershon presents the Holocaust as the conclusion of European Jewish life. I include Gershon in this book precisely because she continued to live and write in a post-Holocaust diaspora, attempting, but never managing, to write the epilogue to the Jewish 'story'.

Many poets deploy Holocaust verse in a similar manner. Rather than express the multifarious experiences of a diasporic culture that lived before the Shoah and has subsequently revived, much Holocaust poetry proffers a single reading of the diaspora as a narrative of victimhood. Such a perspective on the European diaspora as a story of terminal suffering continues to gain adherents. There are at least two anthologies of Shoah verse in English: *Holocaust Poetry* (1995) and *Beyond Lament: Poets of the World Bearing Witness to the Holocaust* (1998).[10] An encyclopedia of *Holocaust Literature* appeared in 2003.[11] Necessarily, the continuous story of the Anglo-Jewish diaspora and its poetry is ignored by those who would view all twentieth-century European Jewish poetry as Holocaust literature.

Likewise, Sidra Dekoven Ezrahi chooses to ignore Anglo-Jewish poetry when discussing the relationship between Israeli and diasporic writers. Ezrahi suggests that in order to perpetuate an open-ended Jewish story, and avoid a debilitating narrative closure, some Israeli writers have constructed the European Jewish diaspora as a place of post-Holocaust 'unredeemable *and indestructible ruin*'.[12] According to Ezrahi, Europe has become for such Israeli poets what Palestine was for some pre-Shoah European poets. As they yearn for a lost way of life in Europe, Israeli poets perpetuate a Jewish narrative beyond the bounds of Zionist closure. There can be, Ezrahi maintains, a fruitful 'exchange between Jewish culture as a *minority* culture, whose paradigmatic experience is exile, and as a *majority* culture struggling with new definitions of time and space and the imagination'.[13] The artist R. B. Kitaj also identifies a creative tension between Israel and the Jewish diaspora in the unforeseen situation of 'normative co-existence [that] replaces the "normalcy" once wished upon the state'.[14] I contend that Anglo-Jewish poetry offers precisely these forms of tense, open-ended narratives that avoid the epilogues proffered by Zionism and the Shoah.

The narrative of Anglo-Jewish diasporic poetry has generated its own internal tradition. Rosenberg may have an heir in Emanuel Litvinoff, who rose to prominence as a Second World War poet with *Conscripts: A Symphonic Declaration* (1941) and *The Untried Soldier* (1942).[15] 'If I Forget Thee', 'Israel' and 'End of an Episode', in Litvinoff's *A Crown for Cain* (1948), are all reflections on the torments of the Jewish people under Nazism, expressing hopes for their future.[16] 'If I Forget Thee' concludes on a Zionist note:

> One day my love will find
> a road over the desert and my joy
> will blossom among you like primroses
> one day you will see me with my hands
> filled with flowers sprung from the desert
> your death made fertile and
> I shall crown your innocent heads
> with twelve stars of Israel.

Significantly, Litvinoff's later 'For a New Generation' (1973) is a Zionist poem written from the perspective of one who prefers to remain in the Anglo-Jewish diaspora:[17]

> Israel is a marriage between youth and the soil
> and *we*, who cannot easily unlearn our loves,
> dream that this land may unburden *you* of history [*my italics*].

Other Anglo-Jewish poets repress their Jewishness and emphasise affiliation with the dominant culture. Like Sassoon, Gilbert Frankau and Jenny Joseph are interesting in this regard.[18] Rosenberg and Rodker may have minority Modernist followers. Harold Pinter's poetry, for example, can be read in such a trajectory. Like Rodker, Pinter writes of slimy creatures, such as snails and frogs:

> But still the snail of love
> Suns the decks.
> At Quadragesima in March
> Bubbles shutter the frogs
> In transparent sacks.

Congruously, Pinter's verse is concerned with 'marionettes' in a deterritorialised, Modernist theatre:

> Once, in a ventriloquist evening,
> When winter scoffed the dummy head,
> Said God your messenger is dead,
> The lines are cut, and all the roads
> Are snaked, I,
> Bullseyed under a mosslamp,
> Verbed a fable to this hymning sound.[19]

The reference to Hebraic 'hymning' here suggests a further affinity with Rodker, whose collection *Hymns* was published in 1920.[20] Moreover, Pinter resembles Rosenberg in expressing empathy with insects and rodents:

> Below the transparent fly
> insect equation quite strides
> the slim glass of word,
> instructs the void.

Pinter's allusions to 'the mouse' and 'the stoat' in poems such as 'Camera Snaps' (1952) are redolent of Rosenberg's deployment of a 'droll rat' in 'Break of Day in the Trenches' (1916), and similarly imply inbetweenness or a 'pause in a no man's time'.[21]

In her collection *Femenismo* (2000), Joanne Limburg explores avenues opened by Elaine Feinstein. Poems such as 'The Nose on My Face'[22] unapologetically tackle the otherness of being a female Jew in England:

> What was it about my nose? Did it
> have a pushy way of forcing
>
> itself into a room, a vulgar
> nose-come-lately, embarrassing
> and overdressed? Did it mark
> its owner as a fleshy, suburban
>
> princess condemned to a life of shopping
> and eating and smothering sons?

This study's presentation of some paradigmatic voices makes no claim to being an exhaustive résumé of Anglo-Jewish verse.

Ruth Fainlight may be right to associate the Anglo-Jewish

diaspora with a sense of 'vertical' rather than 'horizontal' difference. Despite class and gender affiliations in England, she writes of an inherited notion of displacement:

> It needed centuries,
> Millennia, to produce
> Someone who instinctively knew
> The only movement possible
> Was up or down. No space
> For me on the earth's surface.
> Horizontal equates with delusive
> When only the vertical
> Remains open to my use.[23]

Daniel and Jonathan Boyarin champion exactly this 'vertical' Jewishness based on 'family, history, memory, and practice'. They favour the 'vertical' and diasporic over the 'horizontal' Zionist conquest of space:

> With the rabbinic 'invention' of Diaspora, the radical experiment of Moses was advanced. The forms of identification typical of nomads, those marks of status in the body, remained, then, crucial to this formation. Race is here on the side of the radicals; space, on the other hand, belongs to the despots.[24]

Litvinoff says something similar, though not anti-Zionist, in 'Earth and Eden' (1948):[25]

> Where time and memory intersect the sun
> seeds of the wise tree grow about our roots;
> where space and conquest spread upon the earth
> our wisdom is undone.

Possibly, there is theoretical ground here for a continuing dialogue between 'vertical' Anglo-Jewish and 'horizontal' Israeli-Jewish poetry.

Meanwhile, the Boyarins emphasise the 'creative, diasporic tension' of Jewishness: 'Jewishness disrupts the very categories of identity because it is not national, not genealogical, not religious, but all of these in dialectical tension with one another.'[26] Such 'dialectical tension', I suggest, resembles the 'continuous active tension' that Silkin demands of poetry, as well as the 'tension' which he identifies as 'truly Anglo-Jewish'.[27] Moreover, the Boyarins' contention of 'the impossibility of seeing Jewish culture as a self-enclosed, bounded phenomenon'[28] finds echoes throughout Anglo-Jewish poetry and poetics. In his *First Diasporist Manifesto* (1989), Kitaj states: 'Diasporism, one's Jewishness itself, keeps changing all the time. Any exciting life of the mind will keep changing one's art.' Like the Boyarins, Kitaj implicitly embraces Rodker's sense of slippery freedom, Silkin's concept of poetic 'process', and Rosenberg's 'ungraspable' diasporic transcendence which refuses 'to be fixed, to be settled, to be stable'.[29]

Such 'impure, unbounded and diasporic'[30] artistry resonates beyond Anglo-Jewish poetry. Indeed, Jewish poetry offers paradigms for a variety of other minority literatures. Indian, Irish and black writers, for example, may re-imagine their own hybrid situations in England by engaging with Anglo-Jewish literature. Once an Anglo-Jewish poetic tradition is recognised, it will be possible to make comparisons between different histories of acculturation to English society and its literature.

NOTES

1.   See, for example, Jon Silkin, *Out of Battle: The Poetry of the Great War* (Oxford: Oxford University Press, 1972), pp. 130–67 and pp. 249–314; Jean Moorcroft Wilson, *Siegfried Sassoon, The Making of a War Poet* (1998; London: Duckworth, 1999); Andrew Crozier (ed.), *John Rodker: Poems & Adolphe 1920* (Manchester: Carcanet, 1996), pp. vii–xxiv; Romana Huk, 'Poetry of the Committed Individual: Jon Silkin, Tony Harrison, Geoffrey Hill, and the Poets of Postwar Leeds', in James Acheson and Romana Huk (eds), *Contemporary British Poetry: Essays in Theory and Criticism* (New York: State University of New York Press, 1996), pp. 175–219; Harry Zohn, 'Refugee poet', *The Boston Sunday Herald*, 1 January 1967, p. 19; Margaret Byers, 'Recent British Poetry by Women', in Michael Schmidt and Grevel Lindop (eds), *British Poetry Since 1960: A Critical Survey* (South Hinksey: Carcanet, 1972), pp. 74–84.
2.   Keith Douglas, 'Desert Flowers' (1943), in Desmond Graham (ed.), *Keith Douglas: The Complete Poems*, third edition (Oxford: Oxford University Press, 1998), p. 108.
3.   Letter of 11 April 1930, in Hart-Davis (ed.), *Siegfried Sassoon: Letters to Max Beerbohm, with a few answers* (London: Faber, 1986), p. 11.
4.   Letter from Andrew Crozier to Peter Lawson of 27 December 2000: private correspondence.
5.   See, for example, Joseph Leftwich, *Along the Years: Poems 1911–1937* (London: Robert Anscombe, 1937), Gilbert Frankau, *Selected Verses* (London: Macdonald, 1943) and A. Abrahams, *Writer of Verse* (London: William Heinemann, 1932).
6.   Peter Lawson, 'Way Out In the Centre: In Conversation with Elaine Feinstein', *Jewish Quarterly* (spring 2001), p. 69 and pp. 65–9.
7.   John Rodker, *The Future of Futurism* (London: Kegan Paul, Trench, Trubner, 1927), p. 8.
8.   Peter Lawson (ed.), *Passionate Renewal: Jewish Poetry in Britain since 1945*

(Nottingham: Five Leaves, 2001).

9. George Szirtes, *The Budapest File* (Newcastle: Bloodaxe, 2000), p. 15; and Isaac Rosenberg, 'Zion', in Ian Parsons (ed.), *The Collected Works of Isaac Rosenberg* (1979; London: Chatto & Windus, 1984), p. 4.

10. See Hilda Schiff (ed.), *Holocaust Poetry* (London: HarperCollins, 1995) and Marguerite M. Striar (ed.), *Beyond Lament: Poets of the World Bearing Witness to the Holocaust* (Evanston: Northwestern University Press, 1998).

11. Lillian Kremer (ed.), *Holocaust Literature* (New York: Routledge, 2003).

12. Sidra DeKoven Ezrahi, *Booking Passage: Exile and Homecoming in the Modern Jewish Imagination* (London: University of California Press, 2000), pp. 35, 139.

13. Ezrahi, p. 240.

14. R.B. Kitaj, *First Diasporist Manifesto* (London: Thames and Hudson, 1989), p. 35.

15. Emanuel Litvinoff, *Conscripts: A Symphonic Declaration* (London: Favil Press, 1941), and Emanuel Litvinoff, *The Untried Soldier* (London: Routledge, 1942).

16. Emanuel Litvinoff, *A Crown for Cain* (London: Falcon Press, 1948), pp. 53–4, 71–3, 81.

17. Emanuel Litvinoff, *Notes for a Survivor* (Newcastle upon Tyne: Northern House, 1973), pp. 4–5.

18. See, for example, 'Love and Country', in Frankau, p. 2, and 'Patriotic poem against nationalism', in Jenny Joseph, *Ghosts and Other Company* (Newcastle upon Tyne: Bloodaxe, 1995), pp. 24–7.

19. 'At the Palace of the Emperor at Dawn' (1949) and 'Once, in a Ventriloquist Evening' (1949), in Harold Pinter, *Various Voices: Prose, Poetry, Politics 1948–1998* (London: Faber, 1998), pp. 105–6.

20. John Rodker, *Hymns* (London: Ovid Press, 1920).

21. Rosenberg, 'Break of Day in the Trenches' (1916), in Parsons (ed.), pp. 103–4; 'Hampstead Heath' (1951), 'Camera Snaps' (1952) and 'I Shall Tear off my Terrible Cap' (1951), in Pinter, pp. 112, 126, 113.

22. Joanne Limburg, *Femenismo* (Tarset: Bloodaxe, 2000), p. 22.

23. 'Vertical' (1976), in Ruth Fainlight, *Selected Poems* (London: Hutchinson, 1987), p. 28.

24. Daniel Boyarin and Jonathan Boyarin, 'Diaspora: Generation and the Ground of Jewish Identity', *Critical Inquiry* 19:4 (summer 1993), pp. 714, 717–18 and pp. 693–725.

25. Litvinoff, *A Crown for Cain*, pp. 39–40.

26. Boyarin and Boyarin, p. 721.

27. Jon Silkin, *The Life of Metrical and Free Verse in Twentieth-Century Poetry* (Basingstoke: Macmillan, 1997), p. 61; and Jon Silkin, 'The Poetry of Isaac Rosenberg', in *Isaac Rosenberg 1890–1918: A catalogue of an exhibition held at Leeds University May–June 1959, together with the text of unpublished material* (Leeds: Partridge Press, 1959), p. 3.

28. Boyarin and Boyarin, p. 721.

29. Kitaj, pp. 49, 37.

30. Bryan Cheyette, 'Venetian Spaces: Old–New Literatures and the Ambivalent Uses of Jewish History', in Susheila Nasta (ed.), *Reading the 'New' Literatures in a Postcolonial Era*, The English Association Essays and Studies Series, vol. 53 (Cambridge: D. S. Brewer, 2000), pp. 57, 59 and pp. 53–72.

Bibliography

PRIMARY MATERIAL

Unpublished literature

Gershon, Karen, *The Historical and Legendary Esther* (*c.* 1980).
— *The Boy with the Sling: A Life of King David* (*c.* 1984).
— *The Last Freedom* (1986).
— *Manna to the Hungry* (1990–91).
— *A Tempered Wind: autobiography* (1992).
— *Notes of a Heart-Patient and Other Poems* (1993).
— *Love is Not Enough* (undated).

Published literature

Books

Bottomley, Gordon (ed.), *Poems by Isaac Rosenberg with a Memoir by Laurence Binyon* (London: Heinemann, 1922).
Crozier, Andrew (ed.), *John Rodker: Poems & Adolphe 1920* (Manchester: Carcanet, 1996).
Feinstein, Elaine, 'Father', *Prospect* 5 (winter 1961), p. 24.
— *The Circle* (1970; Harmondsworth: Penguin, 1973).
— *The Magic Apple Tree* (London: Hutchinson, 1971).
— (ed.), *The Selected Poems of Marina Tsvetayeva* (Oxford: Oxford University Press, 1971).
— *The Amberstone Exit* (London: Hutchinson, 1972).
— *The Celebrants* (London: Hutchinson, 1973).
— *The Glass Alembic* (London: Hutchinson, 1973).
— *Children of the Rose* (1975; Harmondsworth: Penguin, 1976).
— *The Ecstasy of Dr Miriam Garner* (London: Hutchinson, 1976).
— *Some Unease & Angels* (London: Hutchinson, 1977).
— *The Shadow Master* (New York: Simon and Schuster, 1978).
— trans., *Three Russian Poets: Margarita Aliger, Yunna Moritz, and Bella Akhmadulina* (Manchester: Carcanet, 1979).

— *The Survivors* (1982; New York: Penguin, 1991).

— *Bessie Smith* (Harmondsworth: Viking, 1985).

— *The Border* (1985; New York: Marion Boyars, 1990).

— *Badlands* (London: Hutchinson, 1986).

— *A Captive Lion: The Life of Marina Tsvetayeva* (London: Hutchinson, 1987).

— *Mother's Girl* (1988; London: Arena, 1989).

— *All You Need* (1989; New York: Viking, 1991).

— *City Music* (London: Hutchinson, 1990).

— *Loving Brecht* (London: Hutchinson, 1992).

— *Lawrence's Women: The Intimate Life of D. H. Lawrence* (London: HarperCollins, 1993).

— *Dreamers* (1994; Basingstoke: Pan, 1996).

— *Selected Poems* (Manchester: Carcanet, 1994).

— *Lady Chatterley's Confession* (1995; London: Pan, 1996).

— *Daylight* (Manchester: Carcanet, 1997).

— *Pushkin* (1998; London: Phoenix, 1999).

— *Dark Inheritance* (2000; London: The Women's Press, 2001).

— *Gold* (Manchester: Carcanet, 2000).

— *Ted Hughes: The Life of a Poet* (London: Weidenfeld & Nicolson, 2001).

— *Collected Poems and Translations* (Manchester: Carcanet, 2002).

Gershon, Karen, *Selected Poems* (London: Gollancz, 1966).

— (ed.), *We Came as Children: A Collective Autobiography* (1966; London: Papermac, 1989).

— (ed.), *Postscript: A Collective Account of the Lives of Jews in West Germany since the Second World War* (London: Gollancz, 1969).

— *Legacies and Encounters: Poems 1966–1971* (London: Gollancz, 1972).

— *First Meeting* (Richmond: Keepsake Press, 1974).

— *My Daughters, My Sisters* (London: Gollancz, 1975).

— *Jephthah's Daughter* (Knotting: Sceptre Press, 1978).

— *Coming Back from Babylon* (London: Gollancz, 1979).

— *Burn Helen* (Brighton: The Harvester Press, 1980).

— *The Bread of Exile: a novel* (London: Gollancz, 1985).

— *The Fifth Generation* (London: Gollancz, 1987).

— *Collected Poems* (London: Macmillan, 1990).

— *A Lesser Child* (London: Peter Owen, 1994).

— *Grace Notes* (Toppesfield: The Happy Dragons Press, 2002).

Gershon, Karen with Levenson, Christopher and Crichton Smith, Iain, *The Relentless Year: New Poets 1959* (London: Eyre and Spottiswoode, 1959).

Harding, Denys (ed.), *Poems by Isaac Rosenberg* (London: Chatto & Windus, 1972).

Hart-Davis, Rupert (ed.), *Siegfried Sassoon Diaries 1920–1922* (London: Faber, 1981).

— (ed.), *Siegfried Sassoon Diaries 1915–1918* (London: Faber, 1983).

— (ed.), *Siegfried Sassoon: The War Poems* (London: Faber, 1983).

— (ed.), *Siegfried Sassoon: Letters to Max Beerbohm, With a Few Answers* (London: Faber, 1986).

Liddiard, Jean (ed.), *Isaac Rosenberg: Selected Poems and Letters* (London: Enitharmon, 2003).

Loewenthal, Karen, *The World Was Old* (London: The Bodley Head, 1956).

Noakes, Vivien (ed.), *The Poems and Plays of Isaac Rosenberg* (Oxford: Oxford University Press, 2004).

Parsons, Ian (ed.), *The Collected Works of Isaac Rosenberg* (1979; London: Chatto & Windus, 1984).

Rodker, John, *Poems* ('To be had of the Author, 1 Osborn Street, Whitechapel', 1914).

— *The Future of Futurism* (London: Kegan Paul, Trench, Trubner, 1927).

— *Collected Poems 1912–1925* (Paris: The Hours Press, 1930).

— *Memoirs of Other Fronts* (London: Putnam, 1932).

Sassoon, Siegfried, *The Complete Memoirs of George Sherston* (1937; London: Faber, 1972).

— *The Old Century and Seven More Years* (London: Faber, 1938).

— *The Weald of Youth* (London: Faber, 1942).

— *Siegfried's Journey 1916–1920* (London: Faber, 1945).

— *Collected Poems 1908–1956* (1961; London: Faber, 1984).

Silkin, Jon, *The Peaceable Kingdom* (London: Chatto & Windus, 1954)

— *The Two Freedoms* (London: Chatto & Windus, 1958).

— *The Re-ordering of the Stones* (London: Chatto & Windus, 1961).

— *Nature with Man* (London: Chatto & Windus, 1965).

— *Amana Grass* (London: Chatto & Windus, 1971).

— *Out of Battle: The Poetry of the Great War* (1972; Oxford: Oxford University Press, 1978).

— (ed.), *Poetry of the Committed Individual: A Stand Anthology of Poetry* (Harmondsworth: Penguin, 1973).

— *The Principle of Water* (Cheadle: Carcanet, 1974).

— *The Little Time-Keeper* (Old Woking: Carcanet, 1976).

— (ed.), *The Penguin Book of First World War Poetry* (Harmondsworth: Penguin, 1979).

— *The Psalms with their Spoils* (London: Routledge, 1980).
— *Selected Poems* (London: Routledge & Kegan Paul, 1980).
— *The Ship's Pasture* (London: Routledge & Kegan Paul, 1986).
— 'Seven Poems', *Tel Aviv Review* 2 (fall 1989/winter 1990), pp. 166–76
— *The Lens-Breakers* (London: Sinclair-Stevenson, 1992).
— *The Life of Metrical and Free Verse in Twentieth-Century Poetry* (Basingstoke: Macmillan, 1997).
— *Testament Without Breath* (Manaccan: Cargo Press, 1998).
— 'Four Poems', *The Jerusalem Review* 4 (2000), pp. 174–7
— *Making a Republic* (Manchester: Carcanet/Northern House, 2002).
Wilson, Jean Moorcroft (ed.), *The Selected Poems of Isaac Rosenberg* (London: Cecil Woolf, 2003).

Articles

Feinstein, Elaine, 'A Legendary Hero', in Ursula Owen (ed.), *Fathers: Reflections By Daughters* (London: Virago, 1983), pp. 159–67.
— 'Elaine Feinstein', in *Contemporary Authors Autobiography Series*, vol. 1 (Detroit: Gale, 1984), pp. 215–24.
Gershon, Karen, 'The Tenth of November', *Midstream: A Monthly Jewish Review* 14:3 (March 1968), pp. 17–23.
— 'Journey to the Past', *Jewish Quarterly* 144 (winter 1991/1992), pp. 71–2.
Rodker, John, 'The Theatre in Whitechapel', *Poetry and Drama* 1:1 (March 1913), pp. 43–4.
— 'The Theatre', *The Egoist* 1:21 (November 1914), pp. 414–15.
— 'Theatre Muet', *The Little Review* 4:4 (August 1917), pp. 12–15.
— 'W. H. Hudson', *The Little Review* 7:1 (May–June 1920), pp. 18–28.
— 'Other Books', *The Little Review* 7:3 (September–December 1920), pp. 64–5.
— 'Twenty Years After', in Julian Bell (ed.), *We Did Not Fight: 1914–18, Experiences of War Resisters* (London: Cobden-Sanderson, 1935), pp. 283–91.
Silkin, Jon, 'Editorial', *Stand* 1:2 (1952), p. 3.
— 'Editorial', *Stand* 4:1 (1958), pp. 3–4.
— 'The poetry of Isaac Rosenberg', in *Isaac Rosenberg 1890–1918: A catalogue of an exhibition held at Leeds University May–June 1959, together with the text of unpublished material* (Leeds: Partridge Press, 1959), pp. 1–3.

— 'The war, class, and the Jews', *Stand* 4:3 (1960), pp. 33–6.
— 'Anglo-Jewish poetry', *Jewish Quarterly* (spring 1967), pp. 22–4.
— 'The first twenty-four years', in *Contemporary Authors Autobiography Series*, vol. 5 (Detroit: Gale, 1987), pp. 243–65.
Silkin, Jon and Thwaite, Anthony, 'No politics, no poetry?', *Stand* 6:2 (1963), pp. 7–23.

SECONDARY MATERIAL

Abrahams, A., *Writer of Verse* (London: William Heinemann, 1932).
Abse, Dannie, *Remembrance of Crimes Past* (London: Hutchinson, 1990).
Adorno, Theodor, 'Commitment', in Rodney Livingstone, Perry Anderson and Francis Mulhern (eds), *Aesthetics and Politics* (London: New Left Books, 1977), pp. 177–95.
Aldington, Richard, 'Flint and Rodker', *Poetry: A Magazine of Verse* 17:1 (October 1920), pp. 44–8.
— 'Two poets', *The Egoist* 1:22 (16 November 1914), pp. 422–3.
Alexander, Michael, *Jazz Age Jews* (Princeton, NJ: Princeton University Press, 2001).
Anderson, Margaret, 'Editorial Note', *The Little Review* 6:2 (June 1919), p. i.
Bauman, Batya, 'Women-identified women in male-identified Judaism', in Susannah Heschel (ed.), *On Being a Jewish Feminist: A Reader* (New York: Schocken, 1983), pp. 88–95.
Bauman, Zygmunt, *Modernity and the Holocaust* (1989; Cambridge: Polity Press, 1991).
— *Modernity and Ambivalence* (Cambridge: Polity Press, 1991).
— 'Allosemitism: premodern, modern, postmodern', in Bryan Cheyette and Laura Marcus (eds), *Modernity, Culture and 'the Jew'* (Cambridge: Polity Press, 1998), pp. 143–56.
Bell, Julian (ed.), *We Did Not Fight: 1914–18, Experiences of War Resisters* (London: Cobden-Sanderson, 1935).
Berkowitz, Michael, *Zionist Culture and West European Jewry Before the First World War* (Cambridge: Cambridge University Press, 1993).
Biale, David, *Eros and the Jews: from Biblical Israel to Contemporary America* (California: University of California Press, 1997).
Birkett, Jennifer, 'Elaine Feinstein', in Pamela L. Shelton (ed.), *Contemporary Women Poets* (Detroit: St James Press, 1998), pp. 113–15.

Bodenheim, Maxwell, 'Poems by John Rodker', *Others* 2:4 (April 1916), pp. 212–13.

Boman, Thorlief, *Hebrew Thought Compared with Greek Thought* (Philadelphia: Westminster Press, 1960).

Bonaparte, Marie, 'Obituary: John Rodker 1894–1955', *The International Journal of Psychoanalysis* 37:2–3 (March–June 1956), pp. 199–201.

Boyarin, Daniel and Boyarin, Jonathan, 'Diaspora: generation and the ground of Jewish identity', *Critical Inquiry* 19:4 (summer 1993), pp. 693–725.

— *Unheroic Conduct: The Rise of Heterosexuality and the Invention of the Jewish Man* (California: University of California Press, 1997).

Brooke, Rupert, *1914 and Other Poems* (1915; London: Penguin, 1999).

Burman, Rickie, 'Jewish women and the household economy in Manchester, *c*.1890–1920', in David Cesarani (ed.), *The Making of Modern Anglo-Jewry* (Oxford: Basil Blackwell, 1990), pp. 55–75

Byatt, A.S., *Writers in Conversation: Elaine Feinstein* (London: ICA Video, 1987).

Byers, Margaret, 'Recent British poetry by women', in Michael Schmidt and Grevel Lindop (eds), *British Poetry Since 1960: A Critical Survey* (South Hinksey: Carcanet, 1972), pp. 74–84.

Caesar, Adrian, *Taking it Like a Man: Suffering, Sexuality and the War Poets* (Manchester: Manchester University Press, 1993).

Campbell, Patrick, *Siegfried Sassoon: A Study of the War Poetry* (Jefferson: McFarland, 1999).

Cantor, Aviva, 'The Lilith question', in Susannah Heschel (ed.), *On Being a Jewish Feminist: A Reader* (New York: Schocken, 1983), pp. 40–50.

Carey, John, 'Digging in the sand', *New Statesman*, 20 May 1966, pp. 736–7.

Carmi, T. (ed.), *The Penguin Book of Hebrew Verse* (London: Penguin, 1981).

Carpenter, Spencer Cecil, *Winnington-Ingram: The Biography of Arthur Foley Winnington-Ingram, Bishop of London 1901–1939* (London: Hodder and Stoughton, 1949).

Celan, Paul, *Poems*, trans. and ed. Michael Hamburger (London: Anvil, 1988).

Cesarani, David (ed.), *The Making of Modern Anglo-Jewry* (Oxford: Basil Blackwell, 1990).

Cheyette, Bryan (ed.), *Contemporary Jewish Writing in Britain and*

Ireland: An Anthology (London: Peter Halban, 1988).

— *Constructions of 'The Jew' in English Literature and Society: Racial Representations, 1875–1945* (Cambridge: Cambridge University Press, 1993).

— '"Ineffable and usable": towards a diasporic British-Jewish writing', *Textual Practice* 10:2 (1996), pp. 295–313.

— 'Venetian spaces: old–new literatures and the ambivalent uses of Jewish history', in Susheila Nasta (ed.), *Reading the 'New' Literatures in a Postcolonial Era*, The English Association Essays and Studies Series, vol. 53 (Cambridge: D. S. Brewer, 2000), pp. 53–72.

Cohen, Joseph, *Journey to the Trenches: The Life of Isaac Rosenberg 1890–1918* (London: Robson Books, 1975).

Coleridge, Ernest Hartley (ed.), *Coleridge: Poetical Works* (1912; Oxford: Oxford University Press, 1980).

Colley, Linda, *Britons: Forging the Nation 1707–1837* (London: Yale University Press, 1992).

Connor, Steven, 'Isaac Rosenberg: Birkbeck's war poet', at: www.bbk.ac.uk/eh/skc/rosenberg/ (30 October 2000).

Conquest, Robert (ed.), *New Lines* (London: Macmillan, 1956).

— (ed.), *New Lines – II* (London: Macmillan, 1963).

Conradi, Peter, 'Elaine Feinstein', in *Dictionary of Literary Biography, vol. 14: British Novelists Since 1960, Part 1: A–G* (Detroit: Gale, 1983), pp. 293–4.

Corcoran, Neil, *English Poetry Since 1940* (Harlow: Longman, 1993).

Cork, Richard, *Jacob Epstein* (London: Tate Gallery Publications, 1999).

— 'Isaac Rosenberg: Poet and Painter', *Apollo* (March 1991), p. 204.

Corrigan, D. Felicitas, *Siegfried Sassoon: Poet's Pilgrimage* (London: Gollancz, 1973).

Cox, C. B., 'Patriots and Exiles', *Spectator*, 5 August 1966, pp. 179–80.

Crozier, Andrew, unpublished letter to Peter Lawson (27 December 2000).

Cunard, Nancy, *These Were The Hours: Memoirs of My Hours Press, Réanville and Paris 1928–1931* (Carbondale: Southern Illinois University Press, 1969).

Davies, Walford (ed.), *Dylan Thomas: Selected Poems* (Harmondsworth: Penguin, 2000).

Deleuze, Gilles and Guattari, Félix, *Kafka: Toward a Minor Literature* (1975; Minneapolis: University of Minnesota Press, 1986).

Deleuze, Gilles and Parnet, Claire, *Dialogues* (Paris: Flammarion,

Collection Dialogues, 1977).

Donno, Elizabeth Story (ed.), *Andrew Marvell: The Complete Poems* (Harmondsworth: Penguin, 1976).

Doob, Leonard W. (ed.), *Ezra Pound Speaking* (Westport, CT: Greenwood Press, 1978).

Dor, Moshe and Zach, Natan (eds), *The Burning Bush: Poems from Modern Israel* (London: W. H. Allen, 1977).

Doyle, Charles, *Richard Aldington: A Biography* (Basingstoke: Macmillan, 1989).

Eagleton, Terry, *Exiles and Emigrés: Studies in Modern Literature* (London: Chatto & Windus, 1970).

Eliade, Mircea (ed.), *The Encyclopedia of Religion*, 16 vols (New York: Macmillan, 1987).

Eliot, T. S., *Selected Essays* (1932; London: Faber, 1966).

— *After Strange Gods* (London: Faber, 1934).

— (ed.), *The Literary Essays of Ezra Pound* (London: Faber, 1954).

— *The Complete Poems and Plays of T. S. Eliot* (1969; London: Faber, 1978).

Eliot, Valerie (ed.), *The Letters of T. S. Eliot: vol. 1, 1898–1922* (London: Faber, 1988).

Ellershaw, Henry (ed.), *Keats: Poetry and Prose* (1922; Oxford: Clarendon Press, 1960)

Ellmann, Maud, 'The Imaginary Jew: T. S. Eliot and Ezra Pound', in Bryan Cheyette (ed.), *Between 'Race' and Culture: Representations of 'the Jew' in English and American Literature* (Stanford, CA: Stanford University Press, 1996), pp. 84–101.

Ellmann, Richard (ed.), *Selected Letters of James Joyce* (London: Faber, 1975).

Englander, David (ed.), *A Documentary History of Jewish Immigrants in Britain, 1840–1920* (London: Leicester University Press, 1994).

Ezrahi, Sidra DeKoven, *Booking Passage: Exile and Homecoming in the Modern Jewish Imagination* (London: University of California Press, 2000).

Fainlight, Ruth, *Selected Poems* (London: Hutchinson, 1987).

Featherstone, Simon (ed.), *War Poetry: An Introductory Reader* (London: Routledge, 1995).

Feldman, David, *Englishman and Jews: Social Relations and Political Culture 1840–1914* (London: Yale University Press, 1994).

Fishman, William, *East End Jewish Radicals* (London: Duckworth, 1975).

Flory, Wendy Stallard, 'Pound and antisemitism', in Ira B. Nadel (ed.), *The Cambridge Companion to Ezra Pound* (Cambridge: Cambridge University Press, 1999), pp. 284–300.

Forbes, Peter (ed.), *Scanning the Century: The Penguin Book of the Twentieth Century in Poetry* (London: Penguin, 1999).

Ford, Mark, 'The final extra glass', *Times Literary Supplement*, 5 July 1996, p. 4866.

Frankau, Gilbert, *Selected Verses* (London: Macdonald, 1943).

Friedländer, Saul, *Nazi Germany and the Jews: The Years of Persecution 1933–39* (1997; London: Phoenix, 1998).

Fussell, Paul, *The Great War and Modern Memory* (New York: Oxford University Press, 1975).

Gidley, Ben, 'Ghetto radicalism: the Jewish East End', *New Voices in Jewish Thought* 2 (1999), pp. 50–69.

Gilman, Sander, *Jewish Self-Hatred: Anti-Semitism and the Hidden Language of the Jews* (Baltimore: Johns Hopkins University Press, 1986).

— *The Jew's Body* (London: Routledge, 1991).

Graham, Desmond (ed.), *Keith Douglas: The Complete Poems*, third edition (Oxford: Oxford University Press, 1998).

Graves, Robert, *Fairies and Fusiliers* (London: Heinemann, 1917).

Hale, Keith (ed.), *Friends and Apostles: The Correspondence of Rupert Brooke and James Strachey, 1905–1914* (London: Yale University Press, 1998).

Handelman, Susan A., *The Slayers of Moses: The Emergence of Rabbinic Interpretation in Modern Literary Theory* (Albany: State University of New York Press, 1982).

Harris, Daniel, 'Rosenberg in the trenches: imagining King David's world', *Jewish Culture and History* 5:1 (summer 2002), pp. 1–28.

Hartnett, David, 'Traces of darker times', *Times Literary Supplement*, 21–27 September 1990, p. 1007.

Hassall, Christopher, *Edward Marsh: Patron of the Arts* (London: Longman, 1959).

Henderson, Alice Corbin, 'Rodker's *Poems*', *Poetry: A Magazine of Verse* 6:3 (June 1915), pp. 153–6.

Herzl, Theodor, *Altneuland, Roman* (Leipzig: Hermann Seemann Nachfolger, 1902).

Heschel, Susannah (ed.), *On Being a Jewish Feminist: A Reader* (New York: Schocken, 1983).

Hilberg, Raul, *The Destruction of the European Jews* (London: Holmes & Meier, 1985).

Hobday, Charles, 'Isaac Rosenberg, revolutionary poet', *London*

Magazine (June–July 2000), pp. 42–56.

Holmes, Colin, *Anti-Semitism in British Society* (London: Edward Arnold, 1979).

Hoover, Paul (ed.), *Postmodern American Poetry* (New York: Norton, 1994).

Horovitz, Michael, 'Verses out of curses', *Jewish Chronicle*, 23 February 1990, p. 35.

Huk, Romana, 'Poetry of the committed individual: Jon Silkin, Tony Harrison, Geoffrey Hill, and the poets of postwar Leeds', in James Acheson and Romana Huk (eds), *Contemporary British Poetry: Essays in Theory and Criticism* (Albany, NY: State University of New York Press, 1996), pp. 175–219.

Hutchinson, Thomas (ed.), *The Poetical Works of Percy Bysshe Shelley* (London: Oxford University Press, 1908).

Hutchison, William R. and Lehmann, Hartmut (eds), *Many are Chosen: Divine Election and Western Nationalism* (Minneapolis: Fortress Press, 1994).

Hyman, Paula, 'The Jewish family: looking for a usable past', in Susannah Heschel (ed.), *On Being a Jewish Feminist: A Reader* (New York: Schocken, 1983), pp. 19–26.

Innes, Christopher, 'Modernism in drama', in Michael Levenson (ed.), *The Cambridge Companion to Modernism* (Cambridge: Cambridge University Press, 1999), pp. 130–56.

Isaacs, Jack, 'Mr. John Rodker: literature in the twenties', *Times*, 11 October 1955, p. 11.

Jacobs, Louis, *Concise Companion to the Jewish Religion* (Oxford: Oxford University Press, 1999).

Jacobson, Dan, *The Story of the Stories* (London: Secker and Warburg, 1982).

Jeger, Lena, 'Body, soul, and passport', *Guardian*, 13 May 1966, p. 9.

Johnsen, William A., 'The treacherous years of postmodern poetry in English', in Ann Massa and Alistair Stead (eds), *Forked Tongues?: Comparing Twentieth-Century British and American Literature* (London: Longman, 1994), pp. 75–91.

Joseph, Jenny, *Ghosts and Other Company* (Newcastle upon Tyne: Bloodaxe, 1995).

Joyce, James, *Ulysses* (1922; London: Penguin, 2000).

Julius, Anthony, *T. S. Eliot, Anti-Semitism, and Literary Form* (Cambridge: Cambridge University Press, 1995).

Kershen, Anne J., 'Trade unionism amongst the Jewish tailoring workers of London and Leeds, 1872–1915', in David Cesarani (ed.), *The Making of Modern Anglo-Jewry* (Oxford: Basil Blackwell, 1990), pp. 34–52.

Kipling, Rudyard, *Something of Myself* (1936; London: Penguin, 1992).

— *The Complete Verse* (1996; London: Kyle Cathie, 1998).

Kitaj, R. B., *First Diasporist Manifesto* (London: Thames and Hudson, 1989).

Kops, Bernard, 'Scrawling through the wreckage', *Guardian*, 20 November 1990, p. 37.

Kramer, Lotte, 'Reflections', in Stephen W. Massil (ed.), *Jewish Year Book 2000* (London: Vallentine Mitchell, 2000), pp. 69–75.

Kremer, Lillian (ed.), *Holocaust Literature* (New York: Routledge, 2003).

Kronfeld, Chana, *On the Margins of Modernism: Decentering Literary Dynamics* (London: University of California Press, 1996).

Larkin, Philip (ed.), *The Oxford Book of Twentieth-Century English Verse* (1973; Oxford: Oxford University Press, 1998).

Lawson, Peter, 'Interview: Jon Silkin', *Sphagnum* 11 (1981), pp. 24–33.

— 'The relevance of Rosenberg', *Jewish Quarterly* 173 (1999), pp. 71–3.

— 'Way out in the centre: in conversation with Elaine Feinstein', *Jewish Quarterly* (spring 2001), pp. 65–9.

— (ed.), *Passionate Renewal: Jewish Poetry in Britain since 1945* (Nottingham: Five Leaves, 2001).

Leftwich, Joseph, *Along the Years: Poems 1911–1937* (London: Robert Anscombe, 1937).

— '"Jewish" London fifty years ago', in *1915–1965 Fifty Years Achievement in the Arts* (London: Ben Uri Art Society, 1966), pp. 12–16.

Levenson, Michael, *A Genealogy of Modernism: A Study of English Literary Doctrine 1908–1922* (Cambridge: Cambridge University Press, 1984).

— (ed.), *The Cambridge Companion to Modernism* (Cambridge: Cambridge University Press, 1999).

Levin, Ira, *The Boys from Brazil* (New York: Random House, 1976).

Lewis, Wyndham, *The Apes of God* (London: Arthur Press, 1930).

Liddiard, Jean, *Isaac Rosenberg: The Half Used Life* (London: Victor Gollancz, 1975).

Limburg, Joanne, *Femenismo* (Tarset: Bloodaxe, 2000).

Lindley, David, *Lyric* (London: Methuen, 1985).

Litvinoff, Emanuel, *Conscripts: A Symphonic Declaration* (London:

Favil Press, 1941).

— *The Untried Soldier* (London: Routledge, 1942).

— *A Crown for Cain* (London: Falcon Press, 1948).

— 'A Jew in England', *Jewish Quarterly* (spring 1967), pp. 7–12.

— *Notes for a Survivor* (Newcastle upon Tyne: Northern House, 1973).

Longley, Michael, 'Book of the day', *Irish Times*, 23 July 1966, p. 15.

Maccoby, Deborah, *God Made Blind: Isaac Rosenberg, His Life and Poetry* (London: Symposium Press, 1999).

Marcuse, Ludwig, *Obscene: The History of an Indignation*, trans. Karen Gershon (London: MacGibbon & Kee, 1965).

— *Obszön: Geschichte einer Entrüstung* (Munich: Paul List Verlag, 1962).

Massa, Ann and Stead, Alistair (eds), *Forked Tongues? Comparing Twentieth-Century British and American Literature* (London: Longman, 1994).

Materer, Timothy (ed.), *Pound/Lewis: The Letters of Ezra Pound and Wyndham Lewis* (London: Faber, 1985).

Mather, Eleanor Price, *Edward Hicks: His Peaceable Kingdoms and Other Paintings* (London: Cornwall Books, 1983).

Maud, Ralph (ed.), *Selected Letters of Charles Olson* (London: University of California Press, 2000).

Mayer, Gerda, 'Flight to England', *Poetry Review* 88:4 (winter 1998/1999), pp. 25–7.

Milton, John, 'Areopagitica', in K. M. Burton (ed.), *Milton's Prose Writings* (1958; London: Everyman, 1974), pp. 145–85.

Mitchell, Deborah, 'Elaine Feinstein', in *Dictionary of Literary Biography, vol. 40: Poets of Great Britain and Ireland Since 1960, Part 1: A–L* (Detroit: Gale, 1985), pp. 116–21.

Morrison, Blake, *The Movement: English Poetry and Fiction of the 1950s* (Oxford: Oxford University Press, 1980).

Mulhern, Francis, 'English Reading', in Homi K. Bhabha (ed.), *Nation and Narration* (London: Routledge, 1990), pp. 250–64.

Murray, Peter and Murray, Linda, *The Penguin Dictionary of Art and Artists*, fourth edition (1959; Harmondsworth: Penguin, 1978).

Nadel, Ira B. (ed.), *The Cambridge Companion to Ezra Pound* (Cambridge: Cambridge University Press, 1999).

Neuberger, Julia, 'A growing disquiet', *Observer*, 11 March 1990, p. 61.

New, Melvyn (ed.), *The Complete Novels and Selected Writings of Amy Levy* (Gainesville: University of Florida Press, 1993).

Nochlin, Linda and Garb, Tamar (eds), *The Jew in the Text* (London:

Thames and Hudson, 1995).

'Obituary: John Rodker', *Publishers' Weekly: The American Book Trade Journal* 168:21 (19 November 1955), p. 2127.

'Obituary: Karen Gershon', *AJR Information* (May 1993), p. 15.

'Obituary: Karen Gershon', *The Times*, 15 April 1993, p. 23.

Ostriker, Alicia (ed.), *The Complete Poems of William Blake* (Harmondsworth: Penguin, 1979).

Padel, Ruth, 'Imports in England's lane', *Times Literary Supplement*, 16 November 1990, p. 1248.

Page, D. D. (ed.), *The Letters of Ezra Pound, 1907–1941* (London: Faber, 1951).

Page, Frederick (ed.), *Byron: Poetical Works*, third edition (1970; Oxford: Oxford University Press, 1979).

Palmer, Alan, *The Penguin Dictionary of Twentieth Century History 1900–1978* (Harmondsworth: Penguin, 1979).

Pearce, Joseph, *Literary Converts: Spiritual Inspiration in an Age of Unbelief* (London: HarperCollins, 1999).

Pendlebury, Alyson, 'The politics of the "last days": Bolshevism, Zionism and "the Jews"', *Jewish Culture and History* 2:2 (winter 1999), pp. 96–115.

Pett, John, producer and director, *Stranger in a Strange Land* (Channel 4, 1990).

Phillips, Adam, 'Unofficial modernist: John Rodker', *Jewish Quarterly* (winter 1998/1999), pp. 69–71.

— *On Flirtation* (London: Faber, 1994).

Pick, Daniel, *Faces of Degeneration: A European Disorder, c.1848–c.1918* (Cambridge: Cambridge University Press, 1989).

— *Svengali's Web: The Alien Enchanter in Modern Culture* (London: Yale University Press, 2000).

Pinter, Harold, *Various Voices: Prose, Poetry, Politics 1948–1998* (London: Faber, 1998).

Pinto, Vivian de Sola and Roberts, Warren (eds), *The Complete Poems of D. H. Lawrence*, 2 vols (London: Heinemann, 1964).

Poetry Review: Jon Silkin Special Issue 69:4 (1980).

Pound, Ezra, 'Notes and announcements', *Poetry* 1:2 (November 1912), p. 65.

— 'Foreword to the Choric School', *Others* 1:4 (October 1915), pp. 53–4.

— *Make It New: Essays by Ezra Pound* (London: Faber, 1934).

— *The Cantos of Ezra Pound* (London: Faber, 1987).

Prawer, S. S., *Heine's Jewish Comedy: A Study of his Portraits of Jews and Judaism* (Oxford: Clarendon Press, 1983).

Ragussis, Michael, *Figures of Conversion* (London: Duke University Press, 1995).

Reeves, James (ed.), *Georgian Poetry* (1962; Harmondsworth: Penguin, 1968).

Reich, Bernard and Goldberg, David, *Political Dictionary of Israel* (Folkstone: Scarecrow Press, 2000).

Ricks, Christopher (ed.), *The Oxford Book of English Verse* (Oxford: Oxford University Press, 1999).

Roberts, John Stuart, *Siegfried Sassoon* (London: Richard Cohen Books, 1999).

Roberts, Michele, 'Elaine Feinstein in conversation', *PN Review* 23:3 (January–February 1995), pp. 45–7.

Robson, Jeremy, 'Testaments of Faith', *Jewish Chronicle*, 20 May 1966, p. 26.

Rose, Paul Lawrence, *Wagner: Race and Revolution* (London: Faber, 1992).

Rose, Jacqueline, 'Dorothy Richardson and the Jew', in Bryan Cheyette (ed.), *Between 'Race' and Culture: Representations of 'the Jew' in English and American Literature* (Stanford, CA: Stanford University Press, 1996), pp. 114–28.

Roskies, David G., *Against the Apocalypse: Responses to Catastrophe in Modern Jewish Culture* (London: Harvard University Press, 1984).

Roth, Cecil, *A History of the Jews in England* (London: Oxford University Press, 1941).

Rudolf, Anthony, 'Jon Silkin obituary', *Jewish Chronicle*, 12 December 1997, p. 22.

Ruppin, Arthur, *Memoirs, Diaries, Letters*, trans. Karen Gershon (London: Weidenfeld & Nicolson, 1971).

Rushdie, Salmon, *Imaginary Homelands: Essays and Criticism 1981–1991* (London: Granta, 1991).

Said, Edward, *Orientalism* (1978; London: Penguin, 1991).

Samuels, Diane, *Kindertransport* (London: Nick Hern, 1995).

Satlof, Claire R., 'History, fiction, and the tradition: creating a Jewish feminist poetic', in Susannah Heschel (ed.), *On Being a Jewish Feminist: A Reader* (New York: Schocken, 1983), pp. 186–206.

Schiff, Hilda (ed.), *Holocaust Poetry* (London: HarperCollins, 1995).

Schmidt, Michael, 'Stand: Symposium on "Commitment"', *Stand* 20:3 (1979), pp. 12–15.

Schmidt, Michael and Lindop, Grevel (eds), *British Poetry Since*

1960: A Critical Survey (South Hinksey: Carcanet, 1972).

Scott, Thomas L., Friedman, Melvin J. and Bryer, Jackson R. (eds), *Pound/The Little Review: The Letters of Ezra Pound to Margaret Anderson* (New York: New Directions, 1988).

Scrivener, Michael, '"Zion alone is forbidden": historicizing anti-Semitism in Byron's *The Age of Bronze', Keats–Shelley Journal* 43 (1994), pp. 75–97.

Sergeant, Howard and Abse, Dannie (eds), *Mavericks: An Anthology* (London: Poetry and Poverty, 1957).

Sicher, Efraim, *Beyond Marginality: Anglo-Jewish Literature After the Holocaust* (Albany: State University of New York Press, 1985).

Silk, Dennis, 'Isaac Rosenberg (1890–1918)', *Judaism* 14:4 (autumn 1965), pp. 462–74.

Simmel, Georg, 'The Stranger' (1908), in Kurt H. Wolff (ed.), *The Sociology of Georg Simmel* (New York: Collier-Macmillan, 1964), pp. 402–8

Sinfield, Alan, 'Diaspora and hybridity: queer identities and the ethnicity model', *Textual Practice* 10:2 (1996), pp. 271–93.

Smith, A. J. (ed.), *John Donne: The Complete English Poems* (Harmondsworth: Penguin, 1971).

Smith, John, 'Tragedy and poetry', *Tribune*, 8 July 1966, p. 13.

Smith, Richard Eugene, *Richard Aldington* (Boston: Twayne, 1977).

Sorkin, David, *The Transformation of German Jewry 1780–1840* (1987; Detroit: Wayne State University Press, 1999).

Steiner, George, *Language and Silence: Essays 1958–1966* (1967; London: Faber, 1985).

Steyn, Juliet, *The Jew: Assumptions of Identity* (London: Cassell, 1999).

Striar, Marguerite M. (ed.), *Beyond Lament: Poets of the World Bearing Witness to the Holocaust* (Evanston: Northwestern University Press, 1998).

Szirtes, George, *The Budapest File* (Newcastle: Bloodaxe, 2000).

Trachtenberg, Joshua, *The Devil and the Jews* (Jerusalem: Jewish Publication Society, 1943).

Vital, David, *The Origins of Zionism* (Oxford: Oxford University Press, 1975).

Wain, John, *Sprightly Running: Part of an Autobiography* (1962; London: Macmillan, 1965).

Walls, A. F., 'Carrying the white man's burden: some British views of national vocation in the imperial era', in William R. Hutchison and Hartmut Lehmann (eds), *Many Are Chosen: Divine Election and Western Nationalism* (Minneapolis: Fortress Press, 1994), pp. 29–56.

Wavell, Archibald P., *The Palestine Campaigns* (1928; London: Constable, 1940).

Wilkinson, Alan, *The Church of England and the First World War* (London: SPCK, 1978).

Williams, Raymond, 'Commitment', *Stand* 20:3 (1979), pp. 8–11.

Wilson, Jean Moorcroft, *Isaac Rosenberg: Poet & Painter* (London: Cecil Woolf, 1975).

— *Siegfried Sassoon, The Making of a War Poet* (1998; London: Duckworth, 1999).

—- *Siegfried Sassoon, The Journey from the Trenches* (London: Duckworth, 2003).

Wilson, John, 'British Israelism: the ideological restraints on sect organisation', in Bryan R. Wilson (ed.), *Patterns of Sectarianism: Organisation and Ideology in Social and Religious Movements* (London: Heinemann, 1967), pp. 345–76.

Wolff, Kurt H. (ed.), *The Sociology of Georg Simmel* (New York: Collier-Macmillan, 1964).

Zach, Natan, *Against Parting*, trans. Nathan Zach and Jon Silkin (Newcastle: Northern House, 1967).

Zatlin, Linda Gertner, *The Nineteenth-Century Anglo-Jewish Novel* (Boston: Twayne, 1981).

Zohn, Harry, 'Refugee Poet', *The Boston Sunday Herald*, 1 January 1967, p. 19.

Index

Recently published by Vallentine Mitchell

Portraying 'the Jew' in First World War Britain
Alyson Pendlebury

This book focuses on Britain during the First World War and the immediate post-war period, and examines the use of biblical imagery with regard to representations of the nation and its perceived enemies. The study is constructed around four rhetorical themes: 'crusade', 'conversion', 'crucifixion' and 'apocalypse', and traces these through a wide variety of texts, including public lectures, sermons, press articles, political speeches and memoirs, pre-millennialist writings, cartoons, plays, poetry and popular fiction. The central argument is that in the context of rhetorically constructed 'Christian warfare', religious language took on political significance, and old allegations against Jews began to recirculate. The study examines the religious, political and sexual fears associated by Christians with Jews during and after the war, and discusses the ways in which Anglo-Jewish writers, including G. B. Stern, Gilbert Frankau and Isaac Rosenberg, responded to these developments.